PREDATOR
DOWN

MARCO COTA

SECOND EDITION

Copyright 2011 Marco Cota

ISBN: 1460914651
EAN 13: 9781460914656

Manufactured in the United States of America

Second Edition

0 9 8 7 6 5 4 3 2

PREDATOR
DOWN

The Set Standard
First Recorded Public Outcry for a Rape-Killing Case

....

Four thousand years ago in Israel, a story is documented in the book of Judges, chapters nineteen and twenty. A woman was taken from her husband by a group of "Worthless" men, while lodging in Gibeah. She was raped the entire evening. The man found his dead companion in the morning. He took her body to his home to dismember it and send her body parts to the twelve judging tribes of Israel. The entire countryside avenged him by killing virtually everyone in the area of the crime, since they could not locate the offenders. Over twenty-five thousand died for this rape and murder. There was nothing special about this man or woman. Their identities are not even mentioned. The last sentence in the book of Judges states that Israel had no earthly king at this time, leaving only God as their king and that everyone did what was right in the sight of God.

In a New Testament scene, Jesus was playing with children. When his apostles scolded the children for detaining the most high king, Jesus replied by saying, "suffer not the children to come unto me for unto such is the Kingdom of Heaven. Whosoever shall offend one of these little ones of mine would be better off if a millstone were hung about their neck and they be drowned in the sea."

The Rapist is aware of this and trembles. However...

Satan took Jesus to a high place and tempted him. "Service me and all these things I shall give to you."

The Evolutionist's Awakening of a Moral Cosmos

....

In my dream of life, this passing haze, I desire to leave my mark as favorable. A memory that will not condemn me, one that will show that, even though I was not able in my imperfection to leave my true intent, I was able to make a positive contribution. That desire deep within me and my searching is worthy, certainly what I left searchable by those who wish the same goal. I know there is no true judgment for or against me, as I know the truth. What will be left behind to prove me? The proof has to be shown. I leave my life as my proof. I wish all to advance closer to that which is good and perfect and that no child be left open to damage. I fervently hope that everyone can come to this.

The Hijacking

....

"The timing must be perfect, or the plan will fail. Shaan, you must shoot the guards in the face as soon as the escort vehicle has stopped or when you can get a clean shot. The driver first! In the face, Shaan, no radio communication of the situation must be allowed. If one of them reaches for the radio, everyone must shoot him first. We will be acting like the horse is still alive and that we only want to move it off the road. If the transport truck fails to stop, we must do a mobile hijacking."

"They're sure to stop. How can they go around a dead horse and a group of Mexican farm workers on a two-lane road?"

"We hope for this. Regardless, we will get the reactor. Once the truck has been immobilized, you will take your crew and enter the trailer from the rear. The nuclear reactor will be to the far front. Here is what the crate looks like; everyone look carefully at the photo."

"What are these pipes sticking out around the top of the crate?"

"That's where the acid gets dumped in, if the submarine sinks. It's a safety mechanism. The acid dissolves the plutonium core, which is not currently in place. We have plutonium. Our mission is to steal the compact secret reactor, that's all. Leave the acid. It's far too dangerous to transport. The barrels of acid will be strapped to the inside walls of the trailer. Stay clear of them and absolutely no shooting in the trailer. You don't want this stuff on you. Mustafa, after we've secured the reactor, you drive the truck to Eugene. There, you abandon it in this parking lot and go home to Chicago. They're not expected in the Bremerton naval shipyard until tomorrow afternoon. The GPS system will let them know they're on time for the scheduled overnight stay in Eugene. We will be loading the reactor in Coos Bay. Any further questions?"

"How many escort vehicles?"

"Only one, there is no plutonium present. They don't consider the reactor by itself worth the trouble of a formal escort. We expect four persons; the truck driver will not be armed."

"In the face?"

"In the pig's face!"

Predator Down

. . . .

The definition of "predator" by the evolutionist Charles Darwin: Any animal capable by instinct to track and ruthlessly kill another living entity by any means, including surprise or open threat. The predator has no thought of compassion, as it will devour the raw flesh of the living. The positive attribute of the predator is that he keeps the weak population in check.

The negative attribute of the predator is that everyone is weaker than the king of predators, Man. That brings up the question, "Why does this predator exist?"

The Sentencing

. . . .

"All rise. Judge Leonard presiding."

"Good morning. If the state would please bring me up to speed, as I have just gotten back from my vacation in Mexico."

The Prosecutor, Mr. Hasselman, looked puzzled at this judge's unusual and certainly unbecoming statement. Most were not aware of the real behavior in sex-abuse prosecution courtrooms. The manner in which a federal judge handles a tax case is a dimension of difference from a county child molestation conviction. Perpetrators start losing their hair at this stage of the road to Hell, just from being surprised by courtroom attitude. Hasselman had worked this particular case for ten years and had high hopes that Judge Leonard would be angrily aware. The defendant, Mark Johnson, was the slickest of them in that he had fooled the young district attorney ten years prior by turning himself in after a short flee. Johnson had also gone to Mexico while being investigated for the sexual abuse of a five-year-old child, his own. Hasselman gave Mark an empathetic three-year probation sentence in 1998, since he believed this father had repented. Mark then returned to Mexico for ten years; it was all part of his master plan to avoid offender status.

Now, after being extradited to Eugene, Oregon, Johnson received no empathy from the prosecutor. Hasselman now had to convince Judge Leonard of Mark's evil without being embarrassed about letting him slide ten years before.

"Your honor, of all the cases I have prosecuted, this is certainly the one I regret the most. I believed Johnson was sincere, when he came back from Mexico

ten years ago and knocked on the jailhouse door. I gave him a free ticket, your honor, in that I recommended a plea of attempted sex abuse in lieu of sodomy and first-degree sex abuse that he truly committed. Your honor, the victim was his own biological daughter and was very, very young…"

"Hasselman, you seem to think I am a piece of furniture," Judge Leonard exploded on Hasselman. "Allow me to enlighten you that I do have the five senses!"

"Yes, Sir, it's just that you asked to be brought up to speed."

Leonard, having been aggravated with this prosecutor, abandoned protocol and calmly addressed the defenseless Mark Johnson.

"Mr. Johnson, if you wish to contest this hearing, stand up; do not look at me but turn around and face the people of the state of Oregon. They are your accusers."

Mark stood and momentarily cringed at the sight of the filled courtroom. The eyes of everyone Johnson's knew were on him, and he saw disgust in each. He showed no emotion, other than a slight touch of pride, which was interpreted just as guilty, as everyone there was, yet hypocritical. The judge took charge in his highly experienced and preplanned sentencing.

"Once again, you are in my court, Johnson. Did you think I would forget you?"

Mark turned to look at the judge and to answer. Leonard, however, knowing Mark's resistance to the system, quietly turned him away.

"I told you to look at the people, Johnson; do not think about looking my way again."

"But of course, Sir," Mark answered, turning away.

Leonard proceeded methodically.

"Johnson, you were given a huge break from twenty seven years in state prison in exchange for a plea bargain that amounted to three years' probation. I am appalled and, to this day, cannot understand or try to understand why you were released. The final sentence that went into your criminal history is labeled 'Attempted Sex Abuse,' a class C felony. What a break you managed to purchase by your treacherous but effective deception. I want you to tell the court what attempted sex abuse really amounted to."

Mark resisted in shameful silence but showed a hesitant desire to excuse himself by jaw movement and subtle biting of his lower lip.

"Mr. Johnson, I remind you that your decision to contest the hearing demands you answer my question," the judge said. "Contempt of court will be added to the possible revocation of your probation."

Mark looked over the entirely dismayed crowd and surmised an explanation.

"It means that the State of Oregon has the power to fuck you out of your children for doing what you know is good and wholesome!" he said, revealing himself.

Every eye was now on the judge in fear and curiosity. The prosecutor was in doubt about his position, thinking a dismissal was in the works. Judge Leonard was composed and wore a conservative smile on his unsurprised face.

"Mr. Johnson, the criminal charges that you agreed to in the plea bargain reads differently than what you just stated, in your opinion by the way, that what you did was good and wholesome," the judge said, calmly, dismantling Johnson's statement. "I remind again that you can be cited for contempt of court by lying. I also remind you that, in this court, you cannot hide behind this minimized plea bargain, which, had I known who you really are, I would not have signed. What were the original charges and explicit acts that you confessed to for being granted this remarkable plea of attempted sex abuse?"

Mark looked confidently at the audience of ever so curious appearance.

"I was originally charged with sodomy and sex abuse."

Leonard continued smiling and looked even more satisfied.

"Mr. Johnson," the judge said, "I am happy you only gave a half truthful answer; since you now say that the whole truth of what you did was 'good and wholesome,' and you said it with so much more heart. Now is your chance to tell us exactly what you did to this young girl that you claim to be so good."

Mark had to make his destiny; it was his last ditch position, due to his denial and arrogance, which could not allow him to say he was wrong."

Leonard maintained his cool, low voice and composure towards Mark but demanded that he enlighten the court.

"Come on now Johnson. Let's have it. What is it that is so 'good and wholesome' that made the State of Oregon fuck you out of being a father?"

Mark was highly agitated with Leonard's extreme passivity and postured himself defensively and blurted out his defiant position. "I rightfully kissed my daughter, where she knew it meant that I loved her, and it drew her closer to me. She loved me god…damn…it! She loved me even more after I kissed her there!"

Every eye lit the room by the whites alone. The silence was suddenly broken by gasps of shock and dismay. Heads turned, and the whispers became thoughtless rambling, since no one could put words into real meaning, but everyone knew what the jabbering meant. It meant they wanted to eliminate this man and to quickly move on, far from this disgusting scene.

Leonard brought the courtroom under control and proceeded swiftly.

"Mr. Johnson, you have your opinion, and it looks like the entire state of Oregon has a much different one. We made laws that everyone agreed to and you knew the law. You knew you were damaging your daughter, you knew you were only satisfying your monstrous self. You made things bad for yourself, today, but I planned this. I planned this, since I know more about you than you do. I will always be one step ahead of you, and you will fall many steps behind me, until you can admit you were wrong. I know what you don't, and that is, if you can simply step outside your arrogance and pride, someday you may accept being wrong is the right step.

"I went down to Mexico to see how good you had it. It's time to make up for it. I am revoking your probation and sentencing you to the maximum of eighteen months in the Oregon State pen house, without protective custody. If you complete this term, I am also extending your post prison supervision to thirty-six months. In the meantime, you can tell Bubba how wholesome your actions were. Sheriff Ward, get him out of here."

The Released

....

"Mr. Johnson, I'm Emily Wentworth your release counselor. How are you doing today?"

"I'm ready to leave."

"I'm sure you are, but I wonder if you really are ready for society."

"I did fine before and I will do well again."

"So you think you did well, hmmm. I want to read you something that you told your prison counselor just seven short months ago. Ready?"

"Oh, yeah, sure, go ahead."

"Mr. Johnson you said that in your entire history you never recall anyone in your family hugging you or showing you signs of affection. You said that you were never kissed on the cheek when leaving for school, not even as a young child. You state that all your family members, including your stepmother and stepsister, constantly teased you. You said that this was why you had problems and why you finally wound up going to prison. Your entire file consists of rejection, which is admitting on your part to having a real issue concerning criminal behavior. Tell me, does that reveal anything at all to you about what could become of you? I mean do you really think you did well and will do well out there, based on your own words?"

"I served my time that you all deemed was sufficient for me. You think anything you say now is going to change any one little thing about this whole fiasco? You can't even change the fact that I'm walking out of here in five minutes. Why be concerned? There is nothing you can do now except let me go."

"Mr. Johnson, I plead with you that you please remember this moment we had together. No one can say the words you said without causing others to wonder about what you truly know is right. You can't hide yourself from me. I know you're aware of what good you could be."

"I am what I am. Isn't that what the god of light told the barefoot lawmaker? I am not Moses. I am that I am and I am in charge now."

Prelude

· · · · · · · · · · · · · ·

"Don't kill the dog, Angie. I'll always want to remember that moment."

"The demon is dead in you, Mark?"

"Yes, Fabi. Very much so. I love you, too."

In these moments of madness, the media in the United States was having a heyday with the most publicized serial killing case in history.

"This is *World News Tonight* with Peter Jennings."

"Good evening and welcome. I'm Peter Jennings. The most profound criminal case in America dubbed the "Acid Rapist" has police coast to coast in the frenzy of the Twenty-first Century. On the loose, a serial killer who has discovered the perfect method of disposing evidence taunted police in Los Angeles. A total of five victims so far have been dissolved in a powerful, federally-controlled nitric acid compound and dumped onto city streets and storm drains in Pasadena, New York, Denver, Seattle, and most recently Boston.

"It is said that the Navy uses the acid to dissolve plutonium in the reactors of nuclear submarines in the event they sink. The killer taunted Los Angeles special crimes unit detective Bill Worthy three months ago by telephoning him from the disposal site in Denver, Colorado. There, the killer carefully drained the acid over the base of a metal power pole, which toppled onto a taxicab driver the next morning, killing the driver by electrocution."

"The first site discovered nearly six months ago on Route Sixty Six or Colorado Boulevard in Pasadena had police stymied. It was deemed an illegal

dumping of a regulated substance, which has high disposal fees of nearly two hundred dollars per gallon. The caller posed as New York police sergeant Les Allen, asking Worthy about the acid dumping on Colorado Boulevard, stating that he read about it in the papers. He then made Worthy aware of the dumping in New York."

"It's not clear why the perpetrator made the call, but what is clear is that he knew both Allen and Worthy. Worthy mishandled the situation. He did not properly follow up on the perp's call. The perp sent a blind fax of the Pasadena dumping report to Allen. Allen disregarded the report as routine. In the three remaining months, the killer struck three more times in Denver, Seattle, and Boston. These are only preliminary reports, as the case was brought to light this morning by Paul Harris, an inspector for the EPA, who tested the contents of the dumped acid and determined that it was inundated with hemoglobin, which is the iron in human blood. We have Mr. Harris live from Pasadena now. Connie?"

Chapter 1

The Hadrons Stay

❧

The beast is created and fed as all creatures are. What deviations take place in each human life mold the identity to its present state of tribal status. All deviations in the matrix of diversity conclude that we are creating an enlightened species. A human species of various deviations, which most identities are in the realm of acceptance. The tolerances allowed and demanded from the tribe, however, have definitive boundaries. There is one boundary, when it is crossed, is the blasphemy that even the God's do not allow plea. The masses have also cataloged this broken frontier as unforgivable and labeled for life "Offender ostracized in whom the worm dieth not."

Mark Johnson, age forty-two, fell from grace and was aware that he had. He did not tremble like the demons that compelled him. He went forth, knowing his destiny was to defy those that separated the cosmos from chaos.

As a child, he knew no guidance. His father had abandoned him by never knowing him. The street mother surrogate raised him to see what had only been in his past vision. Being fertilized by dark forces, he chose a cold outer tribe. Recruited by the street mother in Tacoma, Washington fed his destiny of alienation. His personal mentors were separation, shallowness, and selfishness.

Right out of prison for blasphemy, he went straight for defiance and picked his target from a phone booth in Eugene, Oregon, calling his accuser.

"Bare Necessities. This is Vicki speaking."

"Hey, Vicki, is Shea there?"

"God, Mark, you know she doesn't want to talk to you."

"I'm sure she will if you tell her I've got the child-support money. Ya know if she wants it."

"I don't want to relay all this."

"Come on, Vicki. You and I go way back. Hell, you used to do it for me and me for you. Can't forget that, can ya? Yeah, *Mamacita*."

"Not for you, but she does need the cash."

"Thanks, Baby."

"Shea! Pick up the phone."

"Who is it?"

"Hm. It's Mark! He's got the child-support money."

"Why doesn't he go through the courts?"

"You want to take his money or not?"

"Okay, yeah, right, but stay on the line with me. You know how he is."

"Right."

"First I'm going to be frank and make it clear, Mark. I do not enjoy talking to your kind. So you want to start helping out your…ah can't believe I'm saying this…*my* daughter after five years, huh?"

"It's good to hear your voice! I was in jail by the way."

"You were in jail for eighteen months, and that's because you violated your probation. We worked a deal so you wouldn't have had to go in. But no you blew it and went back to Mexico so you could be with your Maria."

"Never would've found me if I hadn't come back and rang the doorbell."

"What? Are you bragging?"

"Not at all. I'm saying I came back voluntarily."

"Not the way I heard it."

"I'm interested in what you could hear fifteen hundred miles away. I still have a house in Cabo. I could bail now, and the cops would never know a thing. Besides, the charges were reduced from a Class A to a Class C felony. They wouldn't even think about extradition."

"You're right. You're small time even to the pigs. Besides that, you probably got kicked out or couldn't make it there. What did happen? You lose all your money to a whore you thought was the perfect woman? Ha. What was her real name? I saw from the police report you married some Maria."

"Didn't really get married."

"Ah, so you did get taken!"

"Her name is Maria. She's fine but got into hitting it."

"I was right. You were forced to return. But I thought you liked druggies. Ha, I'll bet she's a bi case too?"

"Had the best time of my life in La Paz. She taught me a lot. She showed me how to forgive."

"Who do you need to forgive? Maria, for taking all your money? Ha ha!"

"Why can't you forgive this? Did this here thing for you. Came back and turned it in."

"Heather, your daughter, that's why! I should have known you were going to skip out. I'd have recommended the full twenty-seven years you had coming. I'm the one who recommended probation, Mark, but of course I was influenced by your patsy friend Marilyn, who I know you bribed."

"What did she have to do with this?"

"After you came back and turned yourself in, she called me day and night to go light on you. She still loves you, even after you ran back to Maria or your house in Cabo!"

"How could you go light on me?"

"The DA asked me what I wanted to do with you. Now I kick myself. I'd have loved to come to the prison and visit your sorry ass for twenty-seven years. I would have been on time for each and every birthday you had left. I don't think you would've made it to seventy-five in there."

"Didn't work out that way. I actually had the time of my life. Much better times than you had."

"You're right. While I was taking care of your...I mean *my* daughter, you had your whore. You know how hard it was for me to finish the nursing program!"

"You're a nurse now?"

"No! They said I wasn't fit. Wasn't fit! Because I had so much trauma in my domestic affairs. You probably don't know what that means, do you?"

"I know a lot about these things, you know, Shea. I studied some in school to. I learned that whatever a person takes in there is always a little of that something that stays inside us. That little portion can never find its way out."

"What have you got inside you, Mark? Do you know what's inside me or my daughter?"

"Oh yes, I do. You feel so much of it is all about you; even all the love I once gave you is still there."

"You hurt us so much. Now you want to bring back this shit. Why? Do you really think I'd buy it?"

"It's there in you, Shea. You still feel the love. Even the biologists know this. A tiny piece of everything you ever took in is still there. Even food stays in you, Shea. Did you know that some of your mother's milk is still in you? Yes, it's a fine mix in and all about your body. Remember all the times you swallowed it, Shea?"

"What are you talking about?"

"Scientists and doctors all agree a piece of everything you eat, a small part, stays inside you for life. The hadrons never go away. We're connected, honey. A part of me into you forever. Remember all the times, especially that long trip to the desert. You did more than cuddle for ninety plus miles. Oh, yeah, Shea, it's all in and about you now. You swallowed, and it's in you forever. . ."

"You total scum bag, Mark . . ."

"Vicki! I should have known you'd want to listen in. You always did like my gab. Ahead of my class I got delivery now coming out the house. Got it down. Shea's gonna be sick for ten motherfuckers. Yeah, you're a spitter, Vicki, but not Shea. The smut's deep in and all about her. Probably in her tongue. Her taste for men has seriously regressed since I left. Only Shea will cry tonight. It's good to cry, lying in your bed. On your vacant side. Your side of the bed that you made. It's in you, Baby. Mmmm, cry. . ."

"Go to Hell!"

Vicki and Shea hung up. Shea was gagging and began to dry vomit.

"God, I never knew he could. God, how does this guy get to me? I didn't know you were with him, when I—"

"It's okay, Vicki. He was so cool when we met. Together just long enough to do me and turn moron. Damn he's done it again. Help me to the bath."

Shea's thoughts dwelled on Mark's words to the point of convincing her. For days, she would be nauseated, thinking about the long bent-knee drive to the desert with him. This sickened her to the point of nearly drowning in her vomit. She had detested Mark for five years without his direct intentions of unwarranted revenge. He vowed to bring her down. This was the beginning of his vengeance. Mark had always been deadly accurate with his words. Shea respected his mind. She knew he was right, slowly acquiring his desire.

Shea was barely eighteen years old, with one child, when she was seduced in by Mark's bait. The sight of his Porsche 911 carefully posed in her path was but one of the few shallow lures Mark relied on. Wouldn't it make perfect sense that she would take the bait? Mark had learned to break the rules to this point without consequence. The law could do nothing to Mark, but society and the circle around him punished him by rejection that he was numb to.

Shea was a new fish in the tank Mark had purchased off the street. Her hardknock history of neglect and juvenile crime was the recipe for being attracted to the abuser's tack. Having given birth to her first daughter, Quetzali, when she was seventeen, Shea was single and in need. Quetzali's father ran out when he was discovered to be an illegal alien. After his deportation to Mexico for drug trafficking, her family and associates ostracized Shea. On welfare and no hope of

a ladder to success, Mark was good usable meat for her. She thought she knew what she was doing when she said yes. *I can use this account to make mine fat*, she thought. She had no idea what she'd gotten herself into.

The life they tried to live was of high value, with no drugs, little drink, and no cheating. She lived with him as a would-be wife, doing her best to support Quetzali. She was now actually being a good mother. But Mark's veil had fallen, and the true misfit character drained Shea's will to stay. His daily selfishness and use of her body depleted her of the identity she desired, so dearly, but which she had already lost. Shea became mentally traumatized and physically dehydrated of life. She realized she was in the same trolley she'd been in with Quetzali's father and her past.

In Shea's own lack of discipline, pregnancy and Heather came within eleven months. The custody battle was lost to Mark, not by a court but by Shea's inability to manage two children. She left for California when she lost Heather at six months. Mark waited until she was five to cross the chasm and blaspheme her spirit by the ultimate father-daughter-bond betrayal. Shea blamed herself. Quetzali and Heather blamed her. So did Mark.

Mark fled to Mexico following the run-away trail of Quetzali's father, seeking escape. The weak gringo couldn't adjust to that environment. Mexico was for the truly social. He knew prison would be easier in the States. Mark got lucky, as he had no criminal history and the prosecutor was naïve to sex-crime behavior. On the street now, not in his cushy home, the registered predator had it in his mind there was no recourse and no hope of redemption.

Jeremy, Mark's longest known associate noticed him in the phone booth, while driving by. He pulled his 1989 Chevrolet Camaro hot rod to the curb. "Mark! How'd you get out of the hokie?"

"Jeremy! God, where did you come from?"

"Kinda hard to miss a tank like you wearing a beaner shirt like that in a booth! What's up with that?"

"Ah, old clothes from Cabo, you know . . ."

"Get in. Paula's waiting for me at Marie Calendar's."

Mark got into the Camaro, clearly identifiable as the shared family car because of the child seat in the back, Paula's scattered belongings on the floorboards, among Jeremy's crumpled beer cans. Paula'd always been somewhat of a carefree woman, a magnet for Jeremy.

"God, Jeremy how are you?"

"Surprised as hell to see you! Paula's going to have a cow when she sees you!"

"She still working at Calendar's?"

"Ha, working? You know better."

"Yeah, I'd like to see her again. So it's all cool, huh?"

"Hell yes! She knows you got some of that money left, ha ha. You do, don't you?"

"Damn, Jer, you never change. You still banging your head to Metallica, right?"

"I grew out of that!"

"Yeah, well I lost all my CDs, anyway. You remember all the videos?"

"Ho boy, how could I forget video! You sitting in front of your big screen every day and night, driving Paula to save Jesus. Anyway, what's up?"

"Lee's kid is driving big rigs, so thought I'd give it a shot. I'm in school now."

"No way, Mark. Are you gonna drive?"

"Kinda did lose all that money, dude."

"What?"

"I bought two houses in Mexico, but because of the warrants, I had to put them in ah, someone else's name."

"This Maria I heard about?"

"Yeah, you must have heard that from Shea."

"Nope. Trina. She was over looking for some smoke, blabbing away as usual, you know."

"God. She must be a total airhead by now. That's why I punted. She smoked the clover over five times a day."

"Yeah, Mark, but she was the best you ever had. I mean. . . "

"I know what you mean. That girl was good but killed the last brain cell. I don't think she even knew her color.

"She had a number of colors, Mark."

"I did love that chameleon. I think she was the only one I ever loved."

'Still fantasizing?"

"Ah, you know that, but had to drop back. It was out of hand. If she only could've gotten off that shit. Hell, yes, I'd be married to her now. I'm going to hook up again, real soon."

"You'd better forget about the women around here."

"Hmmm, I don't even want to look at a white woman again, especially one from the U.S.A. I love women. Black women especially. Those women are level and reasonable. Shea broke Marcel and me up."

"I remember that. You did bring that young black girl over to my house. Paula and I said you never looked so happy."

"I was, but for some reason, I only loved Trina. I'll find another hottie better than her."

Trina had the look to turn every head in a pageant but only to look away due to her insobriety. "I am kinda wondering why Trina? Couldn't have been her bod," Jeremy said, toying with Mark's head.

"She was the hottest, wasn't she? Man, I loved making out with her."

"Mark, I hate to tell you this, but the local news stations broadcast and flashed your ugly ass on the late newscast. I read the police reports. Shea brought them over a few years back, after you split the first time to La Paz. You're right. It was all hearsay. The report had no evidence in it. I don't care. I hated Heather, since she had everything and didn't appreciate it. If I had all that and my father did something fucked up, I'd have shut up. I have to tell you that I don't believe what I read. Whatever you did do, I don't care. Like I said, I hated her. I think the trucking job would be a good way to get on with your life. By the way, forget about Trina."

"Hard to do. But it don't matter, 'cause I'm gonna get laid tonight."

"That, I don't wanna know about, but as far as Trina goes, I know. Look. Don't be down. We... you know Paula and I don't hate you. Just be cool now. I know you. I don't think you're the plague. You just screwed up in a bad way. Ah shit, you know what I mean. Oh geeze. I can't believe I said that to you. Fuck."

"Oh, that's what I needed to hear."

"You know that guy, Harold The guy from Nigeria that you sold your business to. He lost the whole damn thing in four months, which was every client. I and everyone else knew you were the best. You kept that company together for seventeen years. Hell, now that I think about it, I worked for you one month too! You fired me right?"

"Well shit, when I went to check on you, they said you and Paula left four hours early every day. Like you said, I was good at what I did."

"Yeah, I could never get to that level of ambition. What made you burn so hard at it?"

"God, I dunno. To me it seemed natural to make the big moola."

"I guess. Twenty thousand a month clear. Goddamn Ferrari, motor home, two BMWs. . ."

"Damn, don't bring back those memories. I lost all that to another bitch in Mexico."

"Paula thinks you did all that so you could attract all those young girls like Trina, Shea, and Marcel."

"Yo, Jeremy! Shake that dust off me now."

"Okay, so you liked stock-piling exotic cars! How many Porsches did you have? Ha ha."

Mark's mother died when he was just short of five years old. His father remarried within a month to a dominating woman. His father retreated completely, ignoring Mark while his stepmother was someone Mark had to *deal with*, rather than be *mothered* by. At eleven, Mark realized that his father had murdered his mother. He never let it out. He'd hold onto it to his grave.

Mark failed in his profession as a certified public accountant, due to his fears and antisocial disorder, which did not mix well with the highly professional office environment. He never made it past the initial interviews for job placement at the University of Oregon. He was educated but barely passed the four-year accounting program in five and a half years. The truth was that he could not make it flipping burgers or in any job that required adult interaction. An elementary school teacher in charge of children or a clergy member would suit him well but his education was of a different sort.

The janitorial company was his killing field. He learned the skills in high school, since he could not hold down the burger joint or grocery store jobs. A janitor worked alone in the grip of the night. As a cleaning company owner, he would prosper. The clients were easily fooled by his educational background and the high quality of his self-recruited cleaning staff, with whom he didn't have to communicate. Presently, Mark decided on the truck-driving profession for the same set of qualifications and shortcomings. Mark knew who he was, but there was so much he didn't know.

Jeremy prodded Mark about his short life in Mexico.

"So, what happened down there? We all thought you'd never come back to face this, unless you more or less got caught. You always were so prudent with your...you know, the life you had. Ha!"

"Everything wrong happened down there. You think it's hard to have it going on here, just step into that vacant lot. Everybody is after you from the *Federali* to the burglar. Prison life is better here than being free there. You know my house had a metal door and bars on the god-damn windows! Man, you have to be numb tough to make it in Mexico."

Mark was girl watching as they drove, and he noticed a young blonde.

"Hey, look at that fine babe over there!"

"That's Paula, Mark!"

"Oh, ah sorry, Jer."

"What the Hell is she doing? Who is that guy with her?"

"Oh, man, keep rolling, Jer. Park this thing around the corner and be cool."

Mark recognized the person as detective Rainey, a much-run-into annoyance.

"This way. You want me to go this way?"

"Better to be cool; this could go down bad."

"Why do I listen to you?"

"'Cause you know I'm right, and that guy looks like he could kick both our butts."

"All right, but I'm only laying back for a minute. She's supposed to be at work. We got bills to pay, and I work my ass off. Look, now there's a cop talking to her. That's it. I'm on it."

Jeremy pulled a U-turn and whipped his Camaro to the curb. The plain-clothes officer gave Jeremy a grin, showing that he knew him. "Off work early huh?" Jeremy said.

"Paula acknowledged Mark by ignoring Jeremy."

"Hi, Mark! God it's been forever!"

"Close to it. What is it this time, Paula, prostitution? Ha ha."

"You're the same."

"The truth about you too, huh!"

"God, you guys cut the shit," Jeremy was beyond livid and exploded. "What's my wife doing here?"

The plainclothes detective identified himself to Jeremy. "I'm Officer Rainey. How are you, Jeremy?"

"Identified me so soon, heh?"

"My job, but your wife gave you up. She's here because Marie Calender's got robbed. The suspect is inside and she's the only one who saw him, so we needed her for an ID."

"All right a cop with a sense of humor. Don't you usually do a line up for this sort of thing?"

"Not when the suspect is dead."

Jeremy took a step back, startled. "Christ! Are you all right, Paula?"

"Considering this happened three hours ago and that he had a thirty-eight up my nose, not doing too bad."

"I'm sorry, Babe. I knew it had to be something like that."

"What?"

"What he means, Paula," Mark said, answering for Jeremy, seeing that Jeremy was in shock, "is that he's happy you're OK."

Mark reached out to shake Paula's hand, but she pushed it aside, momentarily looking him up and down then hugs him. Paula wondered what she had just done when she got back her presence of mind. Mark was now convinced of

the security of his position and gratified. She had to continue in that vein, now and did so by senseless verbalizing.

"Are you okay is the question, Mark."

"Better now, thanks."

Officer Rainey, knowing Mark well told Paula she could go. He communicated to everyone by eye contact that Mark was not a model citizen. Jeremy, strengthened by Paula's outward stance, refused Rainey's unspoken message.

"So you want to come over for dinner like old times Mark?" he asked. "It's Friday and Paula just sits around. C'mon, let's delve some Beam black label. Wasn't that the ticket?"

"Ha ha! God, you're tearing this up. You're talking my language now. It's all good with you, Paula?"

"If you're buying!"

Detective Rainey had been rejected and wrote down the license plate number from the Camaro, as well as the Beam black label suggestion.

Paula, Mark, and Jeremy prepared to leave. Paula again gave way to Mark, by getting in the back seat. She slightly questioned herself as to why she hadn't initially refused to have Mark over. She realized her current trauma allowed it.

Jeremy and Mark were as close as best friends meeting as neighbor's twelve years before, in 1988. Through wild parties, Mark's divorce from Sandy, and by shared secrets they absolutely couldn't tell, they had a common interest. Yet, there was a chasm of difference they each acknowledged but nebulously ignored.

Paula filled them in on the robbery.

"Loser had snot running down his chin, and he sneezes this clap spooge all over my face! If I were a man, I'd have grabbed the gun. The look in his eye was like he could do me, but I refused to believe it. His hand was shaking so hard I don't think he could've hit me."

"That would have scared the hell out of me, Baby."

"Terrified me, that's why I didn't grab the gun. I couldn't move. I mean even after he left. You know you see in the movies the bad guy says, 'don't move or get up or count to one hundred before you get up.' That kinda shit. Well, let me tell you something, they don't have to mention that shit. I didn't think I was gonna move my ass for a week. My neck is still hard to move and I don't know if I pissed my pants or I got wet. It was hard to tell, 'cause I just took a piss before he goddamn stuck that thing up my right nostril."

"Jesus, Paula!"

"Jeremy, you think I'm going to swallow this without a full throttle blowout? Put yourself in there. Now I know what it's like to be in a position you damn sure have to be in to understand why my pants are wet!"

"So, what do you think it was, Paula?"

"Was what, Mark?"

Mark chuckled, as he conducted his brash inquisition. "I mean, did you wet or did you get wet?"

"Mark! Man you are as messed up as her, dude. All this disrespect, not to mention the fact the guy was blown away. You guys get real."

"No, this is real, Babe. I can see where he's coming from. Yeah, I got wet! Real sloppy wet. I don't understand it. It was like a faucet got turned on and it wasn't my bladder."

Jeremy was highly agitated now. "Why the hell would you get wet with a gun in your face, Paula?"

"It wasn't sexual, let me tell you. I don't know what that was!"

"You sweat."

"Again, Mark! I always wondered if you were a troubled sleeper. You got bad insomnia, man? Jesus, dude, we're going to go eat now."

Jeremy was hysterical and on the verge of putting Mark out. "What am I missing here? What the…?"

"No, dude, I heard that right before a woman gets raped, her emotions hit the water faucet," Mark rationalized. "It's a body response, like almost disconnected from the head but not. Like an extreme forced-submission thing. Almost as if it was saying, 'okay, I know what's coming, so give it!' It gets wet. Paula, you know our armpits sweat when we get stressed, why not there too?"

"Oh, my God, you guys, let's get the Beam and go home!"

"Sounds good to me," Mark replied, knowing he had overstepped. "What about you, Paula?"

"No sweat off my…well, you know, don'tcha Mark?"

Jeremy and Paula laughed it off, but this silenced Mark. His difference was always showing as the offender's behavior, which he often ignored at costly ignorance. Mark constantly thought to himself about the sweat. He thought about the smell of sweat in the sense of attraction to mate as an animal. He related the odor of the armpit to the vagina. This predator from evolutionary beginnings melded with modern societies' perversions, such as porn deviation contributed to his deviance. Oral sex and a very young female vagina completed his narrowed little world. He always thought of the perfect woman he could delve into. Paula's directed remark of no sweat turned him off. He wanted perfection in the behavior

of a woman, and he also wanted the body young and clean. All the while, in his mind, he sought the powerful dream of taking control of what he worshipped.

Mark had left tropical paradise in La Paz. His money running down had threatened his security. He longed for Maria and was starting a journey that would bring him to do anything for her. His desire for her was the perfection he sought in his mind; it was far from love, but it was close to who he was. Maria was his escape. Meeting her in San Pedrito when he had first fled from justice had saved him from spending the rest of his life in prison.

With international warrants out for his arrest, she hid him well. Everything he bought she accepted in her name. The two houses, the second one used for rental income, since he could not work because of the warrants were in her name. They sold this home two years afterwards, because they needed cash. Maria gladly gave Mark the proceeds from the cash sale, and he hid it away. At the onset of their relationship, he suffered her lifestyle by living between her family and a shoddy third-world apartment. Mark learned a new culture that he came to respect, and he loved La Paz for its reality. He knew she was his only way of survival. Few women in this part of the world ever received the blissful treatment and attention she had.

She loved Mark and felt great sympathy for him. That was exactly the feeling he wanted her to feel. Mark led her to believe he had a death sentence pending in the United States for murdering the man who had raped his daughter. Nothing could have made her protect him more. She had been fooled into believing that Mark's love, simply because he never had to tell her in the first place. That, alone, fooled Maria into believing Mark actually trusted her. That was precognitive during his planning. The truth is that the sex offender is the most cunning and tricky of all criminals. Most do not get arrested; many get caught but not charged. There are hundreds of thousands of adults walking around in society who were sexually abused as children, keeping it to themselves. Many of those become sexual predators, and what's worse, many more who will offend have never been sexually offended.

A true native Mexican, Maria was part of a culture that rebelled against the corrupt system. She was a two-year victim of sexual abuse by her father, between the ages ten and eleven, and this deepened her bond to Mark. He had given her his phony confession about brutally killing his child's rapist, long before she had told him of her father's abuse. Her deeply rooted hatred for rape and fits of rage from the damage done, had been crushing Mark since the day she told him. She gave him detailed explanations of how her father would orally sodomize her and told him that the inmates raped him several times before killing him, after he had

served five years of a twenty-year sentence. This knowledge gave Mark a gastric ulcer and neurosis.

In his self-centered world, it took Mark two years to see how badly damaged Maria was. Her fits of extreme rage directed at him seemed to come from nowhere but, in fact, were being subconsciously triggered by his mere presence. The subliminal character of a child molester's presence and her experience caused her awakening from the temporary dormant Hell in her head. Her instincts were aware of Mark's actual past, but she was incapable of consciously identifying him due to his brainwashing.

Mark believed this rage was his god-sent education for what he had inflicted upon his own daughter. He realized Maria had no real normal social behavior due to her father. Even in the bedroom, he saw her real history unveiled, reliving her father's abuse. She would constantly take Mark's hand to grab her hair (as if he would force oral sex) taking the place of the sodomy she had suffered from her father. Semi-screaming in each moment with detested and confused desire, she begged Mark to continue in this daily ritual, haunting him of his own crime against his daughter. This radical reversed karma seemingly coming from God as payback, slowly disintegrated his unstable being to near psychosis. Sex became unwanted justice. This brought to his unstable mind the idea that there were controlling powers outside the flesh, powers to be revered. He was convinced that the powers of light had focused on him for eternal punishment, by putting Maria in his path.

Finally understanding Maria's condition and reason for being, he felt driven to make the difficult decision to turn himself in. His temporary sorrow for Heather had forced the decision. He drove to Eugene, Oregon, and knocked on the jailhouse door.

After he experienced the inside of a state corrections facility, he made it clear the plea would be not guilty.

Maria had no idea why he left. The revelation that the man making love to her was the same as her father would have been ultimate betrayal. She called Mark's father in Portland, Oregon, and he let her know Mark was in jail. He withheld the reason, causing her to withdraw by blaming herself. She would fervently pray for Mark on her hands and knees in her now empty home. Maria wanted, with every fiber of her being, the one back who she thought understood her.

The original DA wanted to sentence Mark the full twenty-seven years that he had indicted for. Mark could not have timed his first return to justice more in his favor. The original DA was out with a serious injury.

The state was forced to throw the case in the lap of a young, overloaded prosecutor. He had no time for the case because of several high profile cases that were being prosecuted at the time, including the nationally televised mass shooting at Thurston High School in Springfield. The courts and DA decided to release Mark to a three-year treatment and probation program, granting a five-day jail sentence for his timely return for justice. He could be given eighteen months if he violated his probation.

Mark did violate the terms of his parole by returning once again to Mexico. His falsehood and pretentious side of the relationship with Maria brought further disintegration. The fickle and inept rapist returned to Oregon a second time, within three months, to his should-be lifetime home, Oregon State Penitentiary. Once again, the system locked up another monster for the grand total of an eighteen-month Hell and gladiator training. This time, a new monster, reinforced by the system, was released. Now, living with Jeremy's family, the monster loved the system and operated parallel to it, knowing the law couldn't touch him. To him, it was a contest.

And who supports sex offenders? The ones who do not believe it, their friends and family. Paula and Jeremy were prime, real-life examples of how these convicts manage.

Chapter 2

Poison

❧

"Hey why don't you crack open that Beam? There's some Coke in the fridge. I've got to change. Be out in a minute."

"All right, Jer. Got ice?"

"Paula, do we have ice?"

"Yeah, it's out in the freezer in the garage. I'm going to shower. C'mon, Jeremy."

"Can you wait a bit, Mark?"

"Sure, why not? Mind if I turn on the tube?"

"Go for it."

Jeremy and Paula retreated to their bedroom and showered in the master bath.

"Jeremy, we never really talked about Mark. The extent of this thing . . . and you know . . . what if he's . . . ?" Paula asked.

"Paula you know Shea. Don't you ever forget the shit she put you through. Hell, she admitted to filing a false restraining order against him. She even signed a legal document stating that she lied. I've never known him to be sick or violent. Shea's a goddamned stripper for Christ's sake."

"You think she's capable of falsely accusing Mark of sodomy?"

"Look, she lost her older kid. She had to give her up to adoption. She had her tubes tied after she gave birth to Heather. The whole idea of her having Heather was to snag Mark's money. He didn't even want a kid. He got a vasectomy right afterwards. The only way she could get Heather back was to accuse him. For six years, she was gone stripping in Sacramento, leaving Heather with Mark in the difficult years. She couldn't have won a legitimate custody case."

"She's the most screwed up bitch I've ever known. The first thing I really thought when all this went down five years ago was poor Heather. Now she has to live with Shea."

"You really thought that?"

"Yes, I didn't even consider that Mark raped her."

"The reports don't say that he raped her. He. . ."

"I know, and that sounded so weird to me that anyone would want to do a sick thing like that and, what's more bizarre, is visualizing Mark doing it! What was that part about the poison?"

"Shea accused Mark, said that Heather said daddy savored the poison of her... you know."

"God, that is sick. We have to make a decision; we can't play with this."

"Do you really think Mark would go down on his own daughter, Paula? I'm sure Shea made it up."

"How do you make up something like that?"

"Remember how Mark would always tell Heather things were poison, since he had all those cleaning chemicals from his business?"

"I do."

"He labeled everything bad as poison, so she would understand the consequences."

"Yeah, he did do that. It was so she wouldn't lie to him."

"I never got that part, Paula."

Paula convinced herself of Mark's innocence. This was the tragedy of friendship so many people fell into... *our best cannot not molest.*

"Yes, he did. He told her that lying was poison and that for every lie she told she had to tell two truths to wash the poison out."

"Think like a kid! How do you lie, Paula?"

"God, in Heather's mind, with the tongue."

"Mark always said he would lick her if she lied to him or did something wrong."

"Shea did make up this shit. She told her to say daddy licked the poison out of her privates. That's why he didn't have to go to jail. There was so much doubt they couldn't foresee a conviction so they cut a deal."

"No. They offered him no jail time if he pled guilty, but twenty-seven years in prison as a child molester if he took it to court and lost. What would you have done, Paula?"

"There's no doubt he's innocent."

"You didn't answer my question."

"Yes I did. To think after six years Heather was just going to strut up to Shea and say, 'Daddy savored the poison of my privates, Mom.' I can't believe that, in one day, all this bullshit could come about."

"Goddamn, Paula, you've been brutal lately. Anyway he's cool here?"

"Cool? I feel sorry for him. He can stay if he likes. God, that man did so much for us. He gave us a place to live for three months before Shea accused us of doing cocaine and forcing Mark to ask us to leave. She was trying to get Heather then wasn't she?"

"How so?"

"By making Mark look like he was hanging with dope dealers and endangering Heather."

"Yeah, and she was only back in town one week when she tried that, remember? You think she really knew we were getting high?"

"No way. Goddammit! How could I have been so stupid not to see all this? We could have helped him when he called on us."

"No we couldn't. No one would have cared. They wanted Mark. They thought Shea was Ms. Perfect. They didn't even know she was gone for four or five years more or less or that she was a stripper. They wouldn't listen to Mark. He was labeled from the get go. They didn't even really understand that Mark had full custody of Heather or that Shea never paid a dime of child support. There was a witch-hunt on at the time, and the pigs had screwed up when Compton's kid came up dead after many calls of abuse."

"I remember that. The cops never responded to those complaints, so they caught Hell for it. They weren't going to let that happen to them again, even if it was a bogus report."

"You about done, Babe?"

"Throw me a towel. Let's order pizza. I want to watch *Hellraiser*. That last movie you told me about."

"Cool! Mark will like that, too. You know he was a grip in that movie?"

"Then how will he like watching it, if he helped make it?"

"He was in Mexico when it came out. He never saw it."

"All right. Go out there and keep him company. I'm starved, would you order the pizza?"

"Sure. Sorry for not talking to you about the robbery, but you did bring Mark up first."

"Go on, we'll talk about that later."

A few minutes later, Jeremy was dressed and went into the living room.

"Hey Marko what you stealing?"

"Well, I was looking at the *Hellraiser* tape."

"No shit. Paula wants to watch that. I did get the message from my mom about you telephoning her from Mexico to look at the credits. When I saw your name pop up, I thought 'that bastard.' Now you wanna tell me how the Hell you managed that?"

"I was in Mickey D's talking with a babe about the book I wrote. This goofy fella, Vince Palomino just sat down and started running conversation at us. Couldn't believe this guy. He'd made over twenty movies. By the time he chowed his third Mac, I got the job. Anyway, I knew how much you liked *Hellraiser* so thought I'd give Nancy a ring to relay the message to you."

"No you didn't. You were bragging! Your book might have gotten published before all this shit happened to you."

Paula entered the room. "And it was a bunch of shit, wasn't it Mark."

"Hi, Paula. I'm relieved to hear you say so, but do you think so?"

"I know so. I was thinking about something else, too. Isn't Shea's father in prison for murdering her mother?"

"Been there since she was six years old."

"Why didn't all these fuckers understand that?"

"I already told you that they were on a witch-hunt, Paula."

"You guys been talking about it, huh?"

"We had to, Mark. You know that. But we know Shea and we've been hanging with you for twelve years. You ran a good business had a good family. You're educated, funny, and excellent with Heather. Now Shea, that's another story, considering she was a runaway stripper before you met her. She also worked for an escort service. Why you went out with her, I'll never know."

"I didn't know all that. She just walked up to me at the gas station, where Jeremy was working, and introduced herself."

"She planned that, Mark."

"How so?"

"She came over to our apartment every time you left, asking about you."

"Asking what?"

"The wrong things, like how does he afford a Ferrari and a Mercedes, you know."

"She knew I was going to be at the gas station?"

"Yes, she knew Jeremy worked there, of course. That particular day, he was working when you came over to our apartment looking for him. She heard me tell you he was at the station."

"So she came by the station to hook me?"

"Exactly."

"She told me she was on her way back from work and wanted to see what the car looked like. She mentioned something about too nice a Saturday for a Ferrari and a good-looking guy to be hanging out at a gas station. Jeremy was about to get off work and she mentioned that she lived in the same apartment complex, after she heard I was going there. That's how it all got started. I never knew she was scoping me."

"I didn't think you would have gone out with her. I didn't want to pry into your business, so I never mentioned it, after I saw you were happy."

"Mention everything from here on, please."

"So what's up with this trucking job, Mark?"

"You know, I'm really pumped about it. I've always liked to travel and I'm not into another relationship."

"I remember all those camping trips we'd take. Jeez we wound up in the Nevada desert once. Guy just keeps on driving. Whatever happened to that camper?"

"Down in La Paz; parked in back of my real estate agent's house."

"You must have had fun down there."

"Jeremy, I'm not shittin' you, it was the best time of my life. The Third World has the spot."

"I'm confused; you went down there then came back but then disappeared and…what?"

"After I came back and knocked on the jail's fucking front door, the DA thought I'd repented and lowered the charges to Class C felony, attempted abuse. My lawyer Gordon told me they would never extradite me for the reduced charges if I split again. I couldn't see any reason to stay here, when I had Maria and two houses in Cabo. Maria was calling me every day. I had to go back. In time, I ran out of options and money so I came back again and did the eighteen months. So here I am, now, waiting to crack some big dollars but wishing I was back in La Paz."

"Hell, I'd go right now with that waiting for me."

"Screw off, Jeremy!" Paula said.

"I meant the houses, Paula. Baby I'd take you with me."

"Sure you would. I've seen what those women look like when you get way down there in the tropics."

"So have I."

"Let's have it, Mark, is she a babe or what?"

"Damn, Jer, Angie is so fine. She's still got that Third World bone in her nose. Ah, she says things like…well…*pussy* openly. But she says it like pooszy. I'm trying to clue her."

"What does she say, Mark?" Paula had to inject, as she finds it funny. "Come here, Mark, eat my Pooo."

"Gawd, Paula, talk about me!"

"Jeremy, I'm just having fun with him."

"Yes, as embarrassing as it is," Mark replied, "she really does talk like that. She's so innocent that she doesn't know any better."

"Dumb too!" Jeremy puns jokingly.

Mark justifies himself by showing them a photo of Angie. "Here, look at her!"

"God, I guess she's fine. Look at this, Paula."

"That's not a this, Jeremy, that's one woman to beg for."

"God, Paula, sometimes I think your bi."

Paula chuckles gregariously. "I would be if she were here."

"Listen to this . . . Man!"

"She was bisexual, Jeremy."

"Who Paula?"

"No man, Maria."

"Why?"

"La Paz has a seven to one female ratio. But there were other reasons too."

"I don't want to hear it. What the Hell kind of reason is that to come back this time? You had it made and especially knowing if you came back, eighteen months were waiting for you in the big house."

Mark created a story without thinking. "She got into the dope and got really screwed up. Basically she ripped me off."

"It must have been horrendous down there for you to come back and voluntarily face prison."

"She pushed me out. Her Mother turned her against me to get the properties."

"So, why did you leave the camper there?"

"She wrecked the truck on a drinking spree."

"Wow lost it all, you poor bastard. I'd have considered suicide."

"Yo, Jeremy, Mark has enough problems."

"*Had* problems, Paula. I'm doing real good inside. I'm out of the joint. I have friends. Tonight, I feel on top of the world being with you guys. But Jeremy's right. I'd thought about suicide the moment I knew I'd lost Heather."

"So that's kinda another reason you left. You knew Shea would badger the Hell out of you in order for you to see Heather again. You had to give up on that idea."

Mark continued to create his strong illusionary defense enough to convince. "Shea will never let me see Heather again because Heather will break down and reveal the truth. I'm just waiting for the day Heather does it on her own. That was the big reason I came back the first time. I thought Heather would be able to come forward. But they made me this offer of twenty-seven years hard time, if I pled not guilty and lost or zero time if I pled guilty. I couldn't risk it. Who could risk it? That was the fucking dilemma. So, now I'm a pervert because of my guilty plea and Heather never had to testify."

"I wouldn't have taken that risk! Would they have put her on the stand?"

"Well, Paula, that's the part that finally helped me make my decision. Gordon said they didn't have to put her on. They would definitely have put Shea on, though, as well as a counselor that worked with both Shea and Heather. Shea knew exactly what to tell Heather and then relay it to the counselor in a way that would be startlingly consistent. Shea knew this kind of smut well."

"That's just like Shea, too."

"Definitely. I ordered the pizza, Paula. Actually, two, one for the *gran Mexicano*. I still can't get over the idea that you're going to be a trucker. When are you going to start?"

"I graduate this coming Friday then it's up to Grant's. They're the ones Lee's kid works for."

"Old Lee? The guy who used to supervise your business?"

"Yep, old Lee."

"I thought he was dead or would be dead by now."

"He did have all those problems with diabetes, but the old guy keeps on. He's got his own janitorial service now. Self Janitorial as he calls it."

Paula mentioned how Lee was able to clean her bathroom well past her wildest expectations with a product she didn't know but with which Mark was very familiar. "You know he used some kind of acid on my bathroom fixtures at the old house. That stuff made my toilet look spanking new. I need that stuff for this place."

"I can get it for you. I can go over to Nick's at Scott Supply Monday if you'd like."

"We need that stuff here, buddy," Jeremy added.

"All right, Jer. I'll go visit old Nick on Monday and pick up the acid. Here, you go take this. Jim Beam Black and Coke the breakfast of champions. A toast to my old and reliable friends."

Mark easily downed a triple shot of the whiskey, barely diluted by the cola, which he had also passed to Jeremy and he winced from its strength.

"Whoa, boy, you've been in the joint or Mexico. Tame that down a bit. By the way, I thought Mickey D's gave you heartburn."

"Not as bad as Shea has. But I'm about to change all that."

Mark had found a new home with his trusting amigos. Here he would reestablish himself the way he always had. The short-run opportunities had been swarmed to always lead to new territories. He'd learned that getting away was his way and it was now his for the taking. The real truth behind Mark's return to eighteen months of justice was hidden desire for his addiction. He knew that, deeply hidden within the monster, he would get greater opportunities after waiting the eighteen months. The rapist gives up life and limb for the God of desire. He knew that cheating and stealing advanced him much further than an honest day's work ever would. He would now steal life in exchange for the Morning Star's bonuses of a soul. Soon, the gods of society would bow down in a harvest of sorrow and regret.

Chapter 3

Follow the Majority on Monday

~~~∾~~~

"Hey, Mark, I haven't seen you in years. Where've you been? Buying over at our competitors?"

"Yeah Nicholas they always did have better cleaning products than you. Ha ha! This is my buddy, Wayne."

"Hi Wayne. Mark is a tool isn't he?"

"Yes, yes he is. So you know this guy well, Nick?"

"Made me rich, Mark did! He bought more cleaning supplies here for his janitorial company than everyone else combined. So, are you really buying from National?"

"Man, where you been? You didn't hear?"

"Oh, that's right, you turned the business over to Lee."

"No, Nick, I sold the business and moved to Mexico."

"No wonder I didn't know. I don't know a soul in Mexico."

"Nick, you don't know anyone here, except your wife!"

"I don't even know where she is. She left me four years ago about the time you did. Huh."

"Yeah, I took her to Cabo."

"What? Where's Cabo?"

"OK, Nick, it's time to lance back up here to some reality. You got any of that sixty seconds stuff around here?"

"Oh yes. You mean the acid for descaling toilets?"

"Yes."

"Well, I got some stuff here that's a whole lot more potent than that. You see, I ordered it through a fella come out here from Chicago, but it's real powerful. I can't sell it, except to licensed contractors, and even they don't want it."

"Why?"

"Hell, this stuff is so strong it'll eat through concrete. But if you dilute it down, it'll work on the meanest job you got. The only thing is, he stuck me with five hundred gallons in those big special plastic drums over there."

"So, how can we work a deal, Nick?"

"Well you gotta take a fifty-gallon drum, Mark. I'm not pouring that stuff."

"I can't afford a fifty-gallon drum of acid for a toilet, Nick."

"Well I'll tell you what. You take one of those drums and maybe I can get your business back from National."

"Nick, I was in Mexico!"

"Oh, Hell, I don't care who you're buying from; you started with me way back in 1979. I'll get your business back. Go on, take the drum up front there. That rig your driving tells me business must be real good. I don't know anyone driving an eighteen-wheeler in the janitorial business. You used to drive a Jaguar. Nice car."

"It was a Ferrari."

"Still a nice car. I can't believe that ignoramus and lost-minded alarm system you put in the thing. Not too good for the gander."

Wayne is set back by Mark's ownership of a Ferrari.

"You had a Ferrari?"

"Yes he did, Wayne. I went out to take a look at the damn thing one day. I touched it and it screamed at me like a whore out of toilet paper. Scared the bejesus out of me!"

"What the hell?"

"Hey, Wayne, how many alarms you hear go off every fucking day?"

"Enough."

"How many women you hear scream bloody murder?"

"You're mental, man. How'd you do that?"

"Had Shea scream in the alarm recorder. It worked. Kept the goonies away from my bitch. When she screamed, the cops definitely showed. They did once. Told me I had to change it."

"Did you really do this?"

"Yeah, I had her scream free sex into it a million times."

"No, twit, I meant did you just get out of jail? Sounds like it by the way you talk, or did you really do the alarm in the first place? I wouldn't waste my time

asking if you changed it! Incredibly childishly stupid, Mark. I don't think you're going to get this job dick. We about ready to get out of here, Nick? I think this guy's a weenie wagger."

"Oh, your mama. I've heard enough. I'll have Dave come up and give us a hand to load up the acid. It's super heavy."

"Oh boy, why not? I'll keep it at Jer's house. Maybe we'll find a use for it."

"Sure you will. A business booming like yours needs the heavy duty. Be right back. I'll get Dave to help you out."

Mark dropped into a daydream, contemplating his once torture-free past. Wayne easily clued into his problem of sorts.

"You okay, Wagger?"

"Mmmm…huh? Oh, I used to buy here all the time when I had my business. Wayne, thanks for letting me use the trainer rig."

"Sure, actually, why don't you drop me at my place and park it over at Jeremy's tonight? You two can unload it with the EZ lift, right?"

"Sure. That would work out good for me too. I just want to get out of here."

"Lot of old memories come back at the strangest places, don't they?"

"Seventeen years worth right here."

They loaded the acid onto Mark's training rig, and he parked the rig at Jeremy's residence. The visit to Scott Supply ripped at Mark, bringing back years of his livelihood memories. He thought he'd never see the light of a free day after his indictment, but this was torture to him. He had many sudden wake-up calls of his losses, due to his well-understood actions. Life was so hard now. Payback had gotten to him. The pay of labor in lieu of his previous cushy life of hot tubs and unlimited credit is what offenders cunningly avoid all their lives. Truthfully, though, he knew all too well that his life was dung, waiting to blow away. He could only come up with a substitute life now and he was subconsciously working at it full time. Consciously, he would hide from himself, not wanting to but able to face himself. He'd find a way to bleed his pain away. This was the only direction he had left.

Jeremy arrived home only to find Mark attempting to unload the acid from the trailer alone.

"What in the name of John Wayne's ass is going on around here? Parking a Ferrari at my house is one thing but a Freightliner the size of which. . ."

"Yeah, yeah, just help me unload this stuff."

"What stuff? You started burging already?"

"Right. I got the acid Paula wanted."

Jeremy was awestruck by Mark's decision to get the barrel of acid. "Dude! You got that for one goddamn toilet?"

"Only place in town that had it, and I had to take the drum."

"You didn't have to do that, Mark. What am I saying? Are you nuts?"

"Actually, we can find some other uses for it. This is pure and pretty deadly stuff. Clean anything if it doesn't eliminate it."

"Other uses? Dude, your sense of humor needed serious help years ago—but this! Well, what the hell. Let's check it out. You want to keep it here in the garage?"

"If it's all right with you. I mean this is some awfully bad stuff."

"Let's get it in before Paula gets home. What did you have to pay for this?"

"Two hundred, fifty."

"You sure you should be spending money you didn't lose in Mexico?"

"Ha! You still think?!"

"Yes I do. God, this stuff is a bit heavy!"

"Sure is. Let's kind of jockey it. I'm afraid to roll it. Might get away from us."

"I agree. Usually something this heavy is specialized."

"Yeah, they looked up my old contractor's license to sell it to me."[1]

"Jesus, don't tell Paula about this."

Jeremy and Mark maneuvered the acid to the trailer's EZ lift tailgate.

"All right, tailgate going down."

"Sounds like something you were taught to say."

"Isn't that weird? I did say it that way. They do teach us to announce it rigorously."

"Mark, I'm really worried about your normality, dude! It's really getting bad. Driving big rigs to my house and buying drums of acid, plus bringing your work home with you 'Tailgate going down?'"

"Only thing I'm worried about is getting this acid into the garage. How could this stuff weigh so much?"

"No doubt this is at least three times heavier than water. I can't deal with this. I'm going next door to get that scare-me-bad, corn-fed Travis."

"Travis! That's the ticket."

Jeremy got Travis, an oversized Oregon logger, whose looks nearly brings timber down, is amused by the request. Upon seeing Mark, his attitude becomes bovine in his direction, yet quite congenial with Jeremy. When Travis shakes Mark's hand, the hold is too suddenly solid and painful, yet Mark retains his composure.

1

"How the Hell are you!"

"Okay, Travis. How are you?"

"Right on top! Right on top of it. Well, this is a two-man job. Step aside, Mark. Jeremy, let's wheel it clockwise over to the right corner of your garage. I'll support it, you just wheel it."

"Let's go. It's pretty heavy, huh?"

"Goddamn. What the Hell's in here, Jeremy?"

"Industrial acid."

"That explains it. Don't get caught with this stuff in your place. It's illegal as Hell keeping it here. Probably as bad as the crack you smoke, huh, Jer?"

"I shoot it now."

"Damn, don't you make me drop this over, man. Whew. I'd hate to be the guy that works this warehouse. Well, now, is this where you want it?"

"That'll do you, monster."

"Not like some monsters, Jeremy. Gotta get back to the game. Forty-niners are on." Travis looked Jeremy in the eye relaying his message of having no desire for Mark to be living in the neighborhood.

"Thanks, Travis. Don't know what I'd do without your ugly butt."

The air between Mark and Jeremy needed clearing, but Jeremy truly had no doubts. He sensed Mark's dejection and knew exactly how to mend him. "Guy is a total asshole, but I use him for what I can. If he had half the brains he used to pump his biceps, he might get laid once a decade. He's just jealous because you had a Ferrari."

"That's all he ever saw of me, huh."

"Well, what'd you expect. White boy drive's that thing over here twice a week. Makes for some hard stroking for us poor colored folks. Speaking of stroking, bet that's about no fun huh, Mark?! You know if you quit masturbating, so much you'd look a lot better!"

"Yeah yeah. Ha ha. I'll get back to my babe soon enough."

"What babe?"

Mark's slip of the tongue wasn't a giveaway to Jeremy about Maria, but Mark knew the evidence would mount against him if he didn't start being more careful. There were so many lies to cover up, it was as though Mark needed three brains to process all the cover stories. He wanted to lie to Jeremy again, by inventing that there was another girl in Mexico waiting for him. He stopped himself from weaving a tale because of the stress of having to make it all up as he went. All that he was came into conscious thought every time he lied. He didn't want to face this person. It was time to avoid him.

"You know, my jack-off, pocket pussy, Jeremy, what else?"

"Chill, you lummox. You got something on the side I don't know about?"

"No, I guess it's gone."

"You're talking about Maria, right?"

"Well, it's not that I lied about Trina, but Maria was so good to me in the beginning and, considering the circumstances, I'll never be able to put that tropical woman out like I did Trina."

"That's because Maria put you out, dude, and you better get well over it, or you're going to be fucked beyond help. You want to go back to Mexico, back to her?"

Mark considered not being rude. Jeremy realized that he couldn't answer the question.

"You can't go back, man. She'll tear you up. It'll tear you up. You'll have to do five years on a second parole violation. You're here, man. You're here."

That was beyond Mark's comprehension. His entire motivation was to return to Maria. Maria was his only hope. Mark was like a truly faithful follower of Christ. He worshipped her as his only salvation. He couldn't bring himself to reveal that he'd failed as a man in La Paz, and that Maria was an abuse victim. He'd brought back the money from the rental house sale.

Being the extreme person he was, he had buried the sixty thousand dollars in the Eastern Oregon desert on Juniper Mountain. He hoped to make an investment during his short stay in the land of the free, to secure enough income for a life in Mexico with or without Maria. He hadn't worn out his welcome south of the border but, in his mind, there was no place stateside for him. This was his place of exposure. Oregon or any state was hideous exposure to Mark's total being. He could hide in Baja. He needed to hide. He could hide from himself there. Now was his time to get the rest of himself out of his psyche. He could not take this anti-harmony part to Mexico with him. He had to get it out, though only once wouldn't be enough. He was posed to attack many times, as the fuel was topped off. Not until he got close to being caught, would it be time to leave, and not until then. The monster wasn't growing; it had matured long ago. The fuel was the revenge in his mind. The fuel tank could never be exhausted or content.

Now, the monster was educated about how, when, and where to commit the crimes. He contemplated how to avoid more exposure. A child could catch Mark, but not a single, dead, adult female. He had to prove himself to himself and to all he knew. They would know it was him, but he'd be gone without pursuit without evidence, free as a natural born Mexican. Gone.

"You're right, old bud," Mark admitted. "I'm here. I think this job's going to work out fine for me, and I'll be able to start over."

"You got the job with Grant's trucking?"

"Well, he let me take the rig didn't he?"

"Yep, looks like you can start paying rent."

"Oh, man, I forgot. You need some money for that?"

"Where do you get all this cash? You've been in jail eighteen months, and now you're buying acid and who knows what else. I think your shitting me about losing all that money you took down there. What was it, quarter million?"

"All gone, Jer."

"Damn, I feel like kicking your ass."

"Me too!"

"Let's pop this cap open and draw some of the acid out. We need to clean up that bathroom before Paula gets here."

"All right, I have the draw pump in the cab. Be right back, homeboy."

"I'll unscrew the cap. That looks simple enough."

"Got it off?"

"Yeah, it has to be strong. The stuff is making my eyes burn from the fumes. Shit, I can't take this. You're not gonna like this. Need a mask for this one, Marko."

"Why, so you can breathe? Hmm I guess. Stand back a moment, Jer."

"What the hell have you brought home?"

"This is seriously unexpected. I've got a fire mask in the rig. I can draw it out with that on."

"Your call, Mark."

"Hold the pump, Jeremy, while I put on the mask."

"You look like a goon. All this for a bathtub and a toilet."

"Believe me, it's the last time I'm doing this. Get me a glass jar. You got a pickle jar?"

Jeremy got Mark the jar, and he pumped a pint of acid in to it. The fumes were too much for Jeremy, making him retreat. Mark took the jar of acid to the bathroom where he added one more pint of water. He slowly poured the acid around the fixtures and was surprised at how fast it worked. He set the jar down on the back of the toilet tank, with one inch of acid left inside. He removed his mask, only to immediately begin choking. Meeting Jeremy outside the two-bedroom duplex, Mark continued to gasp.

"Don't go in. I'll have to put the mask back on and open up the windows."

"It's that bad?"

"Way bad. I feel burned inside."

"No way. Are you serious?"

"I'll be OK. It was just for a split second, and I didn't breathe it in, just partially. But that fuckin' bathroom looks great. Here I go again, so Paula doesn't beat my ass."

Mark opened the windows for ventilation while Jeremy waited. Jeremy was not bothered by the turn of events; rather, he became more amused with Mark's unorthodox methods.

"All clear, dick?"

"I don't know; let me come out and take off the mask." Mark came out and removed the mask. "What a trip. I can smell it out here. Not so bad now, but it really fumes when it hits water. I'm going in to check it out." Mark returned to the bathroom without the mask and examined his work.

"How is it?"

"A little scent left. It's okay. I don't think Paula will notice."

Jeremy walked in and checked out the bathroom. "Ho looky that. Paula's going to think I bought a new stool. I'm not telling her about this acid. Don't mention that it's here, Mark, or she will go livid."

"I can't blame her. Just tell her I brought home the regular stuff I used to use. I'm going to lock up the rig and clean up the mess." Mark forgot the jar of acid in the bathroom, while he was hurrying to get the mess cleaned up. He closed the garage door, just as Paula drove up. He waved.

"Wow! Is this our new sport utility vehicle?" Paula said, as she got out of the car.

"SUV Paula, SUV."

"Is that what I keep hearing about? Oh yeah, sport utility vehicle. SUV. I get it!"

"You're a true blonde."

"I have so many blonde jokes. I get a new one every day at work, but Jeremy never lets me tell them."

"I wonder why"

"I don't know."

"Hey, quit razzin' my dumb blonde. Get robbed today, Paula?" Jeremy said when he came out.

"Worse than that. My boss had gas and farted all day. I had to tell everyone I had a cold."

"Why were you gagging?"

"No, dummy, I had to wear a food handler mask or I would have gagged. How can anyone shit all day like that?"

"Ha ha, Paula, you have had your moments, too."

"Not like that. He smelled like sewer shit."

"You sure have been agitated lately. Speaking of sewer, go check out the bathroom."

Paula eagerly moved to the bathroom, her place of privacy.

"Oh, wow, you remembered . . . daaamm this looks like new stuff here, man! Thank you, Mark."

"Piece of cake, Madam."

"What's that smell? It smells like something pungent was spilled in here."

"What's pungent, Paula?"

"Jeremy, I know a few words you know! So what's the stink?"

"Take a shower sweetheart."

"I can't now; your mother called and said I have to pick up Jerica. She's been called in to the hospital tonight."

"So, why did you come here first?"

"She wanted her uniforms that I embroidered for her."

"Yeah, Mark, my mom's a registered nurse now."

"I knew she'd make that. She deserves it."

"Well I'm off. Back in twenty. She's sending dinner back with me. Spaghetti and Dad's homemade bread that you got fat on."

"No kidding. Here's ten bucks to stack up some more calories. Stop at the Circle K and get some Pacifico. Isn't that the beer of choice, beaner?"

"Man you guys are being too good to me."

"Who said you were getting any? Ha!"

"I'm going to check out that football game. Do you mind?"

"I'll join you.

Jeremy and Mark made small talk, while Paula picked up Jerica, their eight-year-old daughter. Paula had given her first two children to her ex-husband's mother five years before. Her ex had been sent to prison for a number of petty crimes, including battery on Paula. She met Jeremy at a 7-11 store and was pregnant soon after. Three kids and no child support payments with a nine-hundred-dollar-a-month salary meant facing some harsh realities.

With Paula now working, they had just enough to make ends. Mark fit into the friendship, due to his inability to socialize beyond his small circle and knowing they could use him. His income status in the top ten percent was far ahead of his character. He had always found refuge from his loneliness with them between his short-lived relationships. His money also kept their interest up and questions

down, as he was very generous to them. Mark had to buy his women and friends. He'd never known real love. Witnessing his mother's painful screaming death was the first step in his disorder. His father's withdrawal and a prejudiced, abusive stepmother with a daughter his age both fueled and starved Mark. Fueled for success and starved of personality development, Mark's destiny was set. Paula returned with Jerica who remembered Mark well.

"Hi, Mark!"

"Wow you remember me, Jerica!"

"Not really. Mommy told me, but I do remember that pretty red car you always came over in."

"He sure did come all over in it!"

"Dammit, Jeremy, don't talk like that in front of her!"

"What, Paula? I came the first time I heard the alarm on it. Tried to steal it! Harsh, Mark, and you gotta be gay. Good thing you're not a redhead or then you'd really need to have it going on! Ha Ha!

"Jeremy, I mean it, not in front of Jerica! And besides, maybe he dyes his hair."

"Right. Anyway, Jerica has no idea what I'm saying, do you pumpkin?"

"I have lots of ideas Daddy, and I think you need to say you're sorry to Mommy and me too."

"OK, sweetheart. I love you so much. Come to Papa. I'm sorry my little meadow muffin. Mommy too. Ha ha. Listen to this. Dyes his hair! Paula you must have had a day!"

"Mark would you like to help me with the beer and. . . ." Paula resorted to Mark.

"Beer! Hell I'm on that. Sit down, Mark!"

Paula and Jeremy went outside to the car, leaving Jerica and Mark alone. Mark probed Jerica for Paula's real thoughts about him. Pay close attention to Jerica, he thought, actually labeling his character traits based on Paula's teachings.

"So, ah, your mama told you I was here, Jerica?"

"Yeah."

"What did she have to say about that?"

"She said that you were an inside person if everyone was outside."

"Really? Please tell me more."

"Okay. She said that if people were outside, you might watch them through the window or you would watch TV or something. If people were inside, you would be outside, but if it was raining outside, you'd stay inside, only you wouldn't talk very much. Maybe you would go to your bedroom and watch TV."

"What kind of person are you, Jerica?"

"I like to be outside with all my friends when we play. I don't like to just look at them or watch TV by myself. I would feel really lonely if I did that. It's good to be with your friends. You can talk and play so much you know. I really like talking to my Daddy. He's really funny. Mommy says he's a shh 'a smart ass,' hee hee."

"Well, you're right about that, Jerica. Don't worry, I won't tell that you said that. We can keep all of this a secret, can't we?"

"I knew you wouldn't tell. I won't either, don't worry."

"How did you know?"

"I can tell. I can see it in your eyes. Mommy says you can see a lot from a person's eyes. Why do you like to be inside?"

"Well, I really don't want to be inside. I feel out of place at times. Paula just sees it in a different way. I really would like to go out and play with you."

"Goody, but maybe tomorrow; it's dark out now."

Jeremy entered the living room partially hearing the conversation.

"Cold like a mother-father, too! Jerica, go change your clothes."

"Okay, Daddy."

"Check this out, Mark."

"I don't think this came from your mother's house."

"Paula bought a porno. She sits and watches these things endlessly."

"I remember her doing that on one of our Friday night blowouts."

"Yeah, it was at your house, ha ha!"

"I only had the one."

"She found it, though. Said it was a freaky one. Something about a chick and her brother."

"I tossed it."

"You mean you tossed off to it!"

"I hope Paula bought beer."

"Pabst Blue Ribbon! Screw that Pacifico!"

"You sound just like Dennis Hopper, only not so profane."

"If you hadn't noticed, Paula has given me the ultimatum to tone it down, so I substitute."

Paula pranced gaily up to Jeremy. "Substitute this, Baby. Yeah, gimme some..."

Paula snuggled up to Jeremy, pushing him against the kitchen counter, sweet-talking him for her immediate attention. Mark's attention was also captured, and thoughts of his ripped life raced through his head, always far away from the normalcy of the nuclear family he desired. Not much could make him

feel more solo in his life of pain he could not escape. If only he could get back to Maria with some serious cash. These were his foremost thoughts all the time.

"I know what you want, Baby. You want me to fix dinner for Jerica and Mark, while you go play with the VCR. Watch it in the bedroom, okay? Mark only goes for the real kinky flicks."

"Ha ha. Hmmm aren't we candid? I already ate, anyway. You guys watch the game. Jerica needs to take a bath. I'll get her started."

"All right, but keep it down in there!"

"I don't do anything that disturbing to you, now do I? Just imagine if we were alone tonight what you'd be doing. Jeremy, you have your fetishes too!"

"Alright. I love you, Babe. Go on, honey. I'll take care of it. Yeah, go on."

Mark and Jeremy muffled their snickering, as Paula left, mumbling about her seemingly morbid but harmless indulgence.

"What makes her jump on that?"

"God, I don't know, but she never hid it from me. The first day I met her she mentioned porno."

"Like how?"

"Like if I wanted to watch one."

"Did you?"

"I sort of blew it off. Not like I said no, but we made other plans."

"What other plans?"

"I got her high, and we made our own porno! Well without the camera."

"So she's been into this for all that time?"

"I guess her Dad had a stockpile of skin flicks, but he didn't…you know. She played 'em while he was at work."

"She told you that?"

"Paula tells me things I don't believe, but that's why I believe the important stuff about her. Suppose that's why we're still together. I let her do what she wants. I don't know how she can look at it so long, though. I see a porno and get bored after ten minutes of head and . . ."

"Okay Jerica's in the tub," Paula called out from the bathroom. "Can you kinda keep an eye on her, Jeremy?"

"Will do. You have a real. . ."

"Jeremy, you and Mark have a good time!"

"Yeah, dude, let's cook up the spaghetti and finish the game. This is something I learned a long time ago not to mess with."

"She's serious."

"Very intent. Some people get very serious about their pastimes. But Paula— whoa, I can't tell you. But she's very discreet. Her mother doesn't even know."

"I hope Jerica doesn't."

"Oh, hell no. Paula locks the door and puts all that crap up where Jerica can't find it."

Jerica screamed intensely out from the bathroom causing everyone to flinch.

"Daddy, daddy, mom! Help me!"

Jerica screamed in agonizing pain. There was no doubt that she was in a serious situation. Paula got to her first.

"God, Baby what's happening?"

"I poured the warm water on my hand. It's burning, Mommy it's burning me!"

"Jesus, Baby here put it under the cold water in the sink."

Paula grabbed Jerica's left hand and flushed cold water over it. The skin on her little index finger dissolved off in an instant, exposing the red tissues. The remaining fingers and thumb followed suit. Paula immediately panicked. She threw herself back onto the wall, falling to the floor, then realizing something was burning the hand with which she grabbed at Jerica. Jerica was screaming frantically, shaking her hand, spattering blood throughout the bathroom and in Paula's face.

Jeremy and Mark stood in the doorway, totally dumbstruck. Jeremy, not knowing what was going on was mentally frozen. Mark, however, was completely aware. His immediate fear and sorrow was not for Jerica but for himself. He knew he would be going back to prison for this. Not only for recklessness of leaving the acid on the toilet back, but now his probation officer would know he'd had contact with a minor, in direct violation of his parole conditions.

Jeremy gathered himself. "Paula, get up!" Jeremy shouted. "I'll get Jerica. Let's go Mark. Grab the bath towel for Jerica."

Mark hastily wrapped the oversized towel around Jerica's little hand. They scrambled for the Camaro, intent on getting to the hospital. Paula screamed, as well, signaling that she'd been burned too.

"God, I can't take it. It's so hot! I'm bleeding!"

Jeremy stopped for a split second while thousands of images careened through his mind, like a horror montage from the *Hellraiser* film he so coveted that had come to haunt him. He looked over his own hands, wondering if he would be the next victim.

"It's not happening to me. Goddamit what is this? Let's go, now! Mark, get another towel for Paula. I'm carrying Jerica to the car."

"Here, go, Jeremy. I can't. It's a probation violation. The cops will be at the hospital. Now go!" Mark looked intently at Jeremy making sure his friend understood his message.

"Clean this place up, Mark! Get that shit out of my garage. The cops will come here for this! I'll deal with Paula, but this is a wash with you and me."

"I'll do it. God, I'm sorry. I'm so sorry."

Jeremy raced Jerica and Paula to the hospital, where his mother worked. He knew he'd be in trouble with Paula, if she found out that the acid was a high industrial grade. He was forced to lie that he had it, and it would be his own fall.

"Paula, we can't tell anyone Mark was there. The cops will arrest him. You know it'll mean five years in prison for him."

"I know, just hurry and get my baby there. What is this, Jeremy?"

"I left the acid on the toilet, Paula. It was my fault."

"Don't worry about Mark! You worry about Jerica, or I'll kill that bastard. I should always listen to the majority. I will always listen to what most people think from now on. I'm never taking sides with that small guy again. We let him in, believing his shit. From now on, I'm playing it safe with the majority. I'm not even going to listen to me."

"Paula, get a hold of yourself. I promise he's gone."

"He sure is."

At the house, Mark raced to clean up the blood-spattered bathroom, hoping Paula bought into Jeremy's plea. He knew he couldn't move the barrel of acid, and if he asked someone in the neighborhood to help, he'd be inviting a potential witness against him. He had to risk leaving it and getting Jeremy to help load it the next day. These plans had been formulated in Mark's mind from the moment he saw Jerica's extreme injuries. He had thought, in that moment, how to cover it. Not one moment crossed his mind concerning Jerica. Instead, he blamed Nick for giving him the acid. *It's always someone else screwing me up and everyone is out to get me.* These words always echoed in Mark's consciousness, and he believed them. It was never his fault; blame never required him to suffer the consequences of his actions.

Jeremy pulled into the emergency lane at the hospital. The emergency room personnel were waiting for them, since he had called ahead from his cell phone.

Jeremy's mom Nancy was at the ER entrance. Jerica was in shock and panicking to the point that Paula couldn't hold on to her. Paula dropped Jerica, as

she ran toward the door. Well aware of Paula's past with her first two children, Nancy blows up on Paula.

"Get away from her! You can't do a damn thing right!"

Paula refrained from retaliating in Nancy's environment. She also felt the truth of the moment. "Please, help her. It's acid from... I mean for cleaning. She got acid on her hand."

Nancy and the emergency staff rushed little Jerica into the trauma unit. Jeremy and Paula were asked to take a seat at Billing. Paula was humiliated and tried to hold off on treatment for herself, until the receptionist noticed the blood-soaked towel.

"Are you hurt?"

"I don't know if it needs treatment."

"Let's look, okay?"

Paula opened up the towel, only to find it heavy with blood and fluid. She and Jeremy panicked when they was that the skin was totally dissolved off her palm and the underside of her fingers. They could only think about Jerica's condition, considering that Paula had only momentarily touched her.

The receptionist saw that Paula was not showing pain and realized she was in emotional shock. She kept calm and called for treatment.

Upon entering the treatment room, they couldn't but help notice every available physician grouped and bent over Jerica. The conversation was quiet among them, as if they were collaborating on a plan of action against the offender of this victim. One of the physicians turned his head, locking his eyes with Jeremy, as he and Paula walked to the treatment station. Jeremy could only see the eyes of this repulsed doctor, due to his mask. His eyes, however, carried judgment, which battered Jeremy's ability and desire to protect Mark. As they set up for treatment, the nurse called out for Doctor Dean. The doctor with the accusative eyes walked over, Jeremy winced, knowing that he would give Mark away.

"I'm not Doctor Dean, but I'll do. You've got some kind of problem here. This is nothing in comparison to your daughter."

Paula now responded as a mother, but retained self-preservation. "Oh, my God. What's going to happen?"

"You mean to Jerica or you?"

"Jerica."

"Well, young lady, Jerica is going to lose all her fingers and probably her thumb."

"How can that be possible!?"

"The acid you used disintegrated the cartilage between the joints of her fingers, as well as the knuckle joints. Her thumb had at least seventy percent cartilage loss. There was even some bone loss. Her hand is badly burned, but the heavier tissues and the bleeding protected against losing her hand. There's no reason for me to ask exactly what this was, since there isn't anything we can do about it. All we can do now is treat the both of you for burns. It's a police matter. I think you know that, don't you, Sir?"

Jeremy looked up and made a split-second decision to hold his peace. After having been arrested once, he knew to keep his mouth shut when it came to the justice system. He knew that if the cops found out he'd voluntarily let Mark in and helped him pack in the acid, it would be, at minimum, accessory if not a direct charge.

"Jeremy, aren't you going to answer him?"

"No, Paula, we don't have to put up with this. If he wants to make it a police matter then we only speak to a lawyer, understand?"

"It was an accident!"

"Just keep quiet, Paula. We'll get through this."

"My Jerica! She won't get through this! She's lost her hand! Doctor, why is this a police matter?"

Doctor Adel, who had seen his share of abuse in the ER decided to probe Paula, hoping she would talk. "First of all the lowest level of crime committed here is that the chemical you used is an acid only used in extremely controlled organizations, such as the Navy's nuclear department. This particular type of acid ate right through the hull of a Russian submarine off the East Coast near Bermuda. The sub's hull was compromised, because the acid was highly reactive to seawater. It can only be stored in glass or a special type of plastic fiberglass container. As a matter of fact, it has to be mixed in its final container. Nothing else will hold the acid in its finished form."

"But we didn't get the acid. A friend of ours did, and he said it was for cleaning our bathroom fixtures." Jeremy said, immediately inventing the story to help keep the blame off himself. "Yes, it was Lee Self. He gave it to us some time back. He owns a cleaning service."

Paula looked at Jeremy, wondering why he was so intent on protecting Mark.

"Tell me a little about Lee. How could he get a hold of a highly controlled chemical?"

Jeremy looked intently at Paula, trying to maintain the code of silence. She pantomimed by dropping her jaw.

"He does have a conviction. We knew he had a conviction."

Paula began to understand the gravity of this family's fate. She blamed herself for not taking Mark's situation with the state more seriously. The importance of not letting an offender around children was now all too clear. Jeremy's cool began to get through to Paula, lifting her spirits. She understood that they were clear of prosecution. Lee did have a record and was an incoherent diabetic. They could get away with blaming him for the acid. They were off, and now she would concentrate on Jerica.

"That couldn't possibly matter if he had a conviction, Sir," Doctor Adel probed further, "unless he wasn't allowed to be around you or your child. Is that the case?"

"Naw. He has some kind of driving conviction."

"I tell you what; let's allow the police to take it from here. I've got this guy's name and it seems like you're now willing to talk. Am I right, or should I take this another way?"

"Yes, doctor, we have nothing to hide."

"Good, Jeremy. I'd like you to wait outside. We need to keep Jerica here tonight. Paula will take about thirty minutes. You can visit with Jerica before you go home. She's under sedation now but will be awake when you see her. She'll still be on heavy pain medication. The police have been notified. They are usually slow in cases like this, so be prepared for a long night."

Suspecting there was more to be discovered by noticing Paula's reaction, Doctor Adel stayed with her. His intent was to separate the husband and wife, until the police arrived.

"I love you, Baby. I'm so sorry this happened. See you in a little bit."

"Don't worry; they will take good care of us. Go on now, call your dad."

Jeremy took his much-hesitated walk outside. Knowing Paula's weaknesses, he nervously hoped she remained loyal to his plan. The thought of choosing between him and Jerica was disturbing. Could she understand that, if she changed her mind, she would also be prosecuted? She could lose Jerica simply by knowing Mark was a convicted sex offender and allowing him around her child. Surely she'd know Jeremy would be charged but, given the seriousness of the situation, did she care? Jerica had lost herself, now, not just a hand, he thought. Paula could give in. He had to stay with the plan. His only recourse was to call Mark at the house.

Mark had finished cleaning the bathroom and disposed of everything, except the now clean, acid-free pickle jar. He knew the police would need that as evidence. His only concern was the barrel in the garage. The telephone rang.

Although he usually wouldn't answer it, he saw that it was Jeremy's cell number on the caller identification, so he picked up.

"What going on?"

"Dude, the cops are coming for sure. The hospital suspects foul play. You gotta get that shit out!"

"I've got the place cleaned up. I left the jar here, where she dropped it. What are we going to do?"

"Calm down. I made it look like we got it from Lee. Don't worry. Just get out of there and pack that shit with you."

"I don't know how to thank you, but I can't move the barrel alone. I've barricaded it in the back of the garage with boxes."

"That won't work, Mark. This is going to be investigated."

"They won't come here tonight, Jer. They'll only interview you at the hospital. Let's move it when you come home. I'll park down the street in the vacant lot."

"I can't take that chance. What if they show up when you're there? You get busted and the rest of us do, too."

"They won't come tonight, man! What are you doing now?"

"I'm waiting for the cops to show. I'm outside."

"Look, they can't hold you there. You could get here and help me. By the time you got back, you could just say you had to walk. You know like you were stressed out."

"I am stressed out! Jerica has lost all her fingers, Mark!"

"You're wasting time. . ."

"All right, clear out the garage. I'll be there in ten."

A security guard approached Jeremy. "Excuse me, Sir. Sir?"

"Yes?"

"Your car is parked in the emergency lane. You'll need to move it."

"Sorry. I'll get it out of the way."

"You can park over there in Visiting."

Jeremy took advantage of the moment, believing that this plan was meant to come together. He headed home to clear himself. That was the only thing on his mind, now, besides wishing he'd never stopped for Mark at the phone booth. People like Mark had trouble follow them. He could only think to himself about Paula's remarks about the majority. He understood the truth she brought out in her state of psychosis. Now, to deal with Mark's psychosis for the last time, Jeremy stealthily pulled into his driveway.

"Dude, you better find a new home in Mexico. My kid is a goddamn cripple because of your stupidity."

"I don't know what to say. I can't imagine how I forgot the jar."

"Don't say shit. Let's get this crap the Hell out of my life and you too."

Jeremy's anger was so intense that Mark hardly needed to help him move the heavy barrel. They got it loaded into the semi, and Mark told Jeremy to go back to the hospital. "I can tie it down by myself."

"You sure can. Don't even think about coming back here. You got that?"

"I do. You won't see me again. God dammit, Jeremy, you know the scoop here."

"Maybe that's just what it is, but I'm leaving and you're gone."

"Goodbye. I'll never forget. . ."

"Bye, Mark!"

Jeremy raced back to the hospital to find an unmarked police sedan in the lot, recognizable by the ubiquitous double searchlights. He has no choice but to park nearby, since the lot was almost full. He hurried inside, trying to avoid looking like he was gone. He was greeted in reception by a familiar face.

"Jeremy. Over here."

He turned, losing his heart to the bottom of his stomach. Of all the people and circumstances, only people like Mark brought such trouble. A goddamned robber, now what else? Jeremy's gaze was flat and even unrevealing, unless someone could read his mind.

"I'm Rainey. Looks like you don't recall me. The other day you know. Paula ID'd the stiff who robbed her at Calendar's."

Jeremy was still unable to speak, since Rainey knew of his involvement with Mark.

"It's okay, Jeremy. I've spoken with Paula. We aren't looking at this from an abuse point of view. Lee admitted to giving her the acid, and he did have a license to do so."

"He did, then."

Rainy had not called Lee. He figured it would have to be real or sound like a planned alibi. Rainy used unorthodox tactics that would be his demise.

"I've known Dr. Adel for years, and he's more of a cop than I am. I mean, he's seen a lot. We all kind of work together at this. You guys take care of yourselves. I'm not making this an official report. I'll keep a personal log of it, though, but it won't go into the system or on the computer. Just be careful. I'd recommend

you have people like Lee come in and do the acid washing. You should never do stuff like that yourselves. Even Mark could do this kind of work. I want to talk to you about this guy, anyway. Do you mind?"

"Ah, no. Not at all. What would you like to know?"

"I don't know if you know this or not, but he was involved with another kid a year before you met him. This case went all the way to trail. He won the case by jury trial, because the DA put her on the stand. Her testimony couldn't meet the guidelines for a conviction. Mark also brought in a paid false witness and his wife stuck up for him."

"Sandi?"

"Yes, and they got divorced three months later. He won both times."

"Well, they were married…what…just six months?"

"Yes, and he planned the marriage with her to help get him off."

"He was charged before she married him?"

"Yes. He promised her thousands. She did get a silicon implant job out of it, but that was it. He dumped her just in time. This guy is smart, Jeremy. Too smart to be a good friend. He knows the law well."

"How old was the kid?"

"Five. It was sexual, and we had him on the content of her confession. It was very graphic. I usually don't get squeamish, but this time I did. Off the record, I wanted to drag Mark out to the desert. This kid will remember his sicko words all her life. So will her family. He had the audacity to cry on the stand, as well as in my office. The jury didn't buy it, but when the judge laid out the conditions for a conviction, they had no choice but to follow the letter of the law and acquit him."

"I heard about something similar to this in his daughter's case. The wording he used."

"I know. I talked with Shea. She said you and Mark were good friends. I didn't do an interview with you because Shea felt you might be hostile towards her. We had to win this case. But you're right, he left words as evidence that no child could invent."

"I don't want to know them."

"So, why do you hang with him? He can only bring trouble to you and especially your family. You do know he has a no minor contact stipulation in his parole, don't you?"

"Well, yes, I do now. I mean officially. But I'm not hanging with him. I saw him at a phone booth just minutes prior to meeting you. I really don't know why I gave him the ride."

"That's what Paula said. Best stay clear of him. I guarantee you he's going to prison, and whoever is hanging around will join him."

"I'm really sorry to hear that."

"I am too, Jeremy, but he's never really been caught and punished, per se. He's gotten away with everything, including murder, we suspect. He thinks he can do anything."

"You know he talks about Mexico a lot. You know he lived well, at least he talks about living there."

"I'd like to talk to you about that, but I have to run now. Do you know anything with some substance on his time in Mexico?"

"He talks about La Paz."

"Good, that alone is more than I knew. Do you mind if we get together, then?"

"No, not really."

"Ok, I'll be in touch, but I'll call you first."

"Thank you, Detective Rainey."

"Go on inside. Paula's waiting for you in treatment room 121."

"Great. See you."

As Jeremy walked in Rainey, stayed around. His line of questioning was empathetically good. The fact that Mark was with Jeremy one day and Jerica losing her hand the same week was no coincidence. Rainy knew that Jeremy was innocent, and he knew Mark was the culprit. Mark had gotten enough people into trouble, causing Rainy to allow Jeremy and Paula freedom.

Time was on the side of the good guy was the detective's philosophy. He decided to leave the case open, pending further information. Basic information as to whether Jeremy and Paula were on the up and up. Anyone who would hang with Mark had dark secrets. Rainey took note that Jeremy's Camaro was now in the lot. Time would uncover every lie. Rainy should have gone for the jugular, as he would later regret.

Rainey believed from years of experience that it all came out with time. Any rushed prosecution would blow up in his face, as had Mark's case with Shari, the five-year-old. Rainey had been the lead investigator on the case and it was his only lost case. He wanted Mark, and he knew Mark was going to graduate to a big-time criminal. He knew the type all too well. The loser always knows his opponent. The winner does not always know his. Sadly, in this case, Mark knew Rainey even better.

"Paula, are you awake, sweetie?"

"Yes, they gave me a shot. Feels pretty good."

"Your hand is in a cast."

"It's just gauze. They put some kind of gel inside to help it heal and fight infection. They said I'll be out of work for a month."

"Where is Jerica?"

"In surgery. They're going to try some new kind of regeneration technique, but they said it was a long shot."

"That's wonderful news."

"Where did you go?"

"I can't lie, Paula. I went home to make sure Mark got all his stuff out. I did talk with Rainey. You stuck to my story. I'm proud of you. Things like this prove to me you're—"

"No, Jeremy," Paula interrupted, "it doesn't prove a thing, except we must be straight from the start. No more shit in our lives. I really hope you got that. We paid dearly for this. How can we ever explain this to Jerica? How can we make up this with her? That we let a sex offender in our house and fed him, only to have him take her hand away?"

"I promise I had thought the same way you are now, all the way home and back here. I told Mark as well. He's gone."

"Start thinking before anything like this comes our way again. I know what you're thinking about Jerica. Don't sweat it. I'll talk to her. She won't mention Mark. I know how to do this, whereas you'll blow it. I'm going to stay here tonight with her. I want you to go home but not before saying goodbye to her and taking the blame for this."

"I was going to, without having you tell me. I'm truly sorry for this. Did they say how long Jerica would be in surgery?"

"Oh, my God. I'm not thinking. Probably several hours. I just can't get it into my head this has happened. Go home, Jeremy, you can stop by in the morning before you go to work. Bring me my Washington sweatshirt and some jeans. I may have to stay here tomorrow too."

"I love you. Please tell Jerica. Bye."

Chapter 4

Disposal

❦

Monday evening 9:30

Mark drove out of town to dispose of the acid. He had disconnected the odometer of the truck since he planned to drive two hundred, fifty miles to Juniper Mountain. He buried the sixty thousand from the house sale at this lonely, selfish place of perseverance. It was all that was left of his once high life. He'd driven the route several times to Bacon Camp Creek Road, in nervous hope that no one had found his only remaining cash. He did have his twisted interpretation of love for Maria, and he did want to use the money to make something for her and a life with her. Thoughts about getting the money and Maria brought on his deviant emotions. He stopped in Springfield to call her from a telephone booth. The connection was distant and faint, but Maria heard Mark with a rapture she did not share.

"Angie? Is that you?"

"*Papacito! Adonde esta usted? Te amo Mark, te amo.*"

"I love you so much too, Angie, my Maria. I'm in Oregon but I want to see you."

"Please come home, Mark. I can no more live the life without you. I need you so much."

"I will come soon. I'm staying with the plan we made. Are you okay? I will send you some money."

"I am not okay. There is no Mark in the house to teach me the English and even more, love me. I don't need money, Mark. We don't need money like you want. The life here is beautiful with only you and me. We have our house and La Paz has enough work for a good life."

"That is what I want, Angie, I want that so much. The probation is for three more years, but I promise you I will come soon. I just want a little more money, so we don't have to work so hard."

"The work is not so hard my love, but the love like ours is very hard to find."

"I understand, and I feel the same as you. I want you so bad. I want to be in La Paz."

"I talk to the lawyer, Senor Isquerda. He said the American police cannot come and get you here. You don't have to worry. Immigration does not check. Everything is done locally."

"Really?"

"Yes, all the paperwork is done here. They don't check on your criminal history. We can be married."

"Your English is getting very good, Baby."

"Not so much, I just remember how the lawyer tell me to tell you. I write it down many times."

"You really want me back, don't you, love?"

"All I want is you in my embrace, Mark. I don't care what you did before or what happening with the police, just come home."

"I promise, as soon as I can make a break for it, I will. I love you so much. I do think about coming home to you every day."

"Why you don't answer my email?"

"I'm not in the prison anymore, so I can do that now. I'm going to get the money now. I need to get a computer. I'll get one tomorrow, and I promise to talk to you every day like before."

"You are going to Juniper where you tell me the money is if you are dead in the prison? You know I would never come to get the money if you are dead. I never understand you, but I love you so much."

"Yes, I'm going now. I'll buy a cheap used computer and I will email you every day."

"I learn the Internet very good now, Mark. It helps me learn the English, when I go to the silly American sites. I read the newspapers and so much. You know that one you show me in Eugene, the *Register*. I am so happy you teach me on your laptop computer. I still have it in the house."

"They are silly sites, aren't they? You remember not to open any other email because of the viruses, right?" (Mark was fearful that Maria might open an email from the FBI or other unwanted source.)

"Yes! But don't forget San Pedrito, Mark. That is nothing silly. That is our love. We live in your camper for two months on the beach and make the love always. I am surprised we don't have many babies."

Mark continued to withhold from Angie the fact that he'd had a vasectomy. "I hope I can have babies with you, Angie."

"Then come home. Maybe they don't know you go and you can come back."

"You surprise me, Maria. Even I didn't think of that. It takes five days to come and go, if I drive. Hell yes, I can do that, tropical woman."

"Really!? Please do it."

"I graduate from my trucking school on Friday, the same day I see my probation officer. I won't have to see her again for two weeks. I could see you Monday morning."

"Please do it, Mark."

"Okay, but you have to let me leave on Tuesday."

"I promise I don't make a problem for you. I am very happy, Mark. Please tell me this is true, not a lie."

"It's true, Baby. I need you so much. I want to go swimming with you at Tecalote. You remember what we did there?"

"I never forget anything we do."

"I have to go now, Baby, the phone needs more money. I love you. *Te amo siempre, mi Maria.*"

"I wait for you, *mi amor.*"

"*Si, Maria es muy felize.*"

"Goodbye my messiah." Maria hung up the phone, as happy as naive innocence allowed. Her father's abuse had in fact superficially abated with the time and Mark's eighteen-month absence. The quality of life Mark had left with her was far above the native way, which significantly abated the hell of memories. Angela Maria was on her way to being healed and becoming a real woman. The thought of Mark's past being a mirror of what had damaged her would destroy all that Maria had left. The reality of it would be fatal.

Mark didn't want to drive to Juniper alone. His life was oblivion, even after speaking with Maria. He phoned an old friend from a different circle who knew nothing of his case and criminal history. Now was the time for teen child's play, the way he understood it.

"Hi, is Joe there?"

"Uhh, no I'm afraid not."

"How about Tammy?"

"No, she's in Reno, but she'll be back on Monday. Who is this?"

"My name is Mark. I'm an old friend of Joe's."

"You didn't hear about Joe, did you, Mark?"

"No, who is this?"

"Brandy, remember, you used to give Lynn Ferguson and me rides around town in that bad ass Ferrari."

Brandy had a fixation with cars and riding. Mark knew this and used it. "My God, Brandy. You were thirteen years old then."

"Not any more. I'll be eighteen next week."

"Wow! So, where did Joe wind up?"

"Mark, I don't know how to tell you. I thought you knew. He fell off Oakridge Falls. He was hunting. We didn't know where he was until spring, when the snow melted off. Everything was such a frenzy. Tammy locked me up in the house. I didn't know where you went. I'm sorry. I don't know what to tell you."

Mark knew of Joe's death, a perfectly targeted *known* victim, her father was dead and her mother was out making ends meet. He began to creep inside Brandy's guard. "I don't know what to say, either. I loved that guy. I remember Bill saying something about him getting lost. I never thought anything of it. He loved to hunt."

"I know. So, what were you calling about?"

"I'm driving a big rig to Eastern Oregon and thought he might have wanted to go along."

"You're driving one of those big fucking trailer trucks?"

"Yeah."

"Oh yeah, Mark, I want to go. I love trucking around. Is it, like nice?"

"Actually it's a huge fuckin' Freightliner."

"Please, Mark. I've got some money. We could buy some Jim Beam."

"I've developed a reputation for that. Even Paula remembered."

"I hate her. She's a pervert, but you're cool. I mean just because you hang around her doesn't make you one. So, when are we going, rubber duck?"

"What's the big ten-four with your mom?"

"When will we be back?"

"Tomorrow or Sunday afternoon."

"Then Tammy doesn't need to know. You got a sleeper?"

"Um, yes. You call your mom Tammy now?"

"Hey I'm eighteen. You think I'm going around the rest of my life asking Mom?"

"I'll be there in ten minutes. Give me your address."

"Right fucking on!"

Mark's fantasy was now fulfilled from his desire. His life was meant for this personal satisfaction so few dared contemplate. He was alive now, and blood was moving like fuel in generations of unchecked instinct. What drove some to the cold had warmed this man to complete ecstasy. The past origins of his humanity were consciously shoved aside. He parked the rig two blocks away on a side street from Brandy's street. He walked the witness-free distance and rang the doorbell.

"Hi, Brandy."

"God, have you been in jail or something?"

"I . . . What?"

"You look like you've been on a rock pile; looks good too. Come here and give me one of those hugs. Mmm, you have been working it, huh?"

"Same to you! Look at you, you're a fox! You used to be so skinny, but it all—"

"Developed?"

"Right."

"You still look like you're twenty five. Do you ever age? Remember when the lady at the theater asked to see your ID?"

"Ah, she just wanted my address."

"So do I. No, actually I do. Shit you look good."

"I should tell you, it may be cold over there. Do you have blankets and shit?"

Brandy hastily gathered her necessities as she talked with Mark. "I'll grab my stuff. This is so cool. You know Tammy always takes off and makes me stay home. Are we going to camp in the desert like we used to with Joe?"

"Better than that."

"How so?"

"You don't have Tammy around and, also, you don't have to buy the Beam."

"I should've known you'd have it. If she knew you were doing this she'd kill us both."

"That's why I parked the truck down the street."

"What?"

Mark realized he'd made an inadvertent slip of the tongue. "I parked the truck down the street. I didn't want your neighbors to rat you off," he corrected.

"Still the big brain, aren't you? Let's go."

Brandy handed Mark two heavy sleeping bags. She kissed him on the neck, giving away her intent. This teenager had lost her virginity six months before, waking the woman in her. She'd had a childhood crush on Mark from the first

day she heard him talk and act, five years earlier. She wanted her childhood dream to be fulfilled to further her fantasy of being a woman. Brandy had admirers: half of Springfield high school and every male on the block. Tammy kept the chains on this beauty. She'd had an abortion and scores of midnight callers. Tammy would have gone out with Mark but certainly not allowed her daughter to. Brandy was selective but she had trusted him from childhood.

They silently walked up to the truck to avoid neighborhood snoops.

"I guess it is a big fucking Freightliner!"

"Actually, it's big because it's a trainer rig. They make us learn the hard way."

"You're going to school for this?"

"Surprised?"

"In a way. You didn't quit your business, did you?"

"Sold it for boocoo dollar's, Baby."

"Boocoo, you remember everything. We had so much fun in that Ferrari. Boocoo fast screaming bitch. I'll never forget when you lit up that alarm at my school. Fuck, you can be so extreme. If it was any other kind of car I absolutely would not have gotten in."

"You don't think we're moving a bit boocoo fast tonight, Brandy?"

"You can remember boocoo but can't remember that you told me what you'd do if I were legal. Something about buying me a diamond, wedlock type."

"I remember, and I'm real high right now on the idea that you're here tonight. I wished people could see us together. I'd feel like a king."

"What do you remember most when you and I were alone?"

"That, I can't forget. The time Joe and Tammy went out to get pot. We wrestled on the living room floor."

"I could feel you."

"What?"

"You know what. I wondered if that was normal then."

"We'll talk later about what's normal. But how's about now?"

"I think it'd be seriously abnormal if you weren't up. And by the way, that is the time I was asking about."

"I was sure it was, too; I mean, I was hoping."

They climbed into the heavy rig. Brandy hung onto Mark, as if she'd been his since her fantasy began at thirteen. The ride was long but they conversed freely about what Mark believed to be good old times and the lies about his current life. Brandy was fascinated with his stories of traveling in Mexico. She reminded him physically of Maria, with jet black hair, five foot six, about one hundred, ten

pounds, and busty. Her kiddy love could never be anything more than his wanton vengeance on his only captor. Only a child had caught him. It was time to reverse that in his mind. He had to kill and escape to reverse his capture, to normalize his life, as it had been before he had fallen short. Revenge and an absolute evidence-free killing method would clear him of the pain. Shea and everyone would know, even Rainey, but they would have no recourse.

"So what kind of cargo have we got back there?"

"Nothing."

"Nothing. So what's up?"

"Well, my little accomplice, we're actually going to dig up sixty thousand dollars. I left some of the money on Juniper because I didn't pay any taxes before I split to La Paz. Not like I'm going to pay them now, but you know, I don't think we're going to make it if you keep touching me like that."

"Sixty thousand dollars? Shit, what do you mean touching? I'm the one touched here, labeling me your accomplice. Somehow I know you're telling me the truth. Goddamn, Mark, of all people I know you would be the only one to do something like that! That's why I've always wanted it like this. We had to play before, now we don't. What do you think about that?"

"Like I said, I don't think we're going to make it there."

"What's a matter? Don't have the basic skills they taught you in drivers' school?"

"They didn't teach me like this! I want to park this thing in a bad way."

"How far is it to the money?"

"Counting the dirt road up to the site, another thirty miles."

"You can find it in the dark?"

"God, you're right, but if we tried with flashlights, a cop could see us from Highway 395. We'd be busted for sure. Thanks, Brandy, I needed you on this trip."

"So, let's pull over. It's nothing but desert out here. I haven't seen a car since we got on this fucking, lonely, whatever road 395. This place looks like the devil abandoned it."

"Yeah, it's the least traveled highway in Oregon. Only a few truckers and ranchers take this route. Babe, would you get some ice out of the cooler? Let's have a couple Beam and cokes. I'm gonna slow way down to find a spot. It's freaking dark out there."

"Mmm, I haven't had a drink in months. God, we're going to have some real good time tonight."

"We sure are. I want to tell you, Brandy. I can't think of a better person to be with here in this situation than you. Not many girls would come out here to get high and fool around."

Mark pulled a plastic bag from his front jeans pocket and dangled it in front of Brandy's eyes. Teenage curiosity lit up her interest by the predator's lure. She stepped into the small clearing beside the seat and disrobed. Returning to Mark's lap, she hung her arms around his shoulders, staring at the substance, which she would will lead her to utopia. Mark seemed unaffected by her, as he rolled up the marijuana cigarette.

"Crimson and clover all over, *mi gata vanedosa*."

"I'm pretty sure I know what crimson and clover means now. That other shit you said really don't matter, even though I could tell it was a compliment. That's right, red and green, crimson and clover. Wow, you guys weren't so far out of it back in your day. I just figured that out. You always did like music like that. I swear I would smoke this shit and drink at least seven times a week if I could. I can't wait to be twenty-one. I just want to be high, like so fucking high I never come down. Ever since Joe died and you left, life's been a big bore, Tammy bitch runs my life."

They smoked the marijuana that Mark had rolled into a joint. Brandy's inhibitions were destroyed, and Mark captured her with his words.

"You don't have to wait till your twenty-one. I'll show you the escape you're looking for now."

"How so?"

"You've got me now and forever, as your escape. To me, you're twenty-one right now."

"I really feel what you just said. I do, don't I? I think you knew Joe was gone."

"I didn't really call for Joe. You're the old friend I hoped would come with me. Look, there's a huge turn off. It's all sage brush and dirt, though."

"Mm, I don't care. We'll be inside nice and warm. It's better natural. I remember how you said you liked the smell of sage. I walked with you and Sandi that day. No one, not even Joe, replied to you. It seemed weird to them, as shallow as they were. I mean the way you said it, but I understood you, your feelings. You're so different, Mark. Everyone knows that, but they don't see why. I think you have something very few men have. Some say you're lacking or deficient, but I think you look past all the obvious shit people prioritize. You look for and see things that really pan out. That's one reason why I always wanted to hang with you. Now, I feel that's why you brought me here. I think if we stretched

reality a bit, say Joe was there, and he said I could go with you if you didn't want him to come along, you would have taken me."

"That's more than a bit. That's all of it."

"It's an example of what you would do, isn't it?"

"How could anyone say no to taking you out, Brandy?"

"See, that's exactly you. You don't know that I know the way you think. I tried to get older men, Mark. They all refused me, knowing that I wanted to fuck. Very few forty-year-old men would do this, especially if they knew Joe and Tammy."

"You think?"

"I'm not going to change you. I'm going to follow you. Any man that can do what you have with what's available in Springfield is on it."

Mark, seeing the open door, seductively and passionately replied to build his own ego, because he already had her. Now the predator divulged his wild jungle.

"I lived in Eugene, dip. I learned a long time ago you have to lie to the liars to keep the truth *you want* alive. That means there is no truth. There's just life and there's no *normal* life. There's just life, Brandy, and who can prove where life comes from or goes to? So, if you think you know me, put that away and desire to know me that way. Then you'll understand how far that goes. Right now, how far will knowing that take you, if you have that understanding in you? That's what you need to do, anyway. Just let go 'cause who the fuck really knows anything about our existence or destiny? Leave what's normal for the shallow-minded."

That stopped Brandy cold, disabling her own inbred boundaries and social restraint. It wouldn't matter now; he had her. He drove the rig another fifty yards, deep into the sagebrush. He did not have a plan since, at this moment, all he wanted was to feel some female. She had reached into Mark, pulling away his initial intentions. He would live second by second making his way through the pliable shell she had turned into.

The predator did not always kill, but he loved having his way. The station where the serial killer is triggered is not a place of desire or hunger satisfaction. That element simply does not exist anywhere in nature. The fuel station overwhelms the simple-minded and is triggered by the mere thought of threat. That exists everywhere and is constant, including in you, as all humans are not totally aware. Depending on who you are and what you have learned cognitively reveals your decision that could bury instinct. The cortex functions just as fast as the old brain recognizes your feelings. When the threat springs up, abandon this identifiable panic fear and side with solving. You do have to analyze that threat

and determine what actual difference it would make against you, but always recognize fear and drop it. Always eliminate fear. Fear causes loss of intellect performance, which is usually more functional than physical, except for flight, when it is absolutely necessary.

Brandy found ecstasy in Mark's experience and his absence of women for eighteen months. Mark satisfied his prime fetish by oral pleasures to Brandy. The predator worshipped the vagina while he killed the beholder. Biting the hand of the one who feeds was a well-known natural behavior in his cosmos. Think not that this is abnormal; the percentage of employees that steal from employers is in the upper percent. And that is the threat you make and face at a surprisingly high level every waking moment, especially in language alone! If Mark spoke the language of the mad, what light taught him? What his great hope was that, even he could be untaught or tamed in this threatening jungle. Welcome to the Jungle, the drums are beating.

Brandy danced to Mark's music. "I had no idea you were so into this! No one has ever done what you're doing to me. I couldn't even speak when you first started doing that. God, I only dreamt of this. I always had to do that but I never did it to them, as long as you're doing it to me. I want you up here. You've been down on me for over an hour. Mark! Stop and come up here. God, baby, how can you do that so long? I can't imagine a woman giving you up. Imagine if you were a woman."

"Well, I'm already a lesbian, so it wouldn't matter, Brandy."

"Oh fuck, ha ha! You know I have to tell you something freaky."

"Oh please do!"

"You really like eating pussy; that's obvious! But damn Mark, this is… unique! To say the least, you are unique!"

"Brandy, do you think I don't know that?"

"Yeah, I believe you do, ha ha. But look here, the way you go about this reminds me of a freaky incident I read about."

"Okay let's hear it, but I'm not stopping being unique or freaky, alright?"

"Fine with me, Mark, but I think you will like this true story. A woman in India was in a coma for five years, so she was institutionalized in a huge hospital. She was a rape victim, but she was knocked unconscious after the rape. So, like for five years, this woman was brain dead in a loony house."

"One day, one of the pervert staff entered her room and disrobed her. He licked her pussy, and her body had an orgasm while she was still in the coma, but as she peaked, she was like alarmed or shaken out of the coma, screaming. She thought she was still at the rape scene five years earlier. She started beating the

guy and chased him around, till she collapsed, cause she was weak. The doctors all came to the conclusion that sex like that was so mind intense that her body chemistry frightened her to consciousness. You know like she was being used or abused and had to respond. I guess it was because it was against her conscious will to be sodomized, so it brought her unconscious mind to frightful awareness to wake up and fight back. I mean that was serious, you know, like how seriously damaging abuse can affect someone who is very young. Child innocence is sort of like being in a coma, ya know. But goddam sodomy, enough to bring them out of a real coma! That's some shit, I can't imagine someone licking my pussy, while I was out, but you…"

"Brandy, you ain't in no coma, and if this isn't what you want, then I'm Mr. Fudd."

"Ha ha. Do you know how many times I just came out of coma?"

"Four. Last one wasn't so intense, first one like broke the time barrier, like within a minute. I'd say you were pretty fuckin' awake."

"Haaa! Second was the best though."

"It was that good. Who said a teenager shouldn't be with a forty-year-old?"

"The sheriff. But I'd never have experienced this for years if I hadn't come with you tonight."

"Four experiences."

"God, I could love you forever."

"Just tell me what you want. Don't be afraid to say what's there. Are you in touch with that?"

"Because I said *could*, when I wanted to say *do*. Yeah."

"You said I was different, Brandy. If you want to be different then don't follow what you been taught. You had to say *could*, since that's what others would have said, thinking you were being normal with me. I'm not normal, so you don't have to be normal. I am not embarrassed or ashamed. You said you loved my way enough to follow me. Are you afraid to take that position with me?"

"I love you. I do. I have for five years. I haven't put you out of my heart since you left. But you abandoned me!"

"No, Brandy, I did not abandon you. Remember the way you answered the phone, like I was some distant friend of Joe's and that you remembered me by riding around in the Ferrari? That car was only a two-seater, if you recall. Double locking my front door when you walked in wasn't for security reasons. Taking the bus five miles to my house wasn't on your way home. I don't blame you; you were thirteen, then, and were taught to hide."

"Oh my God, you are so right. I was treating you like you were supposed to be distant. Oh my God, we were a thing, weren't we? Oh, you are so able to unwrap me."

"Then go for me, Brandy, like I did you. Mmmm, you're mine, yes you are."

Brandy gave Mark his wanton worship.

"I can do this for hours now, and I want to."

"We've wasted five years, Brandy. If you had been open then, you could have known then."

"You respected my age."

"No, you were closed, not able to give what you wanted to. The statement you made of respecting your age should tell you what you would've done if I didn't."

"I really would have given myself to you, then. Goddamit, I would have."

"C'mon, Brandy we're having way too good a time. You know you don't have to be hindered in anything from this day on. I'm gonna teach you to break away."

"But it really was in me to give it to you when I was thirteen. I felt like a slut for feeling that way, then. Tammy always taught me this Jesus and Mother Mary shit."

"Humph, Mother Mary. Christ almighty, do you know how old Ms. Mary was when she gave birth to our savior?"

"Probably twenty-one."

"So wrong, some theologians say twelve. The experts say a max of thirteen. Don't weep, Baby, not for that crap, Brandy. You're much too good to follow that."

"I'm not crying about that. I could have loved you when I wanted to. I thought about you every day. I called your number, until it was disconnected. Mary was only thirteen?"

"Nothing makes her different than you. None of that crap matters. If it does matter to you, it means you're worried about going to Hell. Did you know the devil tried to take God's throne? What's to say someone else might just try that again? What kind of security is that to us? Hell, who knows, I might even have tried it, if he let me in the blue. There's no security, none. I have a point to make. God never changes, so all that kinda shit can go on and on. Remember Tammy saying God is the same yesterday, today, and tomorrow?"

"Ha ha!" Brandy blurted out in laughter.

"What, what?"

"Forever!"

"Forever what?"

"It's *forever*, you said *tomorrow*. That's just like you."

"Blow meeee!"

"Mm, you're practicing your preaching, so ask and get. Who do you really think God is, Mark?"

"I am, fucker."

"Mark, don't call me fucker, c'mon, even though you're my genuflect right now. If I were Eve in the Garden of Eden I would have bitch slapped that serpent for trying to tempt me into eating the apple. Things would be different now.

"How different would the world be now, Brandy? C'mon, some story that was. Oh shit yeah, imagine if Eve said no. We wouldn't have a Bible today or any story-type fairy tale at all. I mean, you would totally eliminate Noah and the Ark, flooding, and animals going and coming two by two, Samson and Delilah, oh, what a killing they made. God, I just cannot accept that people really believe that stuff. What's wrong with people?!"

"I really want to know who you think God is, Mark. You fascinate me in your way. I really want to know if there is a Heaven or Hell. Are we just going to die and that's it?

"It will never be it, Brandy. You're an eternal identity. Whether you're the same person next time or someone different, you'll never truly go out of existence. You just have to control your own destiny each time you come back. And you'll come back again and again, forever and ever, trust me."

"How in the hell do you know that when you just said no one knows shit about our existence or destiny?"

"That is what I said. I also didn't say you would know your destiny. I just said you'll always have consciousness of your existence."

"Like eternal life?"

"Yeah, girl, and it can always be like this, fucking and loving and drinking, getting high like ten motherfuckers."

"Okay, prove that to me!"

"Baby girl, you really going to have to put on your little thinking brain. You ready for the lesson of your life; you really ready for this?"

"Ah yeah why not, fuck, man."

"Brandy, think a minute about mathematical odds, you know, like winning a contest; one of those big fucking contests where you win the whole freaking lottery of three hundred, ninety-eight million dollars. Got that?"

"Yes, those are impossible odds, I mean very impossible odds for me. Where are you going with this?"

"I'm going right where you want to be, Brandy, The answer is about one in three hundred million that you will win if you entered the contest. Those are extreme low odds of winning, right?"

"I said that, so c'mon tell me, what's the point?"

"OK. Eternity is like forever, right? I mean it just keeps fucking going on and on. When twenty-nine trillion years goes by, its like nothing because that isn't even the beginning. Its always been and always will be, going further and further."

"Yes, it never ends; yeah that's so cool; forever is so much like love."

"So, thinking right now of all that eternity, what are the odds of you, at this moment in time, exactly now, right now in all of eternity, to be aware of your existence right goddamn now?" What are the odds of that? Now, really think about it concerning eternity!"

"Oh fuck, oh Jesus fuck me, that's the most impossible odds of all odds, or I'm always conscious! I won the biggest contest of them all!"

"Exactly Brandy, the odds are impossible to calculate, because it's a once-in-eternity chance, which is impossible to calculate. One chance in eternity, plus the fact that you're aware right now, which is a separate statistical odd. The truth is that, throughout eternity, all of the molecules that make up your body and mind will find each other again in the grand mixing and you will come into existence time after time. . .you never truly come to a permanent end. You will be in oblivion during the times after you die for huge spans of time, like fifty or sixty billion years, but in oblivion you don't know anything because you're oblivious! So you're only aware when you are, or exist. You have no awareness of the time when you're dead. That dead time isn't even lost time, since eternity makes up for it."

"Ha! Fuck me, that is the most intense philosophy I've ever heard."

"It is not philosophy, Brandy, it's the purest mathematical fact in existence to explain your existence and the statistics of your existence. The only thing it does not suggest is a reason for your moral existence, which I don't believe in. Science can explain the reason for our basic existence but it cannot present a moral reason for our existence. We can make our own reason during life. However, the need for moral reason brings up the possibility of one other inhibitory factor in our existence."

"What do you mean, now?"

"A God could have emerged or could emerge, like the God you asked about."

"So who could that God be: you, me, or who?"

"The first one to cross the finish line, sweetheart."

"What the fuck?"

"We all started out as the same shit, Baby: hadrons, protons, neutrons, electrons, atoms in all kinds of mixtures. Eventually, with so much fucking time, all the mixtures got it right or conducive to us and out of the dark, the molecules got consciousness, you know like all of us. From there, one of those bad boys could have evolved and was or will be the first one to make it to that place of control. Maybe like the spirit. Maybe some being, wanting power like a politician or even artificial intelligence, will make a change and institute change, like cosmic and moral laws. The finish line, Baby, if that's true, and it probably is, we are all gonna make it to some kind of finish line. That isn't conducive to my current plan, but I got to live with it."

"What about Jesus?"

"Apparently, he's the one in the eyes of many who got the blue ribbon, Babe."

"What about the devil? Why is there a Lucifer?"

"If Jesus is true, then Satan has the same origins, not the same road, but a cross street that interferes with the traffic the winning God of science and logic hates. In other words, Satan is the evolved eternity past presence of the majority of beings like myself."

"So then, why the fuck are we here, I mean people?"

"Because that God would be perfectly scientific, so the deal is this whole thing is out of fairness. Gotta give what would have happened, anyway, the fair chance. If we would have been, anyway, do as the ribbon winning first bad boy wants or knows best in his or her opinion or even fact, we get a ticket to ride and stay too. By the standards of Christ, God is in control, no matter how you look at it."

"Jesus fucking Christ on roller blades, that even makes religious sense. But it seems like God would now be an intruder in our lives, mandating we conform to his ideals."

"Exactly, without right to do so, just an intention on his part. That could also explain why the rest of the world functions the way it does, like lions killing their own offspring and weeds killing the nice little flowers off. Everything kills or takes, to stay alive in nature."

"What kind of intent or God would you be, if it was you that crossed the finish line first?"

"You know, I can best say that as an event everyone has witnessed. You ever see a little girl give a little boy a big embracing hug. Then the little boy rejects her by walking away or pushes her off, some sort of thing like 'don't do that to me,' message?"

"Shit, yes, I've seen that lots, even happened to me! What does that have to do with you if you crossed the line first?"

"I would have accepted. I would've never let go of that little girl's embrace."

"Goddamn, Mark, you talk a different language sometimes, but you know how to hit soft spots don't you?"

"Hmmm, language. You know soft spots get started by intimate communication. I mean clear to the point communication. If I were the blue-ribbon holder, I wouldn't have come up with that Tower of Babel bullshit story, about giving everyone different languages."

"What the Hell are you talking about, now?"

"I'm talking about doubt and good reason to doubt all that shit. I mean, if I were God, we would all be speaking the same language, not French and Spanish and the rest of that gook dop wap lin chin shit."

"Oh yeah, well what would you have us to speak then, Jesus?"

"English, motherfucker. It's the straight up clear to the point poop. Look at the word Motherfucker, for example; in Spanish or in Mexico they say *Pinche Madre*, or *chingas tu Madre*, depending again on where you came from. Do you know what that actually translates to?"

"Na, Mark, I really don't."

"It's all backwards, man; it comes out as fuck mother, or fucker mother, maybe fuck your mother, if you stretch it. But it just ain't the same as saying you Motherfucker! My point is that our culture really is our advanced language. Our culture is over and above other countries by far due to our language. How could that happen, unless someone was able to move ahead? Our abilities differ, proving so much. Granted *Motherfucker* is an American invention, but my point is, the rest of the world is fucked up because they actually think backwards. Now that's just plain wrong, man. I think God favored us English-speaking mother-fuckers because he knew we were going to be the Christians, and he gave the heathen bastards backwards-thinking languages. That's why we got the bitching tech, first man on the moon, Baby, because it's English. There are some temporary drawbacks for having such an advanced and exploratory language, though."

"Goddamn Mark brain . . . what are they?"

"The rest of the world thinks we Americans are of a decadent nature or freaky. But that's only because our behavior goes along with our advanced forward-thinking language. We explore all kinds of shit, which Mexicans think is totally nuts, but like I said, it's only temporary, until we advance way ahead of everyone else. Then we won't have all these indecent-exposure freaks, child molesters, and Ted Bundy motherfuckers who rape and serial kill. Hell, we buy

our kids bicycles on their sixth birthday, then B.B. guns on there seventh. Kids are inadvertently taught drive by shootings from every angle! It's all part of super advancement, due to our English. Being number one isn't always pretty. Number one doesn't have to find out first; it just does find out first. That's why all this shit happens in the USA. And that's why God seems to be all fucked up to a lot of people. He's out in front exploring. I mean, who the fuck would have been able to foresee hurricanes and earthquakes more or less creating a rapist who buys his kid a gun? God can't be blamed for that and won't be. We blame storms on nature any more anyway, but the rapist, a storm also, is classed as part of the devil's domain."

"Motherfucker! You think of the most bizarre shit. Well no, that ain't it. I think of things like that, too, but I don't ever go that deep or bring them up. It's like you go there; you're all the way with no inhibitions."

"I don't put my feet under my chair, Brandy, especially at the dinner table."

"Ah, what does that mean?"

"I'll go into that another time."

"I really need the whiskey, Mark. Kill me with your words if you will, but get me that . . . "

"I'll get it! You stay where you are. I got it. Besides, you said you could do that for hours now."

Mark tipped the bottle up, guzzling the whiskey, seemingly only for himself.

"Only for you, c'mon, man! Think you could contribute some more of that to this illegal minor?"

"Mm, you look so right where you are. How can I not?"

"It's straight, I think I'll be needing some coke."

"I'll let you chase it with the coke. Try it. You'll catch a good fast buzz, and then we can forget all this hideous shit to get on with some kind of crazy love."

Brandy naively turned the bottle up, taking it like it was water.

"Oh my God, it burns, gimme the coke. It's too much."

"Fuck no. Wait a minute, it'll hit you."

"It already has! You like the way I do this?"

"I couldn't like it more; you know you have me."

"Damn, you stare at me intense enough to scare me. Tells me your not fantasizing about someone. I know there is someone. You don't stay in Mexico that long without fucking."

"Maria."

"No lie. Why would you tell me?"

"How could I lie?"

"I'm making the best of it, you fucking bitch. You're a demon."

"Imagine when you were pushing on me five years ago."

"Shut up!"

"Oh God, you're going to make me come again. I'm Brandy and I'm thirteen. I'm pure thirteen."

"God! Your driving me crazy, I'm off. . ."

"I love you, Mark. I've always loved you, and I've waited five fucking years for this moment. Five fucking years! Lay still on me now. Just lay me."

"I can't stop. You got to me. How did you know to do this?"

"Because I knew you would have fucked me then. I can see it in your eyes. It's so obvious to me. You want attention. I know you want to be seen."

"Fuck it, I'm letting it all go. You have got to be that demon; you aren't Brandy."

"Sit down in the driver's seat Mark, yeah go! Put your hand around your cock. See my eyes on your cock. Imagine back to the day you first touched me years ago."

"You are incredibly good, Demon Brandy."

"Look at my eyes. Look at this female's eyes, seeing your worship, Mark. Now come!"

"Yeah! That was the fulfillment of my forty-four year existence."

"I believe you're spent now, forty-four year old. That was what you always wanted to do. You did it and you feel incredible about it."

"I believe you know more than you should for being one week shy of eighteen. You mind if I have a cigarette, you fucking tease?"

"Me too! How old is Maria?"

"Twenty four. But she doesn't have the tight body and freak mind like you. Shit, she certainly never talked to me like that!"

"How could she, Maria's not seventeen."

"God, Brandy, how could I take you to Mexico and replace her?"

"Why do I need to replace her? Why can't we just go there?"

"She's living in my house that I put in her name."

"What's her name, her real name?"

"That's it, Maria."

"What about the rest of it?"

"Maria de los Angeles."

"What the fuck does that mean?"

"Maria of the Angels."

"Ha ha, that is so lame. Hi, I'm Maria of the Angels, weeho, a burrito up my angelic taco ass."

"Why, you little shit, you don't think I have feelings for a woman I trusted with my life?"

"Your life? What do you mean with your life?"

In Mark's dreams of living free and acceptable he suffers a harvest of sorrow over his crime. The over-the-shoulder ghost of his hideous actions will never free him. He suddenly realizes Brandy will discover his "past record" with Heather. There would be no long-term relationships in the homeland. She would most likely bend away from him and turn this night in as a rape when she became aware. Brandy, not taking him seriously, lay on her stomach smoking the cigarette. She continued to smile and caress him. Mark made his plan.

"You like to have a burrito way up your ass, bitch, and such an ass to sodomize."

"No, Mark, let go of my wrists, don't do this. No, ah fuck you! Please . . . take it out."

"No, I think fuck you! Take this, you freak, seventeen-year-old freak. Feel like you have to shit don't you, freak. And you thought I was spent!"

"What are you going to do, Mark? I won't say anything; please, let me go."

"Right, you'll tell the cops."

"Oh God no! Mark, that's not what I meant! That's the furthest thing from my mind. I swear! I meant about Maria!"

"Yeah, of the Angels, you shallow little cunt. My love Nuestra Familia would kill you for that. She'll be honored in the next life, knowing I sent you to Hell. Mexico is real, girl, and we don't play!"

Mark had entered a space he himself could not comprehend, his mind illusions.

"Mark, I couldn't be more sorry. Oh God, please no. I'm bleeding inside. I feel it. Oh god no, it has crossed over"

The powers of darkness ever so present in his mind seemed to combine with Mark. He felt another dimension, losing his own. Brandy did not say that it had crossed over; she was gone; it was Mark who heard and experienced this, as he had crossed the line of no return.

Brandy's frail body went limp after minutes of brutal rape. Mark didn't notice. He was engulfed in the rage he'd waited for all night. He just needed an excuse, just one excuse to turn on her. She'd given him the total *looking* attention he wanted; however, the rapist was in pursuit of other desires. He abused her corpse for the time it took her body's nervous response to wear off. The rapist's

rage would not stop, as he slammed her head to the wood floor in one last stroke of revenge on the tattletale of his failure. Now entered the justification of mad light, or guilt he could not view. He verbalized away his burden.

"Now she's paid—bitch! Die! You're dead forever, not tomorrow, forever! Seventeen-year-old freak. You don't talk like that. I talk like that. I'm the fuck who talks. I savor the poison, you fucking wanna be. Armpit smelling whore! And what the fuck did *it's crossed over* mean! I wanted to vomit. My Maria never made me sick. God, Angie, please hear me, I'll be there. I love you; you're so clean. I did it. I finally did it. It was too fast. I didn't have enough time. I didn't see her eyes. I wanted to see her eyes go!

"There will be others; there has to be others. All I have to do is get away with this. Shit, what am I going to do with you? I don't have a shovel. Fuck, I got nothing. Get a hold. Okay, clean up this place. Fucking bitch. There's no blood. What the Christ *were* you talking about? Crossed over? What does that mean? Still, I have to get all the evidence out. Hair, prints, fibers, everything. That's the easy part. I watched the Discovery channel, Rainey! For years you fuck! Just your body; that's all I gotta hide, just your ass, Brandy. Love hurt so good tonight."

Mark was very thorough in cleaning, which had been his profession for seventeen years. He was well educated. The DA's office had contracted with him for crime scene cleanup years prior to his run in with them. He learned every last detail of evidence removal. Nothing was left of Brandy, except her body now dumped in the sagebrush. He taunted her dead body, believing she heard him on the way to his ultimate destiny.

"Like the smell of sage, you cunt! Oh, you could tell that I could see past it all. What a homer of a woman. Homer of Springfield, Oregon. Look at you. Trust me? Any seventeen-year-old going out with a forty-four year old can't see past her pocket book. You didn't think I'd catch the part about any man making it in Springfield as if I had to be in on it? On you, definitely. Nobody gets my money, not even Angie. Fuck all this. I got you and you're dead. Time to get rid of the acid."

Mark opened up the back of the trailer, to try to remove the evidence from his first crime. He had forgotten about Jerica but not the consequences. He turned on the trailer interior lights and noticed the barrel had something attached to its side.

"What's this? Says, 'Polyfiberglass siphon hose to be used for dip cleaning.' What the fuck is dip cleaning? Dip shits can't even give instructions if I needed them. Fuck, I gotta get this thing moving. Shit, it's too Goddamn heavy. What the hell am I going to do?"

Mark continued to strain at the acid, only to stumble over himself, falling flat on his face. Opening his eyes, he saw fine print on the bottom of the barrel. He read it aloud to himself. "*To dip clean larger objects, remove seal ring at top with nine-sixteenths box and ratchet only. Upon removing barrel top, lay top in side-storage ring slot. Dipping large objects will require siphon hose to be installed in side port. Use nine-sixteenths box only, turn counterclockwise to extend pipe. Insert siphon hose over extension pipe when out one inch, cinch down hose by turning clockwise. Dispose of acid in glass-lined container only.*"No shit, the acid will flow out if I throw in rocks and . . . time to get rid of the acid? No, time to get rid of . . . *Brandy*! Oh boy, I made it to the big time now. No one's thought of this before!" Mark rolled over on his back in laughter. He saw another surprise attached to the trailer ceiling.

"This is just perfect, everything always seems to work out if I work at it long enough. A pulley, it was meant to be! I can lower her in. Shit how long is the hose? Come here, Baby. What you got? Beautiful, it's wrapped around the barrel ten times! Let's see, pie is three point one four times the diameter, the diameter looks like eighteen inches; oh Hell, there's at least thirty, no there's forty feet here."

Mark rigged up his escape from the death penalty, the one chase he coveted as his trophy. To beat the death penalty by complete escape was his satisfaction. He could prove himself as capable of restoring his confidence that Shea had taken. To kill was the vengeance, but his reckoning with vengeance couldn't be satisfied. He did not know that his illness of unwarranted vengeance was self-perpetuated in his mind.

By finding a way to dispose of Brandy, he credited himself. He used tie down hemp rope carried in the truck to tie up and hoist Brandy by her ankles over the now open barrel of nitric acid. There were hooks on the wall of the trailer to tie the rope to, as he hoisted her one-hundred-ten-pound frame. He lowered her head partially in, slowly, and tied the rope off on the wall. The acid began to run out through the hose that he'd slipped through a hole in the floor and buried three inches deep and thirty feet out into the sage. It was a painstaking job only someone like Mark could do. Well-concealed between the tandem tires, a trooper wouldn't notice this bloody drain.

He retreated for a cigarette. It wasn't that he couldn't handle it. He demanded it, but his body was exhausted. He began to hear the boiling of the acid and laughed sinisterly. It was now nine thirty a.m., and he wasn't concerned about anything. Those who traveled highway 395 kept on going, especially if there was trouble. Except if it were their trouble. He heard a rig coming that was in some serious need of help. It slowly got louder. He recognized a blown

head gasket. They would have to stop here, since it was the only turn off for the last thirty miles. Mark hesitated to go back and lower Brandy all the way in. He knew the acid wouldn't work, unless there was a certain amount of external exposure to the air. The sounds of the ailing truck got louder. He dashed for the trailer doors indecisively. There was no more time, as the truck pulled in. Mark hastily locked down the trailer and, in thoughtless panic threw the keys into the sage. The driver and wife dismounted and walked straight for Mark, as if they were bounty hunters collecting.

"Good day to you, Sir, having a bit of trouble yourself?"

"Ah, no! I was camping it here last night. I was about ready to roll till I heard you."

"This is my wife, Jean. I'm Eddie."

"I'm Robert."

"Which way you headed? Looks like your rig is empty."

"I'm just going down to Lakeview and back."

"Good, were from Canada, by the way, and our luck has been the shits. Our refrigeration is out and we been packing perishables for fourteen hours that way. We didn't know until a few miles back. Our relief truck rolled in the Santiam pass. You'd be doing us a big favor if we could transfer our load to your trailer."

"Honey, we need to pay this man for that. Were going to be out thousands if we don't deliver by noon."

"I tell you what, Rob, we'll give you five hundred to get us one hundred miles. Now what do you say to that?"

"I can't let anyone in the trailer. I'm carrying sensitive material. If it weren't for that I'd oblige you."

"My god, son, no one will ever know. I give you my word on it."

"You don't want to know what's in there. It doesn't mix with food at all. You'd be in deep shit if you went along with me, I gotta tell ya."

"One thousand dollars, Son! I'm begging you, Robert!"

"Please, young man, we'll lose bad. We didn't insure our load."

All Mark wanted to do was finish with Brandy. He was plotting any way possible to get rid of these two snares. Eddie walked to the trailer, looking under its frame to see the stress load. In extreme haste, Mark surprised himself with what he considered genius.

"Ahh, Eddie, I have an idea to keep you and Jean legal, for the thousand, take my tractor. Let's unhook it and do the switch. That's easier than doing a load transfer. Have it back by three or it's two thousand, which is the deposit."

"You got a deal! You yanks ain't so bad after all."

"I don't know about that, Eddie, but we'll both be happy."

"You want to pull up along side of me, Robert?"

"Why?"

"So your trailer won't sink in the dirt man! Let's set my tractor under it. Can't you see that you got lightweight jacks on that thing? They don't have large enough platforms attached. It's not designed to carry a heavy load. The weight of your trailer alone will push you down in this muck."

Mark was internally livid. Eddie was right; the ground was soaked and the jacks on the trailer had no platforms. It would go down like a lead balloon. Again, he attempted his only escape.

"All right, but let me go use the great outdoors here first. Gimme five."

"Whatever you gotta do, Son."

Mark frantically traced down the end of the hose to pack it up and coil it under the trailer. The view was wide open. Both Eddie and Jean would see him pick it up and walk it back. His only hope was to cut it under the trailer. His pocketknife was all he had. Would it cut the fiberglass? He grabbed at the hose with his left hand, holding it upwards, making a kink in it below where he laid the blade. He intently thought of the acid and Jerica's hand. The acid should, for certain, not be flowing now, as it had been at least fifteen minutes. Brandy's head could have only displaced one quart.

The knife was barely fraying the hose, in his desperate stroking. He grabbed the hose tighter and pulled as hard as he could, for this was the moment of penal escape. The knife penetrated slightly, then the remnants of acid helped break down the outside of the hose. Holding the knife with the blade downwards, droplets of reddish acid immediately corroded the metal. In crying fright, Mark systematically continued.

Eddie shouts over and starts walking. "Hey Robert, I've got a heavy crank handle if you need it?"

"Yeah, ah just gimme a minute here…ah I…"

"Right up here on the runner, got the runners too, do you?"

"Sort of like to run away."

"Ah, don't be embarrassed; happens out here. Back in a second."

"Take your time."

"That bad, huh?"

"Can't cut it."

Mark was about to give in; he felt beaten. His remark of can't cut it was a premature confession. In his world, it was over, he was busted. Even if he had cut the hose, Brandy's body would swing about in the trailer as he moved the rig over

the pot-holed turnout, spreading blood and acid throughout. He couldn't clean up this forensic expert's dream of evidence. He heard Eddie walking around the side. Mark let go of the hose and dropped the knife.

"Son, you look terribly ill. You're white as Casper himself."

"I'll be OK, it's over."

"Have spells do you?"

"Oh yeah, this is the witch's spell all right."

"I tell you what, kid, I'll just drive my tractor over here and set up. I have some planks I can set under your jacks. I'll set my rig to your trailer quick like so it won't drop in the mud."

Mark was immensely relieved, briefly, only to go deeper into his nauseated panic as Eddie made one last request.

"Got your keys?"

"Keys?"

Mark slapped at his pockets. "Oh shit."

"Ha ha, you must have dropped em when you lowered your britches. Well, Son, you know that spot. I ain't going there. I'll be back."

Mark tried to recall his position when he threw the keys into the sage. In his panic and nausea, nothing gelled. But he knew now that all he had to do was find the keys and it would be home going. He came out of it and collected himself, thinking that a rational criminal is a successful criminal. Mark frantically searched for where the keys should be. Time began to run out, and Eddie was returning. If he saw the exposed hose and smelled the acid, it would be over.

Mark looked out into the sage to see faint small plumes of white smoke from the end of the hose. He quickly went over to see the acid had pooled in a low spot. Its red tinge gave Mark another shock of neurosis. Brandy's total blood volume had drained, flowing out the top relief vent. The acid didn't have full effect, as the blood flowed over the top of it, directly to the relief vent. The acid was acting on her blood in the pool outside. Mark took off his jean jacket and tented it over the pool, by draping it on the sagebrush, hoping to keep the visible effects down. He hastily walked back to where he had been searching.

"Hell kid, you got more problems then we do."

"Jesus, I'll say."

"Can't find them, huh?"

"I will."

"Well, let me help you, but that should include a ten percent discount, you know."

"You got it coming."

Eddie noticed Mark's Jacket.

"What the? There son, that's your jacket. Your keys have to be over there."

"Oh, no, I took it off over there. I didn't . . . there."

"I'll get it for you, then. You keep looking."

"No, please don't. I can."

Eddie was within five yards of Mark's jacket, when he stopped, looking straight down. His face became flushed.

"All right, Kid. We got a problem here."

"What are we going to do about it?"

"You don't have a gun, do you?"

"No, that's one thing they don't let me carry anymore."

Jean walked up, looking over the odd scene and questioned her husband. "Eddie, what the dickens are you doing?"

"Quick, Jean, get the shotgun."

"Now wait a minute, there's no need for that," Mark frantically pleaded with Eddie. "I'm not going to do anything."

"You're right, Robert, but I'm going to have to."

Immediately, Eddie jumped to his rear and raced toward his tractor.

Mark followed suit to cut him off. Eddie stopped a few strides later.

"Now see, you don't need that old shotgun, Eddie!"

"Not this time, but those diamondbacks usually don't back down when you're that close."

"What?"

"The rattlesnakes out here are much more aggressive."

"Oh my God. Are you serious? You saw a diamondback?"

"Surprised to see me move like that, weren't you."

"This is incredible! I'm saved."

"Shit, Robert, it was twenty yards from you. Go get your own jacket. Hey, what's that on the mound behind you? Looks like the keys."

"Oh my god, yeah. You're right, Eddie, it is. We're back in business!"

"You sure got better quick."

"I'll say, been a real bad morning. Anyway, let's get going."

They moved the tractor trucks, and Eddie left with his wife. Mark would stay behind to finish his gruesome, but now paid task, of removing Brandy from existence. He had only to reverse the hose and start the process of elimination, the perfect removal of evidence.

Mark opened the trailer door to his own dismay and fright. Brandy's body was curled up into a tight ball with her chin touching her knees, which in turn,

were bent tight. Her skull was dissolved away from the acid to the bottom of her ears. Her cranial cavity was empty. Her spinal cord was showing through the opening. The nerves had signaled her body to contract. He lowered her in the acid up to the rope line. Brandy was gone in an hour. He felt like she had been erased entirely. He pumped the remaining acid out through the siphon hose. His plan was to dispose of the barrel on Juniper Mountain. Juniper was a desolate desert mountain, so far off the beaten path that even land management rarely frequented the stark site.

Mark knew of the place from his own search of places to hide stolen goods. For months at a time, he had left stolen merchandise worth thousands of dollars in obscure view, covered by tarps. The actions to go to such extremes years before to hide evidence was Mark's solo style. He often pondered on these extreme measures to self determine his conformance and mental state. So few went as far as he did, but no one was as successful in the criminal arena. He was ahead of the norm. He had more and had never been caught, whereas everyone else had been. He had never been caught, until Shea came along. His total being was to defeat it, defeat his one-time loss.

What Goes Around

❦

Westerners have adopted a linear approach to both thinking and living. Westerners, as in the United States, view life as a line from birth to death. Time is essentially viewed as a line, years past and into the future, having a beginning and an end. In that timeline, plans are made for the future, such as having enough money to survive into the future. Events seem to be thought of as one-time occurrences with one-time endings. I challenge this thinking as untrue, selfish, and dangerous.

Most of the world thinks quite differently. For them, all of life and existence is a returning cycle. This line of thought came from observation of the real world, rather than through religion. There are even more beliefs that follow the cyclic view, rather than the linear view, such as Buddhism and Hinduism. I would like to focus on one that is more of a science than religion, the Mayan belief and calendar. I am just one of millions of people from Latin America who speak a language with a Spanish accent that stupefies five-year college students, when they come to Mexico. You do not know how many times I have heard tourists say, "Wow, I really thought I knew my Spanish, so this has to be an off dialect." Trust me, there are no dialects of Spanish. There is Portuguese, but it's just bad Spanish.

Today, throughout Mexico and Central America, a language passed down from the Tolteca or Maya is called Zapoteca. It is not taught in schools and is forbidden to be spoken in schools or in public, because it is sacred. Zapoteca is passed down almost always by the indigenous mother to her children. We speak it everywhere and, surprisingly, enough is all we speak when we are alone in North America. This is the language that allowed the Zapatistas to defeat the Spanish and release the Indian people back into a free Mexico, unlike the Indians of North America, who are still being assigned to reservations, even today. What

I am about to tell you does not come from a western book of second-diluted opinion but rather direct from the record and Calendaro Maya.

From observation, the Maya noted that nothing had an end and nothing was linear or straight. What westerners call hurricanes, they called cyclones, something that is circular and travels erratically, but which spins. They noted that water did not go straight down, but swirled down. They saw seawater take on cloud forms and cycle to mountaintops as snow or ice, and then it melted to rivers, which went back to the sea from which it came from. Everything to them was a cycle. They noted that every year was the same at certain times, with only minor variations. They recorded that the four seasons were always constant. They noted the Moon, Earth, and Sun were round or spherical. They noted that the Moon circled the Earth, which in turn circled the Sun. They surprisingly discovered that the Sun circled the center of the Black Mass as they called it, or the center of the Milky Way Galaxy.

They reveal in the Mayan calendar an astonishing fact to modern-day astronomers that the Sun and Earth will be ecliptic and in perfect alignment with the center of the black hole in the Milky Way on the western date December 21st 2012 for, this 26,000-year cycle completion called procession. This has been recently confirmed and, for that, they deserve recognition to apply cycles where applicable. Incidentally, this date is not the end; it is only another cycle within greater infinite cycles, and they explain that, as well. The Maya knew this thousands of years ago, by intense study through direct observation year after year. This is the basic premise of *Predator Down*, solutions by facts from actual observation and the way we behave due to our cyclical history. The Maya observed the stars year after year and upgraded the world's most accurate calendar to near perfect, more than two thousand years ago by this method.

The calendar is three in infinite and of circular form, such as an analog wall clock; it is not linear. This calendar still exists today and is a repetitive calendar, with variations within each infinite cycle. They have proved from observation that cycles exist in life and the cosmos. They recorded these cycles and events past and *to be* in the calendar itself, intentionally *to be* verified.

A strong message is conveyed that, if something took place in the past, it was sure to happen again and again, throughout eternity. There is no indication that everything that is possible that could take place will or should. If there is anything to be noted about possibilities, it is along the lines of warning us, which indicates that there is a sense of doing what is best for the cosmos. That means the avoidable is, in fact, avoided if you are aware. These humans ascended to the order of gods with that thought.

To be or not to be was discovered here, long ago, and was intended to mean eternal cyclic being. There is no word for "end" in Zapoteca, as it simply does not exist. There is a word similar to "end," which is interpreted as *not ready yet*. What that means is that, if someone or something is preparing a thing, we have to wait to consume it, but it has to be re-made beforehand, so we do not consume it all. This is true patience to those who give, but it is a nightmare to those that want something or something done. That is the first point of cycling favorably, so I would like you to identify yourself here. What do you want *to be* done? This is where the Maya went wrong years later, by powerful individual priestly belief. These religious leaders, by going ballistic toward the linear, unknowingly created beginnings and endings, which gave birth to something new to the people, called "impatience." Impatience is completely anti-cosmic and unnatural. Impatience suddenly became a desire to get things *to be* done, leading them toward a failing linear direction of acts, such as human sacrifice and child sexual abuse. We can avoid decadent failure today, by staying with a fact, discovered by the majority and not wanting to end something that is going *to be* by getting it done. Don't be concerned, I will explain.

Long before the decline of the Maya, they began to notice that the make-up of life itself was cyclic. The heart was found to be the center of a cyclic circular blood system. It was then very clear to the Maya that everything was circulating by cyclical means, having no end, rather than linear and having an end. There was nothing straight and, to them, nothing had an end. They were further convinced when they saw the cycle manifested in human behavior. They then realized that life was strongly interconnected to the physical workings of a cyclical cosmos.

Brain surgery became a curious practice, which revealed that the tissues of the brain and nervous system were also interconnected to think and perform in cyclic patterns. Today, we know that the brain is so highly interconnected, it out connects the most recent advances in any computer technology, or any technology. The brain processes information through billions of neural connections in a cycle that allows us to explain ourselves in detail.

A computer does not have nearly the connections and can only give responses without cyclic thinking. Each individual neuron in your brain has around five connections that really connects to all other parts of your brain and body. The connecting numbers are staggering and the brain's abilities are awesome. Information does not go in one ear and straight out the other, ending the thought. Information gets cycled billions of times, bouncing around in your file system, while you are deciding what to do with it. That *you* part is the greater character of likes and dislikes in the rest of your brain and its cyclic connections

throughout your entire body and being. The bouncing goes on, until you decide on the place you would like to store it.

Your first decision is going to determine the long-term cycle position, whether it's difficult to get out of or easy to set aside. It would be wise to set the bad cycles in your "don't do it" folder, as soon as you recognize them. It could be said that your decision to put it in the "desire" folder is, in fact, your decision to perform the act.

The one thing the Maya found about cycles is that they are hard to break, once they start. People in the West are aware of that, but the proof of a brain storage and thought-cycle process is the point, as I have demonstrated *why* in *Predator Down*. We have found out why we do what we do. But the point is it's dangerous, if you enter a cycle that is even close to sexual abuse. If you had never tasted sugar, you would not have a desire for it. Your brain would never know what chocolate was, until you dove into a cherry and double chocolate swirl topped with sweet cream. Once your brain (you) likes sugar, and right now being triggered, you are sure to be at least recycling the taste it in your memory, if not thinking about checking out your kitchen for something similar.

Your memory alone is enough to set off cycling, not to mention when you naturally get hungry or have something ignite your memory. That is the second point of cycling, the memory triggers are absolutely everywhere and impossible to avoid causing what is known as a "vicious cycle." Once a person engages in sexual abuse, and the brain likes it, that's called the start of the repeat cycle. Once you taste it, look out, watch out, since it is too late to find out that even thinking is wrong.

Your brain and the real world coexist as one, in a cycle that the Maya proved thousands of years ago. There is a factual basis for your very real physical connection to the world. If you did something once that you liked, you are sure to repeat that act. Not only that, but if you dwell on a thought of something you have not done yet and foresee that you would like it, you will likely do it. The reason for acting equates to the file cycling. The separate memory brain file intensively cycles this information over *to you,* again and again. It does this as a mechanical program would in the same way the brain needs nutrition to stay alive and lets you know by hunger pangs. The joys now become addictions to the program files in the old parts of our brains that are highly functional and relate excessively to sex. These are very powerful addictions when related to the procreation of oneself or enjoyment. There are many remedies to close that file, I will discuss.

If you are thinking about the ten-year-old child next door, or a child any-where, you are powerfully chemically cycling this information, over and over, to the state of acting on it. The brain will only cycle so much, before you act, especially when hormones drive the thought. Simply put, it is overwhelming to the weak average human. This is you being the chemical cycle entity that is every bit connected to the cosmos in the way things naturally work. If you put water on the stove that is cycling heat, it is going to boil, and you are no different. You are no different than a growing flower or an exploding star or a cyclone, in that you will obey the laws of physics by acting on what you are cycling.

You are one hundred percent tethered to the laws of nature, and your brain is the weak, unaware medium of this connection. This is the *why* of it all. The brain does not think of a subject once and then let it come to an end. That is where people are fooled; they think that it has an end if you only think about it. The hurricane or cyclone builds to an intense force, cycling and destroying everything, until the damage has been done, and the energy that was spent doing damage causes the cyclone to cycle down. Remember that nothing has an end to it; once it is in your brain, it's there. Once you have thought of doing something, that very thought is in your memory and will stay there. But you have the power to change or put that thought into an "undesirable" folder. That is the thinking cortex, which has the power to choose and change. You can file it as, "I choose my destiny and I am going to change my mind, because this cyclic thinking leads to a bad decision which will only make me worse." File it away and cycle-think into something good right away.

The key and the answer is your intellectual intent and strength. Remedies will be discussed later. Right now, I remind you I am not talking to people who have offended. This book is not for them but for those who have not fallen. Your awareness as to why you feel the way you do and the alternatives you have to avoid self-destruction are paramount, right now, every day, forever. Finding alternative cycles that are better and safer is the start of finding the rest of life you are likely not aware of right now. When you do find it, you will see two things: how wonderful it is and the connection will be so incredibly visible that you will know how to hook up. Wherever you go, there is always something better, and there is not an end to that, either. You can reason with yourself intel-ligently with this awareness. You can advance yourself and many others, when you have good friends who desire to think that way, cyclically. Make friends with yourself, make friends with your neighbor, and you will be able to safely play with all the children happily without end.

Always have it in your mind that in this cosmos, what goes round comes round, around you. It really is Physics 101. These cyclic interconnecting cosmic laws are far above man's law that no one can escape. You can think of the good cosmic laws that, as well, cannot be escaped. You can choose to not cycle-think of the bad ones that allow your escape. Many call it your conscience, but there are those of us who just say, that's the way it is.

Disrupting the Cycle

I offer a short but common example of breaking a cycle to gain understanding of the difference between straight-line thinking and being in a more desirable rhythm. Everyone has had insomnia for no apparent reason. I am not talking about chronic sleep problems, just a case of not being able to get to sleep. A few people have inadvertently found a solution. Those that have not found the solution try to drudge though the night by straight-lining the effort, by staying in bed, thinking that, if they get up, this will waste sleep time. Try to associate that with a forceful beginning-to-ending belief. If some night you can't sleep, try getting up and doing something very restful, but different, such as sitting in an upright chair and staying peaceful; but have different positive thoughts than you had when you were in bed. Maybe get up and go to the bathroom then sit at the kitchen table for a few minutes putting your feet up.

What you just did was disrupt a mini vicious cycle. Now, go back to bed and be surprised as to how fast you get to sleep.

Soon, you will realize that your body is like anything else in nature and goes through cycles. Keep in mind your presence of mind, over all, will enable you harmony. Now, recall that the mind has the most connections, enabling endless cycling. Cycle down by moving out of the linear thinking, and you will find pre-changing "put the predator down."

Interlude 2

Dwelling on the Obvious

Many good people have countless questions about sexual abuse, the most common being "how could someone molest a child?" Then, "why would they? They knew what they were doing didn't they?" The "knew what they were doing" part is the purpose of this interlude. Some of the people who ask these questions are older and don't realize that the art of moral upbringing and family bonding is disintegrating. Some are people who are truly astonished and unaware of sexual abuse, due to their true, healthy state of mind. But a disturbing reality is that many more of the people asking such questions are being pretentious, in that they know how close they are to children in ways that are not personally disturbing to them. The purpose of this book is like no other—*prevention* of sexual abuse, not *rehabilitation*, and certainly not trying to bring back the good old days of moral teachings. Those teachings have not proven to significantly help stop sexual abuse or crime in general. This book transcends morals and goes into the awareness of self-destruction and why we do what we do. The premise is that history is who we are, and history is why we do what we do. Once we can truly understand why, we can factually and methodologically change behavior by high awareness. This book is about a new self-awareness, derived from historical evidence that has been shamefully avoided.

We only have after-the-fact rape rehabilitation programs, and they are only for the offender, not the victims. That's right, we don't have a prevention program. Such a prevention program is expected to be taught to us by our parents, families, church members, and bishops. Do you get my point? Prevention isn't even taught in public schools. Why? Because no one truly knows how to prevent sexual abuse from a scientific or sound and acceptable method.

Many people who speak of morals, laws, and respect, sexually abuse children at the same rate as everyday people do. The secret of this book and prevention is

that we all have to step outside of ourselves to see and realize, for the first time, that facts are answers, not untrustworthy opinions of people who have desires. This comes down to our origins and everything that has occurred between then and now. In other words, it comes from our history of conditioning what we know for sure to be true. The second obvious point is that people do know what they are doing when they sexually abuse a child, except for the obvious consequential facts. There is a reason why people put the consequences out of mind while committing a crime. That shortcoming has to do with what people had been doing in our past, without consequences to their illegal actions.

I will discuss the past without consequences, much later; I will dwell on the obvious consequences of today's world, first.

I'd like you to think about a very simple model. Think about fingernails. The longer your fingernails are, the more likely you are to damage them or someone else with them. They cause extreme pain to our fingers when we break them. Do longer fingernails seem to get in the way of everything, or do they simply get in the way of everything? Why? Factually, they would be sticking out excessively into places they should not be. You'd think clipping them would be the solution, an opinion leading to where? Or you could decide to do nothing with your hands. Which opinion leads to a fact? The truth is, having no fingernails would be the answer if you didn't want them to cause problems. Can you *eliminate other things about you* without consequence? Get ready, we are going swimming where no one has before and it gets deep.

The Facts or consequences to: First the victims.
From a non-traditional point of view but from updated studies and fact finding.

What is abuse and sexual abuse? From the root words in Latin on which English is based, "abuse" has a very specific meaning not revealed in English. In Latin "abuse" takes on the form and meaning of <u>bucear</u> *Bajar, Abase, Abusar*, meaning down, to lower both physically and in the sense that something is lower than something else, under, dangerous, or *bucea*, meaning someone else took you to depths under the surface.

The actual intent of abuse in Latin means that something or someone is being reduced or taken down by a means not invited. Abuse does not mean minimizing, especially minimizing verbally someone's characteristics but, rather, it is an actual reduction or taking down of the person. The reduction in this case of *bucear* is damaging reduction that requires aid or repair. For example, a case of scuba diving or *bucear* can be demonstrated here. A strong man taking a weak

person to the bottom of the ocean, where the weak person suffers an aneurysm and lung damage. The damage done requires medical treatment. In this case, the aneurysm causes irreversible damage to the brain, in turn affecting that person's thought processes for life.

Sex in Latin defines a person's identity in many ways that almost totally encompasses the person's entire identity as a human being. Combining abuse or "taking someone down" to the point of needing repair and aid with their sexual identity can imply that one's entire being has actually been reduced to levels of damage from serious to deadly. It does not mean that the victim has been reduced to a lower status than the rest of society; it means they have actually been reduced and damaged. This logical realization by the victim more often leads them to believe that they are less than what they had previously been. Some victims believe that the offender is better than they are, due to the offender's position and ability to take them down. This position heightens the negative effects of sexual abuse into extreme depression and worthlessness.

Change in Physical Neural Function and Human Behavior by DNA Alteration Caused by Trauma.

Conventional and traditional western medicine have long assumed that the brain is hard wired at birth or at least by age five. Recent observations have proven these assumptions to be absolutely inaccurate.

A possible example of immediate brain change is well documented in ancient Mayan history. This documentation is at levels comparable to many modern-day findings that include aid in sexual abuse therapy to both victim and offender.

Mayan hunters who took adult deer as prey left the few dependent infant fauns to die; however, the women took the deer in as their own children, even breast-feeding the fauns, or they would have died. After they had nursed the fauns to a level of self-dependence, the now grown deer were released into the wild, at an age that the men would have killed them. These deer did not want to leave human populations. Most became more like dogs, protecting the owner's premises. Those deer that did leave left us with an astonishing finding. The immediate following generation of fauns no longer had any fear of humans and would approach the hunters who were carrying weapons. This behavior changed the entire way the Maya cultivated plants and animals to the time of their demise and defeat by the Toltec.

I compare this Mayan example to modern-day scientific findings, especially those from McGill University in Montreal. An intense study by Dr. Meaney

at McGill finds that abuse appears to alter genes. For years, psychiatrists have known that children who are abused or neglected run a high risk of developing mental problems later in life, from anxiety and depression, to substance abuse and suicide.

The connection is not surprising, but it raises a crucial scientific question: Does the abuse cause biological changes that may increase the risk for these problems?

Over the past decade, researchers at McGill have shown that affectionate mothering alters the expression of genes in animals, allowing them to dampen their physiological response to stress. These biological buffers are then passed on to the next generation. Rodent and nonhuman primates, biologically primed to handle stress, tend to be more nurturing to their own offspring Meaney and other researchers have found.

Now, for the first time, they have direct evidence that the same system is at work in humans. In a study of people who committed suicide, published in the journal *Nature,* Neuroscience researchers in Montreal report that people who were abused or neglected as children showed *genetic alterations* that most likely made them more biologically sensitive to stress. These findings bolster the Latin meaning of sexual abuse to be a real *actual change* and reduction in one's entire identity, which is much more than a nonmaterial metaphor of minimizing one's emotions or hurting one's feelings.

The obvious revelation from these discoveries is that now we understand sexual abuse to be a much more damaging event to an actual syndrome the victim carries with him or her in the physiological sense. Scientifically and medically, these discoveries reveal a serious oversight, in that traditional current treatment is insufficient. With that, I submit *Predator Down* as just one of many preventative measures to come. Prevention, not rehab and not treatment, should come first, starting right at home with your own.

Consequences to the abuser:

We will talk much more about victim consequence throughout the book. The purpose of *Predator Down* is to get the mind of the potential predator or abuser thinking about his own future, a horrific destiny. Again, this is intended as a deterrent to sex abuse, or prevention. The focus of this book is on the potential offender, someone or anyone who has not yet offended . The design goes a step further and admits who we truly are. I define these hunters as every human male who can read or who can have someone read this book to them. Making

everything clearly obvious is the design of this book. You can either be offended or accept the truth. Can you accept the truth that you have raised your voice, or yelled at some point in your life? Have you never been angry? Have you never felt like retaliating? Have you never felt the need to say you were sorry, or did apologize? I am certain that most males are not sex offenders however I can prove men have something women lack. We carry traits that can lead us to places we are not willing to admit. Some of us have a hard time with that and still others have a very difficult issue of controlling those traits. I ask that you truly open your mind from this point on and try not to be offended.

Obviously, there is a hunt on for sex offenders. There has been for a long time, but never as it has been in modern times, starting in 1991. The sex offender is no longer ignored. What does that mean?

If someone thinks they can get away with sex abuse against a child today because they knew of girls in the past who were abused, say, by their fathers, and the child told of the abuse, and the relatives just silenced the child—that era has ended. Now, when a child says her father touched her vagina, the world's red flags go up. He is caught! What does that mean?

The sex offender is ultimately going to hell on Earth for the rest of his life, in every respect possible. Forget about anything he had. It is gone, especially if he had peace.

They most likely will go to prison for a minimum of twenty years, more likely between twenty-five and thirty-two years in the worst state prison. They will be forced to do hard labor for more than eight hours per day, under extreme duress from everyone, including staff, counselors who won't visit them, guards will yell, hateful, violent inmates will torment. (If he is white, the risk of death or torture is very high, including castration—and men in prison who have been castrated, usually do survive, but eventually either commit suicide or get killed on a second assassination attempt.) He will be labeled the low life of the prison. He absolutely cannot wander off by himself, yet won't be able to hang out either. He will be monitored 24/7. He cannot stay in his cell all the time. Most likely, he will have to go to the kitchen and clean the huge, metal cooking pots with a very dangerous Latino community, also working there who traditionally hate child molesters.

They have knives in the kitchen, and for that matter, just about anywhere they know there is a predator. But before all that happens, they will ridicule him in front of the entire population; he is going to be famous for a while. Then they will make him pay rent, will give the boss all his money, which won't be much,

since he had to pay a lawyer a minimum of sixty-five thousand dollars cash up front, then the fees get real high, after knowing he's going to pay! Then there will be an order to pay restitution to the victim and family, and then they will sue for a million or so, on top of that in civil court. They are guaranteed to win, too! The sex offender will be broke for the rest of his life.

If he manages to survive prison, he won't have any place to go. All relatives will have already abandoned him, and they will hang the phone up on this one. He won't be allowed to rent any decent apartment or even ghetto housing. All property managers now have access to sex offenders files on the Internet and special channels that include child molesters, and no one rents to child molesters—no one.

No one loves or even acknowledges a child molester these days. That will include the mother in her grave, rest her soul, because these mothers don't live so long, after one of her boys goes to jail for molestation, especially of their granddaughter. She dies of stress much earlier than she should have, and she even commits suicide for bringing a monster into this world who will be alone, completely alone.

But there is one place that will accept him. It's called the Mission. At the Mission you have to get up early seven days a week, at five a.m. You have to be out by 5 30 a.m. with no shower. You had to take a shower the night before with four hundred other homeless, filthy, sick, coughing, gagging people all in a long, mandatory line with absolutely no clothes on, a penis or two will find your rear quarter, and you will be bumped into by someone who has Tuberculosis. You will catch something serious. He has to be in the Mission by seven p.m., or stay on the streets and then go back to prison for violating his post-prison supervision agreement. If he has not yet felt totally horrible about himself, he will at this juncture, because realization sets in that prison was better and we know that is most likely what will happen. His parole officer, who wants to see him every week, will send him back to prison for not having a job, not being able to pay supervision fees, for not being able to pay for State and Federal court-mandated sex offender treatment fees, that he does have to pay for (a minimum of $90/ week). No insurance company will pay for it. That bill usually adds up to about two thousand dollars by the second month. They have to do all kinds of testing, not including the lie-detector test polygraph, which costs more (at least $210 per test), and near all will most likely fail that, since they ask every question imaginable and applicable to putting them back in prison. Yes, back in prison!

Most sex offenders get five to ten years of what the Department of Corrections now calls Post-Prison Supervision or PPS, when released from pre

hell. PPS is the big monster, because the prison they came out of runs it, and they want them back! Why do they want them back? Because they were making money off of them at the hard labor prison job and they hate sex offenders too! Most will go back to prison at least once, after thinking they were free. The second time is worse, because everyone knows them there, and since the sex offender was free is a crime to them!

By the way, sex offenders don't tell anyone their release date, if they even get one; that's a guaranteed death sentence on the yard or anywhere else. When and if they get out of prison the second time, they know what to expect this time and try something different, usually something illegal. This will put them away for life, as all states now have something called repeat-offender laws, which can get anyone ten years for stealing a loaf of bread. But sorry to say, he will be so desperate he will commit a more serious crime, like burglary, and a child will be in the home. Then they will charge him with countless sex crimes. The prosecutor, FBI, police, and all law enforcement will be following this one the rest of his life, before he slips up, and some will design it so. This is the new cultural imposed and accepted justice for sex offenders. Yes, agencies do put incriminating evidence such as child porn photos in sex offenders belongings.

The IRS will become the sex offenders worst enemy. They know all about him, as directed by the District Attorney who put him away and wants him put away forever. Think he will be able to pay child support? That will become a new charge against him, and yes, that is a criminal charge. He still won't have a job and if so, it is a minimum wage dive such as a drain cleaner.

Most released sex offenders are irrational by this point and absolutely cannot make a correct decision. Some of the symptoms of their irrationality are complete delusion, paranoia, neurosis, fear, abandonment to the extent of pure separation loneliness. That means he will feel like a worm compared to everyone else and wish to die. Then someone will inevitably read him a scripture from the Bible, after he thought God had forgiven by conversion to Christianity. That scripture will be a line from Jesus, "It will be better in that day for a man to be drowned in the sea than to have been born." Just exactly what does that mean? It means that when people are drowned, they die. If it will be better for you to be drowned, then that means you won't die, but wished constantly that you could die; now that is horrible!

Does he believe in God or not? It doesn't matter at that point as nobody believes in him because he truly does live in Hell and life just is not worth living, unless he is a Polar Bear. What does that mean? Male Polar Bears kill their own cubs; that's why female Polar Bears take off after inception. She knows to

protect her babies. Polar Bears don't feel bad about anything, but humans are not strong Polar Bears. We are weaker human beings who will crumble to sorrow and shame for these crimes. Those will feel total rejection, even from within.

Just when the offender thinks it's time to move on, something more frustrating to his advancement will arise; actually it already had, but it got worse, his physical health. So far, I have only warned of very few plagues to mental health. His physical health will soon begin to deteriorate, then exponentially, into a very serious and debilitating problem.

Most become quite nervous, hair falls out in clumps. Their skin takes on a myriad of rashes and discolorations. Internal organ problems arise due to the stress that the brain has multiplied by releasing the wrong hormones and other chemicals into the blood. This will increase blood pressure, sugar levels, urea, and several other imbalances, which cause both physical and mental problems. The normal thought processes won't be up to par, and he will make crucially wrong and devastating decisions.

One noteworthy physical trait of child molesters is that they constitute a very large number (by statistic) of lower back problems, especially ruptured discs in the 5th lumbar section, nearly debilitating the individual. Why this is, no one knows, but you can check this bizarre and questionable statistic. Regardless, physical health will deteriorate, due to all the overwhelming stress. Most of all, appearance will be as a sickly sheepish person similar to that of a dying cancer victim. That is how I would describe a child molesters future, succumbing to the worst form of cancer. The victim actually feels good about that and, when he becomes aware of that, he gets worse. Much of this stress-induced health failure is from the rejection he will face from everyone. Once the predator is down like this, that is when he offends again. All of us have to put the predator down, before we ever offend at anything to include being offended by this material. Having troubles with that? Want to know how to put that down? Read on.

You question, Predator? Predator...me? Yes and three billion other men who emerged from our shared and biologic DNA learned history on this planet.

The Hunter-Gatherer and You

❧

Being a male, by nature, you like to do things outside that most women don't. Most men, even boys, like to hunt and fish. Why? You don't save any money at it and you really have to work to get that six-point deer or bear, or whatever you are going after, or properly put, hunting down. It's all ready for you in the supermarket where you can buy anything that you can hunt for, without needing a license or gun, and it is so much easier and cheaper to obtain.

Let's take this a step further. Who usually goes to war and does all the killing? Who usually starts violence? Who starts gangs? Who usually goes to jail for fighting? Who usually goes to jail, period! Why? Do men like to go to war? Do men like to fight? But do they like to go to jail too? In the next few pages of this book, I will make the correlation between this and the question: they knew that what they were doing was wrong, didn't they?

It is a societal failure to think that the offender knew what he was doing was wrong. That question really is totally irrelevant and leads nowhere helpful. Society says that a person knows better than to fight, steal, lie, or molest a child. This is enforced through the recent laws, installed into a very old human infrastructure. The truth is that the sex offender knows more about what he is doing instinctively than the people who made the laws against this behavior, especially the required lying! Telling the truth would be against their nature, but we all know that. And by knowing this truth, we can fight crime much more successfully; so let's get started. Remember now, if you are a male, you most likely love to go fishing, hunting, exploring, finding something new, looking for a…hmmm.

What is meant by "recently installed laws?" Laws against criminal behavior have been around for at least three thousand years. You'd think that is anything but recent; however, when you take into account the true age of human behavior, you discover that these laws have come about so suddenly that the average male, in his two million years of instinctively evolved existence, does not completely grasp this culturally imposed behavioral change. That means it was very difficult not to break laws, and today, it is still a task to obey. Instinct overpowers a law that requires you to *submit to* something contrary to what you have been doing freely for so long. Especially when you have been doing it for a million years. Your natural instinct hates change, especially when the change is against your historically enjoyable behavior.

Evolutionary instinct does exist. It is the instinctive behavior that made us most survivable throughout time. Great minds such as Steven Hawking make statements, such as, "If humans could put down Instinct and think into reason, we would have a chance at surviving." Hawking knows how powerful human instinct is. This instinct is by far stronger than imposed societal, cultural, evolutionary imposed change, which is actually resisted by humans. Total cultural evolutionary change actually does not exist yet. It is partial to the point of being a small fraction of what it is thought to be. There hasn't been enough time for it to function. Fear, the force behind primal instinct, does exist in full form and function.

Fear functioning is not safe. I will get into fear and the alternate to fear, later. For today's sake, let's redefine fear as *respect*. We must have respect for the unknown variables in life, as we at least have the awareness that the unknown could harm us. In our evolutionary history, we were always looking over our shoulder for dangerous threats. Those threats were the predators that were hunting us. The fact is, we respect those who can outdo us. Therefore, we have to use a form of fear or respect to create a reasonable prevention package. What does societal or cultural evolutionary change mean, anyway? Let's go back to the idea of natural evolution. Natural evolution often takes tens of thousands of years, just to make subtle changes in our human physical and behavioral makeup. For example, if you take African natives out of Africa and place them in a radically different environment, such as Chicago, how many generations or years will it take for their skin color to lighten, due to the lack of sunlight? (It is a scientific fact that African natives have dark skin to protect them from the sun's harmful rays, due to their historic location, and Caucasians have lighter skin in order to collect whatever rays are available in these sun-ray deprived areas, such as Chicago. Scientists believe we evolved over great epochs of time, in part due to

our local environment). So, with that in mind, societal cultural change cannot exist in the humans (yet), due to the fact that time and awareness are insufficient to enable it. We are still predators by factual scientific definition, and we shield that fact, since it is embarrassing.

Your first step to awareness is to fully accept who you are by the pure fact of where you come from. You came from the earth, and you learned to stay alive on it by whatever means were available or, what and who you could *overpower*. When you can accept that, you realize a mind-provoking thought. That thought should be that this is who you still are. Yes, you are battlefield-equipped to do serious damage. The equipment is in your head, and it is not going away; you are going to live with it all your life.

The answer I can give you is to first accept it, then learn to overpower it with reason. You may think that is easy, but that is the fallacy. To overpower your-self and your historical passions by yourself is impossible. Besides, by yourself you don't want to throw down. You want to enjoy yourself. If you are really hearing and contemplating any of this, you may just be feeling doubt and many fears, including the fear of change. I will tell you something to be afraid of, not recognizing *who* you really are and not changing. Don't doubt that. Don't doubt that change is good when you are able to reason. Why would you want to remain a spear chucker, when you could be a space explorer?

By the way, for you "creationists," don't stop here. I take an equal approach to sex abuse prevention from a clearly creationist point of view, later, as I am one.

Dwelling on the obvious again, you should know where I'm going with all of this, yes. However, let's, proceed with this line, and then we will get back to the novel. To put the predator down, you must know what the predator is, to recognize his often-rising face.

If you are driving in excess of a hundred miles an hour and a wall suddenly appears a hundred feet in front of you, what options do you have, besides dying? A perfect being would look for a fast solution, maybe drive faster and go through the wall unscathed. But you aren't perfect; you make errors. The truth is that, if you are not making errors, you are not making anything. The truth of the matter is that our legal system, which did not exist in your evolutionary-conditioned history, has put a sudden sexual behavior wall up in front of you and you are going ten miles an hour too fast through this part of life. At slow speeds like that, that could kill you, only if you are totally unaware, and that would be rare, such as you committing a double homicide. You really didn't evolve with influence from anywhere to commit senseless murder or senseless acts.

What this 10 mph speed and wall can do is severely damage you. This 10 mph speed is your caution, which has been inbred into you while you were hunting. What? Why? While you were hunting two million years ago, or for that matter, ten thousand years ago, you were aware of other creatures hunting you, such as a big cat, the chief predator of your day. Yes, the lion is the most powerful land predator alive. Recall the fingernail model now. The lion has fingernails, or more correctly, claws—long ones—for every aspect of survival, both for escape and to kill.

The lion cannot and does not desire to clip his nails, as he has no choice. But suddenly put him in a zoo. The male lion kills anything that even could be a threat to him, including rarely eliminating his own children or cubs. So, simply put, evolution has given you a yellow flag or cautionary device that allows you to be alert for that lion, and that safety to look over your shoulder can be directed to see the prosecuting attorney's law, and power over you. It is similar to, but it is not a zoo, in that the change is as quick and you are being *asked* to control yourself. You realize that it is time to put the Predator Down.

Now you say, "Oh, a cheap answer to a complicated buildup." I did not give you an answer yet, but I will, later. Read it again; it says, "You realize." That's the first step in eliminating the million-year conditioning of the predatory tendency or choosing to go a different way. I am going to help you find that way. This is the problem, many people do not know the alternate way and don't believe it when they hear of it. That is the second step, the most important, since you will always go back to step one and before, if you cannot see the alternate. Trust me when I say the alternative is better in the sense it is really an advancement in yourself. This advancement that I will discuss soon is actually a real change in your physical brain. Anyone that can read this can make this wonderful transformation with a little work.

When you realized the lion was tracking you ten thousand years ago, you escaped him, since you respected him in your fear. You hunted elsewhere, since you had to. What I'm doing here is making you realize and especially become actually aware that you are an evolved hunter-gatherer. As a hunter, your history spans millions of years, and you cannot realistically conform to sudden changes, such as the law, without total awareness of that matrix of change and your history in that change. It was not illegal for you to rape ten thousand or even two thousand years ago and, as difficult as it is to believe, it is still acceptable legally to orally sodomize your own children in many countries. In Guatemala, it is considered affection.

Humans have been abusing children since the beginning of our primal existence, and we have been getting away with it, reinforcing our current behavior. We now are, in fact, living in a zoo of sudden cultural and evolutionary change. A zoo is nothing more than a controlled environment of both safe and dangerous animals. You cannot realistically quickly change in this culture or man-made zoo for many reasons. You are evolutionarily programmed or conditioned to only accept slow change, except in special circumstances, such as cataclysmic emergencies. This is why so many people take some things that you consider unimportant as the most important issues of their survival or an emergency. We will class sexual abuse there, in that emergency folder.

Evolution has provided us with a mental ability called adaptation, as our past environment has never been stable. Humans are the best at adapting, a tree cannot run from a forest fire, but a human runs, since he has been conditionally brought to awareness, mental awareness of surroundings or environment. Awareness is the key to rapid adaptation. That is science, or fact, not theory, you cannot fool yourself about the need to be aware to adapt. Adaptation and awareness have been partially lost in the last 2000 years, due to life becoming more stable and constant. This is the key as to why there is so much human error recently concerning moral issues and the law. We truly do not know what is going on as societal laws have moved constantly too quickly.

Adaptation through awareness is the key to succeed in avoiding molesting a child, even though one may desire to do so, with that same emergency sense. That same evolutionary urgency one may have to procreate or have sex has factually given you the same level of urgency to abstain or run and look elsewhere. It has simply been lost, or better said, *misplaced* in the move toward modern, civilized man. This mechanism has been labeled "fight or flight." However, flight is easily recoverable when you are made aware of who you truly are. So how do we find out who we are? History has those answers. If you can accept those facts and swallow modern-day pride, you can advance further than you ever dreamed. "Predator" has been labeled as a terrible word, but housecats are predators—those nice furry, fluffy, loving, playful, purring ones that many of us love! Hm.

What does it mean to be a gatherer? Basically, it means you gave up the hunt as a survivor in the sense that you ate alternative foods, such as fruits and vegetables and picked up what you could peacefully to make your life as comfortable as possible, when hunting was out of the question, e.g., no deer or fish around. Your desire would still be there to kill and eat it, but over time you began to enjoy the mangos and blackberries. The potatoes and spices were especially to

your taste; then you expanded your cultivation to include cows and chickens, which were also more convenient to eat.

So this first section of *Predator Down* is about learning to manage your primal instincts that brought you to this place in time from your origins two or three billion years ago. Yes, we have advanced from that first cell that swallowed up what it could to survive, to a modern-day human, who now has alternatives to simple survival and to live very comfortably. The basis of that is to truly know where these instincts come from and to know the consequences of allowing your instincts to remain in use over our more advanced societal thinking. So obvious, now isn't it! But how do you manage it? I'm sorry to say that it does take some work; that work is called "reconditioning."

Your body truly responds to exercise and becomes healthy, or healthier. Recall that I talked about people who had been abused and their DNA or genetic material revealed that it had been altered. We now have proof that the brain is not stuck in its final form. The brain can and actually does change its physical makeup. We call this Brain Plasticity, a term you can look up to discover what I am telling you is fact. What I am relaying is that a change of attitude is not always and does not have to be just a change of one's opinions.

You can exercise your brain in a way that it will actually change its physical-visual makeup and become healthier, in the sense of you feeling incredible, happy, competent, and capable of excellent socializing. You will be able to deal with stress with surprisingly easy solutions and no fear. You will not become sick as often in your body, and any mental illness would be very difficult to acquire. Your brain in a high state of health will allow you incredible ability. That includes great ease in learning and understanding difficult issues. This reconditioning is called change of form and comes through brain plasticity exercises. How do you do that? It could be embarrassing for some of you tough guys. It means getting happy, no matter what is in your way, including bad physical health.

It starts out by imagining everything you are involved with is truly positive based. You may have put a negative imprint on it before, but now you see it as something you can be pleased with, without taking any action on it or him/her, with the exception that you are tethered to it all, or part of it all. You really are.

The second step to a very healthy brain is pleasure. Pleasure also carries that attachment of things and people. But most of all, it is that attachment to yourself and seeing everyone else the same way. Let's find some pleasure!

Find something that you like, love, or adore that is legal and do it over and over, as much as you can. Learn it as an acquired taste. Redevelop your character,

acquire yourself, reacquire yourself to the liking of other people, when they like you, love them and really love yourself. Become a part of everyone, as you are a part of yourself. You will never get bored with yourself this way, and your new character will allow you many friends that enjoyably bring you more safe pleasure.

Pleasure is always taken over anything that is not pleasurable. Don't think that pleasure wasn't around 300,000 years ago; our ancestors truly indulged in such things as art or enjoyed food. They enjoyed making love, and many others enjoyed sex at will. Keep that in mind. They enjoyed eating food with those who helped get it. The pleasure then graduated to talking about how good it was, which led to social pleasure in itself. I am placing evidence here that pleasurable social behavior was a strong a part of our evolutionary past, as was the not so pleasurable necessary predatory hunt, which led us to social bonding in the first place. So what I am saying is that we had to remain predators but, to survive together in groups, we had to become mentally and socially separated from the chaos of the wild. This was the greatest single advance in human history. This is my evidence that the civil, evolved gene does exist in us as equally powerfully as the wild predatory gene, since it was placed in our "self-controllable, decision-making" folder. And the truth is, it is all contained in our biology and psychology. We are teachable, pliable, and convincible humans that can and must change to reach higher goals.

One problem is that the pleasure gene is easy to cover up, since the hunter was aggressive, long before he found pleasure. There is a solution for that, how to uncover pleasure, even though you will never be able to terminate the hunter or predator of the past. You must maintain the pleasure to recondition your brain. This is a goal. Goals prove to be greater pleasure rewards than say sex and ice cream. Drugs and alcohol are temporary pleasures that one can indulge in, if the quantities do not cause brain damage. But Drugs are not goals, so let's discuss the need for goals.

If you have no goals, you are choosing that half of history in your DNA, which is predatory or antisocial. Why? Because that is the natural forward-moving line where we are in our evolution, which is connected to our chemistry of well being. You will think in terms that are wild rather than civil, if you do not set your upward evolution with others. This self-chosen behavior will then be furthered chemically by involuntary brain function, to revert to primal instincts. This boils down to pure body chemistry, which will be difficult to recognize in the early stages as deviant. The math is in our chemistry, which cannot be refuted. It is stored as genetic memory.

Our predatory memory is much older and more established than our recent social instincts. The human brain has many older layers, such as the reptilian seat of aggression, as opposed to newer social, cortical layers. We pack around with us excess old baggage that still works as good as it ever did two million years ago in our heads. That is what *Predator Down* is all about, not using those old reptile parts of the brain, recognizing them, and reverting to cortical thinking processes. So what is the greatest goal you can attain? The goal of becoming connected with yourself, the cosmos, and most of all, people. Be social!

This is why I give the only viable solution, continue with social evolution by using the cortex more or socialize with good goal seekers. This is good, scientific, factual advice for females; allow your boyfriend or husband the social bonding without the stress. Allow him to go out and have some fun, and you should be able to verify that it is with good people. It is clinically proven that many fathers who abused their own children suffered great stress, due to scant outside social bonding. If you are serious and moving towards depression, you will make bad decisions. The more serious your mind becomes, the more you can trick yourself into doing normally unthinkable . . . crimes. Thus, the premise of *Predator Down* is set with unwavering position, based on proven science, real life, and all of our history.

The human spirit as a whole, when moving together, is very accurate, positive, and goal seeking. Individual humans can work harmoniously together with the accuracy of a computer; this is proven in singing groups, such as Celtic Woman singing. The lead singers and choir performed in absolute, perfect timing when they sang "Orinoco Flow" in live concert. The reward to those watching and listening was immense pleasure. This leads to positive desires. The singers themselves have the rewards of great accomplishment, not to mention all the other points that help them. The point is, if you were in any type of group, you would be noticed immediately if you were out of sync.

When you detach yourself mentally, with secrets, the limits of failure are far greater than that level of success had you never crossed the line. That means you will never attain success again, if you abuse a child. The district attorney did not make the current zoo we live in; people as a whole did. Our current zoo or society has its problems for certain, but if we all participated to make it better, there is hope for a safe and bright future for all. That's where the complicated answers come into play, but the truth is, the more people that get involved with each other, the more answers we obtain.

I cannot give you any specific answers concerning your social behavior, but I can assure you of something; happiness and social bonding with others is

guaranteed to keep you out of trouble and advance your life, especially when you focus on Brain Plasticity and continue to get your brain in shape. This chapter is condensed to this: smiles, laughter, joking, playing, and doing it all with friends. I am cutting this subject short to have an impact on you, as it absolutely is an answer carved in stone. It is solely up to you to make the decision. You already have everything to succeed. I was once asked, "What do you need to have paradise on Earth, Marco, mansions, money, brains, charm, women, what?" I replied that I only need one thing and I already have it; it is life. I have life and from life, nothing can be held from me, when I share my life with others. My brain just got healthy sharing that with you.

If you had ten friends that were working towards a common goal, you would have a solid base for success in bonding with them. The wonderful thing about friends or a social group is that you can ask them for help, and if you can get up the courage, ask them for help in this specific area. Of course, everyone is going to pitch in their two cents worth, but as a whole, you can get remarkably good directions. If you act alone, your mind is certainly going to deviate from the normal thinking process of those ten people, and this will lead to you acting out on decisions where you could cause damage. This is the meaning of deviation or deviance. This leads to alienation from the group, no matter whether your decisions are legal or not, but *if* they are.

Molest a child, and you will cause hell on Earth for many, right? You will be punished forever, right? If you still don't think so, please read on. It will become obvious. We will explore the facts. For those of you who are past this, I truly apologize to you for the insult. Trust me, however, there are those who will put their hands in the fire believing nothing will happen, and there are even more who will put there hands in the fire, knowing exactly what will happen, but they will do it anyway. These are more than the defiant; these are the ones I'm talking to. Please listen. You are the ones who want a better experience and future. You actually do, and you want a shortcut to get there. Keep that in mind, along with alternatives or adaptations, awareness, consequences, and respect are truly better than your current desire, as we proceed with *Predator Down*.

The Hideous Avoided Obvious

Children seem, to most parents, to have a separation of mind and body. The body does so much that the mind can't possibly be directing it to do all those activities, especially those things that seriously annoy the parent.

This is a very serious reality when it comes to sexual abuse. The sex offender finds that out in his illegal laboratory of molesting children, children seem to enjoy sex. This fuels the predator to continue his abusive behavior and justify it by entering this frame of mind, which accepts that the child loves the sexual abuse. This is what therapists call "thinking errors." Thinking-error therapy is a misnomer, as the two-million-year history of humans has evolved in an environment of almost no right or wrong decision-making processes, concerning moral behavior. Even the word *thinking* itself should tell you something, if you are to understand these actions. The truth is, the predator doesn't think; he acts on his genetic memory or instinct. The child is also acting out on DNA memory or instinct. How can one be thinking and making errors of such a nature, when there are no errors to be made concerning this nature? Are four-year-old children really making thinking errors concerning body response? Do adults suddenly morph into know-it-alls at some specific point in time, to know all the possible errors that could be made?

Would Hitler have benefited or changed his plans, knowing he was error thinking? What if he could have been shown who he really was and the future results of his actions? I will not support the therapists' failed attempt at thinking-error therapy, as it should be refitted as deviant-thought occurrences. Thinking-error therapy permits the offender to excuse himself daily with such things as forgetting his car keys due to the thinking-error unawareness. This gives him too

much room to avoid facing his deviance. Thinking-error therapy is not condescending of itself, but if one were to daily apply error thinking, it would eventually degrade the human spirit to an error himself. In other words, it's like saying, "Fuck man, what am I for sure going to do wrong today so why do anything?!" It should be more like, "Don't worry about it, since there are no errors," because we are just constantly cycling for the better. I will uncover instilled-thinking processes, based on our human history of conditioned behavior.

I will prove that it is our history, fear instinct, and conditioned behavior that struggle against modern societal law. It's not that we are making errors; instead, most of us are thinking about what had been acceptable up until recent time. Many of us are still doing what was acceptable, for the same reason it was acceptable in the past.

I am talking about reconditioning or rapid-emergency change to protect yourself. A death move that many label an error would be to walk into a lion's den. This has nothing to do with morals, especially when a person is unaware of the den, so he or she would not be thinking about entering. A thinking person does not do things like that unless he or she wants to die horribly. The truth is, we humans are unaware of too much to classify low awareness as *error*. Conditioned and learned behavioral actions, tried and proved over time, with high awareness, would be to try to get away with stealing the lion's catch, when there is low risk. Another example is having sex with a fourteen-year-old child you normally could have two thousand years ago.

There was no connotation of error concerning sex abuse two thousand years ago, since there was no deterrent or punishment. In reality, there was a driving force for these actions, in addition to the hormones, and that drive may still be of the highest magnitude ever known, as life or death. Think of that concerning driven human behavior connected to sex crimes. Evidence has shown that, throughout ancient history, humans had more depth and strength based in driven fear or respect for oneself than they did for morality. This developed into a long-term cycle that is hard to break. The sudden grouping of societies during the last four thousand years converted fear and respect into moral issues. Punishable crimes against children were not been made into law until very recent times. Fossil records of many societies from the Mayans to modern-day religious sects prove that human sacrifice and child sexual abuse were acceptable worldwide. Parents of atheist backgrounds to Archbishops in the church still seem to think the same way from their actions against children.

You then have to ask, what about the stiff laws we have now? I will answer with the hardest truth I can. If we had no laws, eventually only the very strongest

and smartest would be left alive. Crime and chaos would eventually be the norm. What does that tell you about all those people who would kill and who, in fact, exist in vast numbers? It doesn't tell you anything pleasing, except that it proves why we made laws. We know people will cause harm without the law. Many commit crimes despite the law, so that proves humans are in fact predators that need to be in a controlled environment, if they are to do more than survive.

We would never have made it to the lunar surface or invented the light bulb without the law. If you think about it, that is why we have had a great explosion of technology and knowledge in the last one hundred years. Laws equal order, which allows advancement. Laws are the number one reason for our current exponential advances. Think of how you can use the law to your advantage, rather than taking advantage of someone.

It's going to take more than fifty thousand years for humans to naturally obey the law by culturally-imposed evolution. Your present day adaptation hope is that you change your approach to a way that is legal, yet for it to be as pleasing as if it were illegal. One of those approaches could be to not believe a societal norm that you have to have lots of money and have a hot girlfriend! In other words, escape away from *beliefs* that come from lawmakers and the society of phonies. That is the historical backdrop of the law-enforced society, which is condescending on the poor and incompetent.

There is always going to be noticeable and distractive levels of competence in an enforced society. The low level is the problem to society. So if you see where I am going with this, the obvious answer is to work at advancing your mind away from primal urges to civil actions. The error of operating alone is the number one precursor to deviance or crime.

So, does the criminal really make thinking errors when he molests a child? Not according to history. All he is really doing is something that just existed in life—with no "wrong" or "right" attached to it. There was no normal life; there was just life. There were no laws against orally sodomizing your own child. So what is the father doing, then? He is doing what predators were conditioned to do. Something more horrid to divulge is that the children became trained and conditioned to accept sexual abuse. Now, it's incredibly horrid and unbelievable to many people due to the law. The law has changed the way people think who have come to high awareness. These people spread this emotion over the population, but they don't realize it isn't always taken quite so seriously. Why? Many men relate to the predator within them, and they don't want to let go. Children actually display this instinct more openly than adult males. It frightens many to

know what boys are aware of. It is time to realize that six-year-old boys are very predatory.

In 1962, a mother placed a tape recorder in her daughter's room. The daughter was six and she had a new stepbrother who was also six and a-half. The stepbrother was kissing the girl's vagina. The case was well investigated, and there was absolutely no prior sexual abuse or knowledge of sex. The child psychologists revealed the young boy had asked his stepsister if he could kiss her somewhere. She replied, where do you want to kiss me, on my face, my hand? He told her and she said no. After a month of persistence, the six-year-old boy had committed oral sex on the six-year-old girl. The girl experienced what is labeled as the "separation of mind to body response." The shrink jury is still out on cases like this. I say we have to take the position that sexual behavior is naturally instilled as instinct, especially since there are frightfully staggering numbers of cases identical to this worldwide. These thousands of cases have naturally been hidden away carefully, due to our shame.

Again, I suggest that we put away shame and replace it with honor recognizing our ability to change and advance from instinct to cognition. The facts exist in our history; the ability to admit who we are enables us to put the predatory traits down through true foundations of awareness that allow true change for the better. This solid, truthful approach to development by teaching who we are and who we can be could be the greatest advance in the history of crime prevention.

So, what is the solution to preventing sexual abuse against children? I have been talking about the law and what happens to criminals. But let's forget about the law for a minute and say that everyone is allowed to do what he or she wants to do. So, now you can go do exactly what you desire. Now imagine where you and the rest of the world would be in a very short time. What did it do for you? Are you going to sit with your family and discuss it over dinner? There wouldn't be any dinner table is my answer. You see, if it were legal to sexually abuse, everyone would hide from it. Everyone would self-destruct from it. Everyone would eventually die from it. We would, at best, revert to the stone age. So let's talk about sex abuse.

A father who commits the crime of oral sex on his daughter at the very young age of two to five years old will justify in his mind that his child loves this act. What he thinks he is doing is trying to seduce the child into full sexual activity. I select oral sexual abuse in these cases, as it is the statistical starting point for most abusive fathers. Clinically, it is proven the child will actually return to the father and ask him without fear to do this act, after the second or third violation. This will lead to other acts of sexual abuse by the father. But, what the

father does not understand, is that this child's body and mind, together, is not a uniform, functioning organism, yet, and this act is mixing up the child's mind in horrendous ways. The child, not by nature, but by teaching, knows this is deviant behavior and in her mind is very wrong. She trusts her father and is trained to do so. However, the rest of the world she lives in teaches her this is the most horrible and most hideous act in existence. This destroys her from within in so many ways there is not space in this book to explain it fully. Children that experience sexual abuse don't turn in their offenders, and they are torn between being misunderstood, having self-imposed guilt, juxtaposed with the enjoyable physical response of their bodies to the sexual stimulation.

The body is a chemical-response entity, for example drug addiction. Once the addict has become dependent on heroin, the mind does not have too much choice in the matter. The body's chemistry has taken over. Just as a child's body should never be exposed to addictive drugs, as this will kill the child's body and mind, the child's body should never be exposed to premature sexual stimulation, as this will deviate and confuse that part of the normal developing mind in modern-day society.

A specific case exists of trained childhood abuse impact and lifelong deviation that started when a girl was five. The abuse was limited exclusively to oral sex committed on her. She developed a lifelong fetish, focused solely on oral sex and never desired intercourse. Her I.Q. was high, but her well being was almost zero, and she never held a working position. Her suicide note read, "There has to be more to life than this constant memory of my father asking me if I came."

The message in this interlude is to the potential sex offender; yes, you can get a child to do just about anything, and they seem to love it. Make no mistake, they are too young, mentally and emotionally, to understand. When they get older in today's society, however, they will understand things in such a different way than you expected, and you will experience everything negative that has already been discussed in previous interludes. Abuse victims turn in the offender, when they get older, just when he thought he had gotten away with it. During the interim period of ages eight through seventeen, and even beyond, in many cases, the child can actually take back control from the father, knowing she can incarcerate him. This threat dangling over the father's head to obey an eight-year-old's every request or else she's telling mommy is just the beginning of the punishment.

Adaptation awareness is the answer for the predator of today; that is to replace crime with legal passion, rather than feeding the million-year-old conditioned behavior. Predator down is the answer; read on to find out.

Oh, even though that child has temporary control of Dad, she has less a chance of recovery than he does, unless of course, if God. . . .

La Visita

· · · · · · · · · · · · · · ·

Higher Order Intel Observation, a story of aliens visiting Earth to study the human species. Characters Kiko and Chavo from Galaxy M31, planet Perfect.

"Kiko, do you note this deviant behavior among these oficias and aware beings as being unusual?"

"I will not answer that question. I will say that they fight it pretentiously from the male side. The female wants to put an end to it but she doesn't know how to get through to the male. They are missing information vitally needed to achieve this goal."

"I agree, Kiko. They are dismissing why the male acts against his identity. They do not understand that the reason why is the key to unlocking this problem. We must devise a plan to solve this problem they suffer from greatly, as they have become aware of advancement. This species or any species like ours cannot advance with deviance, or it will eventually self-destruct."

"Chavo, they are aware of the double-helix storage median."

"Yes, but their history was inadequately documented. They do not have all the facts of the helix memory. They need to know why they do what they do, in order to move to the acceptable step of instant-requirement behavior change. They need the answer *why* for two reasons. The first one is the premise that a building cannot stand if it does not have the right foundation. Their foundation is not only misunderstood, but in many cases, horribly hindering and untrue. The second reason is that they need to know how to be secure within ranges of contentment with life itself."

"Then we must give them proof to show the *why*; we need to select an animal that clearly displays the helix memory."

"Yes, Kiko, that would be a good starting point. They have what is called a domestic house cat. This species has completely retained all its DNA memory and has learned also to adapt to living with the humans for security and comfort."

"Very good example, Chavo. The cat has learned that it must obey the human's rules or it will not get unearned food and shelter and all the care of attention, giving the cat a longer, more enjoyable life. The consequences to the cat would be hunger and homelessness."

"Excellent, we will show the humans that the cat has retained helix or DNA memory, or what they call instinct. We will prove the cat has unlearned behavior, compelling it to act out these instincts."

"Yes, Chavo, and the best instincts to tell them about is cats are very territorial and defensive. The cat always instinctively buries his waste. No cat was ever taught this, but all house cats do this. All house cats instinctively hunt, even though they are well fed by the humans."

"Don't forget that the male house cat will also sexually engage any female cat. We know that the male will engage in sex acts with his own offspring, while they are only a few months old. We noted that correctly."

"Yes, we did, so we will include that in the sexual instincts of the human male, as well. I am surprised the humans have not discovered this correlation."

"Chavo, what the human male has trouble accepting is that he has humiliating difficulty accepting he even has instincts. He has trouble that he has a background so abasing."

"Then we must show him that he will be more than humiliated, if he continues to reject who he is; he will destroy himself."

"This is not an easy task, now that I think about it, Kiko."

"Yes, this is why most civilizations snuff themselves out at this stage of advancement. But if they had the answers now they could be saved."

"Why do they do the crimes? They simply think it is because they want to and can."

"Chavo, you must then tell them why they do crimes, Chavo."

"Yes, Kiko, they do the crimes, not because they want to or can, but because they are compelled to do them. They need to be correctly informed so they can be freed of their DNA memory or instinct. The million-year history of DNA memory in their bodies and minds compel them to do these acts. The instinct is stronger in some humans than others, depending on where they evolved. I will not focus on where they evolved, though, Kiko. I will tell them that their actions of crime are close to what they call passion, or crimes of passion, a very strong force from within that explains why they are so compelled to do the opposite of what the situation demands.

To defeat it, they must understand why this is such a strong force. They must understand how they used it to protect and preserve themselves in the past. Then they will understand why this same force changed so quickly in the modern world, or they will destroy themselves with this same compelling behavioral instinct. It is time to tell them to put the instinct down and think with the cortex. They are smart enough to understand that now. They just got caught up

in mystery, since they never knew why they were compelled to act as they did. They invented reasons."

"You must give them very clear examples to be able to prove it. This is a species that requires proof."

"What about the six-year-old boy who did oral sex to his six-year-old stepsister?"

"That was not a unique case; there have been countless cases in their history like that one, where the children had absolutely no sexual learned behavior before that."

"Yes, we know that this is instinct, but how do we prove that to the humans?"

"The same way it was proved to us."

"Yes, we saw the boy kiss the little girl on the vagina. We investigated and found that the boy never learned this act. We asked where this behavior originated. And we found that it originated from *within* the boy. We then asked where the boy originated. We found he originated from the DNA, which was passed down to him from a very distant past. We found that, in this boy's DNA he had a strip of DNA or chromosome the female did not have that contained this compelling set of instructions to act on as soon as he was able to. We found there was no control mechanism on this chromosome, except his neural deciding factor, which was actually set up to propagate this compulsion. But it can be reconditioned to put the PREDATOR DOWN!"

Thinking with the Cortex

....

"Hi, Bob, you just get a new vehicle, man? You finally got rid of that old clunker?"

"Yes, the other one did get old and couldn't keep up in traffic, overheated too, and was getting dangerous. Its suspension wasn't designed to handle and brake as fast as these modern, antilock vehicles do that are connected to new processors. It was simply outdated; I could have gotten into an accident and hurt someone, even my own family."

You know how to tell when you're driving with the old brain? Ha. I didn't mean the old brain in the sense of being cool; you have an old section up there that actually dates back about two million years. It would still be very useful if you lived five hundred thousand years ago, and with the addition of a current new processor, the cortex, you would have been the richest ruler of all time if

you had wanted. But I can tell you how to know when you're thinking with the old brains; being *afraid* is the number one giveaway.

If you are concerned about something, you are using your cortex; concern involves intelligent problem solving solutions. Asking "why?" is evidence that you evolved a cortex, so you could make safer decisions without the irrational destruction of Mother Nature herself. You are an integral part of it all. This is a wonderful ability to help you think with the cortex and not the Tyrannosaurus Rex brain that you have sitting under all that! Yes, but I am not reluctant to tell you this embarrassing fact: we are part dinosaur. We are also part dog, alligator, and monkey. That's right, you have all those brain layers in you that function today as they were intended to many years before all of us were born. The good news is we can avoid using those old parts of the brain with awareness that we have new brains that outperform the old parts. The trick is to shut off the old parts by using the new ones.

Some new thinking parts are the frontal lobes. These are actually the high-speed brakes of our new brains. When working properly, the frontal lobes shut down irrationality and anger. We know from Magnetic Resonance Imaging or MRI brain scans that people with under-developed frontal lobes have little braking ability. These people cannot easily calm down or rationalize. We know that people with well-developed frontal lobes are very capable of controlling anger and fear.

Your question should be, "How do I use the new parts and not the old ones?" The truth of that is very simple and has been obvious to many people for many years. Since the majority of humans have evolved correctly, the new parts have mostly blocked the old parts. This is not true of many people, however. We know the connections are there but not as well wired as they could be. We also know that awareness of these facts is helpful, even to the point of equal functioning of the best brains out there. That is proven to be true as the Cerebral Cortex is capable of a wonderful intervention beyond instinct, which is learning. We can learn to know and recognize ourselves completely by becoming aware of who we really are. This is true even in brain-damage cases, since various areas of the brain can relearn.

Many people say the first step of correcting behavior is that you have to want to be good or not want to be a criminal; in other words, make a commitment to obey the law. This stance means you must be willing to be socially acceptable and to not get out of line. I challenge this position as being the most ignorant, misleading advice ever given. I will compare it to putting a five-year-old boy behind the wheel of a Mack truck and telling him to go as fast as he can through the city

center. What I am saying is that you cannot commit to doing anything, unless you are aware of the machine. You must be aware of what you truly are capable of first, both good and bad. You have to recognize where the bad decisions come from. You have to be able to shut the bad ones down early. You have to know why you need to shut the bad ones down, aware that, if you act on the bad ones, they will result in your failure as a human, as we have already discussed.

So, how do we become aware that those instincts will cause us to fail in today's world? First, a modern human must recognize his own negative energies that came from our instinctive, distant past. Now, I will inject that no matter how serious or horrible the situation is, there is no room for any level of your instinctive anger or fear. I will condone fear only when you rationally figure out, quickly, a situation when you need to flee, but keep your fear balanced, as you will need to think of an escape route, as well.

So, to recognize the instincts that will hinder you, first be aware that reason is trying its best to get to your consciousness. You have to learn how to listen, especially if you have developmental problems, but it is there. It usually reveals itself with a very quick possible solution, without anger, fear, and attack. Ignoring the quick solution, your brain will revert immediately to the lower layers, just as an alternate computer would take over programs in even the most sensitive cases, if the primary computer did not respond. In other words you do have a failsafe program to revert to the old one, if you don't act on the first one. You've heard it said that your first decisions are the best ones; there is some validity in that if you are thinking and wired into the situation.

Men having problems with women in domestic affairs will only succeed if they outsmart the situation with fact. Men that do not think with the cortex when having problems with women will revert to the alternate and will react with anger and fear and will attack. These responses will override the thinking cortex from the more powerful, million-year-old instinct, which does not recognize consequences to oneself. It will be manifested in that moment, as "I don't care what happens to anyone, even myself, because I am going to get my way right now."

When I said that a man can outsmart the situation, it could mean he has to realize what the woman is mad about, especially if it is something he did wrong, something he doesn't want to admit to. If that is the case, his instinct is already in operation, since he won't admit to wrongdoing. It would be good to be aware of that type of situation, right then. These are the tricky situations where you change the facts for lies, which enable the lower parts of your brain to fool even you. So what I am saying is that honesty is an indicator that will enable you to

identify which part of the brain you are using, and dishonesty is a red flag. Lies and deception come from the predatory past in how we tricked our prey, as well as our women. If you are lying to your woman and thinking you can rationally think with your cortex, forget it. It isn't wired that way; it is wired to be connected to your heart, as well. Polygraphs proved that years ago.

Fear, anger, and the desire to attack or sexually offend a child all come from the inadequate old brain. Especially be aware and recognize anger as quickly as possible, put the brakes on, and work yourself through with intelligent concern. If you don't have the intelligence, do not revert to impatience; look for someone who does have the knowledge to help you through. Remember, working and living together with your group of friends is the absolute best measure to your success. Sometimes, we are alone and cannot solve a problem. That is why many women will go away for awhile; try doing the same when you cannot do anything else. It is better than fighting and failing.

And that is exactly where I am going to leave you, as there are so many good books out there to tell you how to find yourself in your cortex! Try Dr. Phil or Oprah's list; they are wonderful!

The solution remains and is found in the "Why," and I'm going to do it in reverse. Why would you need to be afraid? It does you no good to be afraid; if anything, it makes you nervous. If you are nervous, you cannot perform. You then make deviant decisions. Being afraid is a simple response, an easy one, without much thought, that comes from that million-year-old, outdated vehicle we now call instinct. I hate the word *instinct*, as it absolutely says nothing. What it means to humans is that, before birth, you were conditioned over great expanses of time to be equipped for survival. That's why babies cry, so they can alert someone. Instinct is why babies suckle breasts without being taught. Instinct is why human predators still exist. Predators are instinctive and are born that way and we cannot blame them for being born.

Instinct is all about why we do so many irrational things. We always ask, why did you do that? I need a reason, tell my why! The answer is simple; we used to do it to stay alive. Now we do irrational things, since we incorrectly think from instinct that our actions will keep us alive. Thinking about that should tell you this is the most powerful force you have. The instinct for staying alive is fused to sexuality, whether deviant or not. So, if your sexuality is in fact deviant, you're contending with a monster force in today's society.

Now, let's take it a step further. Why would you rob a convenience store? Because you were afraid you wouldn't have money to support someone or yourself. Why would someone rape a woman or molest a child? Because they

were afraid of *not* answering the compulsion that has driven them all their life. Why? Because they were not commanding their thoughts with the cortex, which allows you to intelligently use and direct the compulsion in safe avenues. Have you ever seen a giant, fat, ugly brute with a beautiful knockout woman and wonder why she is with him? He knows why! He is using his skills! That's why! If you are having problems with that, then you need to understand the need to fascinate and impress women with your cortex. That is the way it actually was in our history and will most likely,,, always will be. Something of great importance is that you can allow women to do the same thing, fascinate and impress you with the remarkable brain she also possesses. Opening up to her is a good way to learn about yourself and also protects yourself by something called empathetic realization. That in short means you have come to an aware thinking position, enabling you to truly identify with her to the point it is very difficult if not near impossible to hurt her as she has become a part, (person) maybe a part (Person) of you.

There is nothing plastic or fake about authentic fascination. It means there is something admirable about yourself, and the number one fascination to women is a man who is simply REAL! There is absolutely no limit to your successes, but if you resort to the simple-minded fear response of "I cannot be with the best people on the planet," then you will humiliate yourself in a thousand ways. Your fear was instinctively installed on your DNA a million years ago by the forceful male who could take women with his brute strength.

If you tried to get the best woman, you had to fight him (just as wild animals still do) and one of you was going to die for her. If you couldn't have sex with the best women or women, period, you had sex with whoever was available, since they were for the taking. Hence, this is where the sexual predator gene began, and this is where the fear of failure was also born. This is exactly why all this shit happens today. This is 2011. You don't have to do that anymore, and you are smarter than your predatory ancestor ever was. Women have evolved too. They're probably smarter than men, since they have had to sit in the back seat and observe all this squirming throughout history. Women are very keen, too, especially concerning intuition. That's a very good thing if you are real with them. You are as good as anybody. All you need to do is get away from the old and explore the new.

It is time to take an unwavering position; yes, you can argue with me on this firm position. I am asking if you will stop and think of all the good this position could do, especially if you can be convinced to believe it. Think about that for a moment. Imagine putting the doubt and mysticism away that causes so much

confusion. Our existence from the fossil record alone is a fact, not a theory; the only theory is if God set it up that way.

Our history is engraved all about us and in us. It seems that denying it would be harmful or, better said, has been harmful. What could believing in all of this harm, who could it harm? If you think about that, who could blame you for being born with specific behavioral traits? Thinking about it further should be a relief to you for other reasons; the grandest is you cannot feel half as bad, and that is more than the half of it all.

The truth is, it is all you are and, from that, you can get satisfaction from a key point. That key is you have the opportunity to better yourself and your children through changing who you are. Cats do it, since they have to; you could do it since you want to. And just maybe this is the way God wanted humans to learn. This is what *Predator Down* and settling down is all about: Learning. Fearlessly keep it real.

<blockquote>

"But Mom, why?"

"Cause I said so!"

The Why, Why it is so important to know Why.

</blockquote>

So far, many of you may be frustrated, because you don't see the reason or need of the subject material I have brought to you. This page hopefully will answer those questions and bring you that awe and ultimate satisfaction. This page is absolutely the most important page in this book. The trouble is, this page is *possibly* an after-the-fact rehabilitation matter.

It is essential for a child, especially a very young child to have real answers in her instinctive way to be able to understand. If a child understands something, he or she is on the way to success. Children need answers even more so in the way they were taught and saw the world before they were abused. We adults only need to know why, so we can let the children know. Of all the answers a child gets, *how* is actually the least of them. He saw how it was done; she saw what was done and who did it. But this child is always wondering why this was done to him or her, or to anybody, or at all! It can be said that a child's wonder is a strong force.

If a child's mind is going to be set in a sad, guilty frame of mind, wondering why, why, why, what's going to be the outcome? The *why* is going to hang around causing more trauma until it gets answered. The sooner it gets answered the better. The reason I took the stance of *why* wasn't so much for therapists and pre-offenders, it was to give the child his or her first step at healing.

Incorporated into the reason for *why* is for those many who say, "We don't care why!" That type of ignorance will assure us of one thing. We will all become monsters, eventually, and create more pedophiles, rapists, and serial killers.

That's why this book was written, for the child to know why. Once he knows why, he or she can heal. That's better than not knowing why. Why? Because all children need to know why; that is the wonder of being a child, transforming into an adult. The trouble is we adults forget how important it was for us as children to wonder and be able to understand, or know why. Just going around answering, "because I said so," creates more monsters—*that is why.*

A point to pass along

....

Adaptation is a word you've heard a bit from me. Mark seems to adapt very well in every circumstance. That's the danger of intelligent people. They adapt, alone, into their own design, especially if they have something invested in the original deviant plan.

Let's imagine two ships at sea, both are run by the same company but with different captains. Captain A takes a northern route to deliver his vitally needed cargo. Captain B, acting alone, takes a tropical route and enjoys a stay in a sunny port. What's wrong with that deviant course Captain B took? What if he didn't stay in the tropical port and did get to his destination on time with Captain A? Suppose Ship A hit an iceberg and was sinking and that ship B had stayed the course? Suppose Ship B started sinking if it were on its lone, deviant course?

Now suppose there are one hundred ships on this northern course and that one captain who knows about the lovely tropics decides to take the deviant southerly route? Who's the most likely to fail?

Your family is the two-ship example, the rest of the world and you are the second.

It's better you take your family to the tropics when you go on vacation, not alone while your...adapting? Deviating alone. Captain, yes, Captain, are you on course?

Chapter 5

Recovery

⟲

"Hi, Robert, sorry about the delay. I've got something I need to talk to you about."

Mark was afraid that Eddie had found something in the truck relating to Brandy. Eddie was two hours late in returning and Jean was not with him.

"We have to hurry and switch rigs, Eddie. I'm late in a bad way."

"I understand. This won't take a minute to explain, but you're going to have to think about it for some time."

"OK?"

"My boss contracts out, you know, real good money. He doesn't require proof of nothing—not insurance, license, nothing. He knew we were in trouble, but there was no physical way to get to us out here. He wants to repay you in a big way. He wants to give you the contract for Oregon."

"Contract for Oregon. What's that?"

"We have a produce warehouse in Portland. We truck everywhere. Ah, there's been a few problems with our truckers in the past, but nothing serious. Unfortunately, our contract with an Oregon trucker is tits up. That's why you seen me today. I'm just filling in. You saved us thirty-five thousand dollars, Robert, and we'd like to show our appreciation for saving us. It'll net you ten grand a month. I put in the word for you myself. He wants you. Think about it, won't you?"

"I have until when?"

"Next two weeks."

"That would be perfect. I was planning a trip to Mexico for five days, starting Friday night."

"So, what should I tell my boss?"

"He's got a new trucker."

"All right."

Mark and Eddie exchanged information, Mark left his first name as Robert but correct Christian name. Mark was not being careless; the thought of getting caught for any evidence left at the scene was ludicrous. The news that he was on his way again financially would actually fill his void. He began to realize that a normal life could become his with his status returned. What was there was almost always there, and Mark didn't want to change, which was Mark's enigma. He just wanted to feel like he shouldn't have to.

The success of life, the status of being on top and in power was sufficient to keep the desire for change at bay. The power would be difficult to satisfy. This position was ever moving, changing, weaving through the woods of desire. She was the power; she would weave away from Mark every moment, leaving him at the edge of nothingness. She had put him there, taking all he had. The rapist is a product of his programmed degradation. Convinced from childhood, labeled early awareness, called by his opposition as loss of innocence. His stepmother was everywhere; she was all around, every day.

He drove his truck to find the money that would bring him close to her. The money always brought her close to him. It brought Shea close to him, Sandy, Vicki, and Brandy, all of these women were his stepmother, his free to go stepmother, since he never spoke up. But she spoke of him: the vengeance, the mockery. He didn't know to tell anyone. He knew only to listen. Now, it was stepmother's time to listen. She was everywhere and needed a better teacher of awareness. The money for a new, shiny truck would collect and educate step-mother. It would be so easy now; the plan came into his head the moment Eddie mentioned the trucking contract. Nick had nine barrels of the Nitric acid. Maybe he could stretch it to eighteen uses, he thought. The money on Juniper waited through the silence of this desert's desolation. Taking his place as Satan entering the court of God, he dug up his money.

"Yes, Jesus loves me," he mocked. "Yes Jesus love me, for the money sold me so. Ha, all here, I love this place. Someday, dear lord Jesus, I'd like to repay you for not revealing to the Jehovah's Witnesses, that this Goddamn money was here. Because you're my witness, all sixty-one thousand, five hundreds and twelve apostles is hharr! I've got enough to buy old man Johnston's Peterbilt and trailer, plus I'll give five grand to my Maria across the border, across the line. Brandy was right about one thing, I did send her telepathy, that's proof. Maria, can you feel me? I feel the pain now, but I look up, 'cause I'll be there in a week. I know you hear me; I have proof. God, I love you, Maria, across the line, my tropical

paradise. I long for La Paz. It's the peace across the line. Time to go; it's getting dark here. Maria, feel me, I know your pain."

Mark kicked the nearly empty barrel off a ravine, into heavy brush and Juniper trees. The lid flipped off at the last minute, partially spewing the hemoglobin-tainted acid on the desert sage.

"I'll be long gone when they find you: no invoice, no proof, you're gone. That old man Nick doesn't know what he has, some horrible shit that acid. Next victim goes down a storm drain in Los Angeles. They're going to be lit up down there. I always hated those damn signs, 'don't pollute; this drain empties into the Pacific.' Don't those assholes know how much oil, rubber, gas, and God knows what else, washes down every time it rains? Throw some of their blood down it, doing them a favor, useless fucks. Pasadena sucks, Colorado Boulevard, drive your Mercedes, beach babies."

Mark returned to Springfield and met up with Mr. Johnston who owned the school, a retired trucker who took pride in his profession. Mark had met him at the school giving an equipment class. Johnston used his prize possession, a 1996 fifteen-ton Peterbilt, loaded, with custom airbrush paint. Mark knew this was his ticket. He knew Johnston was on the Internal Revenue Service's collection plate.

"Hi, Mrs. Johnston."

"Oh, I remember you. Good Sunday afternoon to you. He hasn't sold it yet, and I want to tell you something. We need the money, so don't let the old man scare you off with the bologna, you know what I mean, Son."

"Who you yakking at out there, Mom?"

"It's Mark, from school, Dad. Come on out here."

"Hey, buddy, I think I got an idea what you want."

"Good afternoon, Bill."

"I heard you, Mom. What do you want to sell it for?"

"If we don't have twenty-five thousand by Friday, the school goes into oblivion."

"You think I can let that go for twenty-five grand?"

"Mr. Johnston, if you want I can come back later."

"If I don't have it sold Thursday, you see, I have no choice."

"Thirty thousand now, with the trailer."

"Thursday, Mark."

"Mr. Johnston, on Thursday I'll have another rig, I'm taking a contract for Canami foods. Besides, did you know by the time someone makes a decision

and gets financing for one hundred thousand, your school will have had it's last class?"

"He's right, Bill. By the time any bank around here approves and disperses that lot, it'd be a week late. You waited too long, Dad."

"Are you sure about that?"

"You had any offers on the rig?"

"No."

"The school is our whole family's livelihood, Bill. Every son of ours will be out of work."

"Goddammit, write out your check."

"I brought cash. You got the title?"

"I damn sure do."

Mark drove away in his new home, equipped with a TV and bathtub. On and in every side of it, he knew how to cheat life and old folks, good old folks. On Friday, Johnston was offered one hundred, twenty-five thousand from the bank for the rig to keep the family school open. Mark had graduated two hours earlier. Four days before, on Monday, Mark had completed his plan, the reason he had to get the truck from Johnston in all haste.

Mark returned to Nick at Scott Supply for the rest of the acid.

"Hi Nick, what the hell you up to, taking your wife back?"

"Well, not after she went to Cape Canaveral with you!"

"Cabo, Nick."

"Cabo, Wabo, who gives a shit?"

"Damn, Nick, I didn't know you were on the up about Cabo."

"I been on the up before you had a daddy."

"Hmm, God, you're old!"

"How'd that acid work out for you?"

"That's what I wanted to talk to you about, Nick. You got the name of that guy who sold it to you?"

"Well no, Mark, it was a shady deal, you see, I met the guy . . ."

"OK, Nick, this is some serious shit. I mean we're talking about a federal control violation. I had to give that acid the dump. You see, a crime was committed, but accidentally. Can you keep a real secret, secret?"

"Secret, secret?"

"Jeremy's kid lost her hand from this shit. It took it right off. If the cops find out you got this shit, not only are you out of business, but Jeremy, more likely Paula, will sue your old black ass right off. Plus criminal charges will be filed, on all of us, but you especially, since you're the illegal vendor."

"I saw the clip in the paper; damn, poor Jerica. I didn't know until now I was related to this."

"This was in the paper!?"

"Tiny clip, but they said she permanently lost the use of her hand."

"Fuck no."

"How the hell was I to know, Mark?"

"You should stay with legitimate vendors, then you'd know this crap wouldn't happen."

"I got nine barrels of it here and one at my place."

"Really, you do have one more?"

"Yes, now I gotta dump it."

"Bullshit, Nick, I'm not getting busted for this. I brought my rig and we're going to load it up. I'm sorry, but I have to make sure this goes down right."

"I'm losing all right."

"You're going to lose everything if you try and sell any more of it. And I tell you what, if Jeremy or Paula breaks down to the cops, I'll have no choice but lead them to you as the vendor. You will be out. My way, I know the acid is gone and you know my lips are sewn shut."

"Calm down, that's actually what I want to do. I'm willing to pay you. Where you going to take it?"

"Way the fuck out in the desert."

"You do know that place."

"Give me the money now, while no one is in here. I have an electric cart with a scoop lift. I'll pick it up myself tonight. Be here at seven thirty, alone. Then we go to your house."

"Here's five hundred."

Mark reached in the cash register and cleaned it out. "And here's four hundred more. Be here, Nick."

"This is robbery!"

"You ever heard the old saying, Nick, 'Tell it to the cops!'"

As Mark walked out the door he snickered to himself.

"Shit, came in here thinking I'd be paying. That's twenty nine hundred in three days; poor Eddie didn't get back in time. I'll have another Ferrari in a week, this way."

The plan with Nick worked out exactly to Mark's demands. Nine barrels went with him back to the far eastern side of Juniper Mountain. One stayed specially set up in his new trailer. In this place, Juniper Mountain, five years before, Mark had prayed to God on hands and knees that he not be allowed to hurt his

daughter. Upon returning home that weekend, he learned from the police that he was being investigated for sodomy and that she had been removed from his custody. He was as close to reformation that day as it would come. Now, he blasphemed. The illness had been there for years, waging war with some real self-dignity. For lengthy times, the little-developed Mark would win, having a woman and semi-clear libido.

But the *stepmother* Mark was the dominant one, the stronger Mark, the Mark who had been shown early awareness, loss of innocence. The disease grew to proportions that even his counselor would not acknowledge the confessions, even if Mark did. But he did not confess; he had a rebellious belief.

When he started his janitorial service over twenty years before, he could not compete. He could not contract one fifty-dollar-a-month account. The illness that he had was now obtaining misaligned courage from his received abuse, needing application of his childhood. What we learn we have to apply sometime in life to justify our spent time.

He had what he thought to be an external drive, his demon alliance. Some "experts" label this as the "subconscious," which either justifies or condemns the desire—even both. He contacted the demon by obeying his desires and the compulsion. Only then would his business thrive, convincing him of a belief in powers, rather than circumstances. The evidence was clear, he had rewards of twenty-six thousand dollars per month, and no worries about being identified for his deeds to the demon. He crossed the line of societal norms and did that which he felt was his right. This demon gave him his dignity; there was no loss as a man. Without the demon, he was a loser. The more crime he did, the more rewards he received, which reinforced his belief.

Whatever you are engaging in that you think gets you ahead through these channels will end up in sorrowful destruction. This is only a misguided thought process. Belief can be devastating in that you continue to believe a fantasy, even after you have been imprisoned for following those thoughts. Some men think that committing various sex crimes will bring them gain due to powers of darkness, believing demons reward each and every deed. These sex crimes vary from indecent exposure, masturbating in front of a female in some public place, and moving onto rape and murder. The prime reason that these offenders believe in this fantasy is that they believe a demon was allowed to enjoy the sex, by borrowing the offender's body with his permission. The demon naturally would give rewards to the offender afterwards, and would take it back if the offender

did not "continue" to please the demon. A person believing like this must accept that his demon, by scripture, is about destruction and lies, and that is what will eventually befall the believer.

Extreme special note. The Belief is the Power, especially if it is a religious belief from childhood.

For those who think that using dark forces, such as Satan, demons, or the mystic is absurd and ridiculous, research the true case, "the Son of Sam" serial killer. This seemingly harmless man swore under oath that the demon spoke to him through his neighbor's dog (a black Labrador), audibly telling him to kill, in exchange for a great reward. This is a very typical phenomenon in thousands of cases. Belief is a driving force, the likes of which can destroy all of mankind in the mind of one bio terrorist. I reiterate who I am writing to, for prevention's sake. Closing your mind to these fantastic patterns opens a niche to other predators who will continue to use these hidden unexplored pathways.

The therapist would be alarmed to know that, right now, a potential predator reading this is afraid being self-exposed. That is exactly the purpose of this book, to expose himself to himself, the awareness thing. Open your mind to them, and you expose a path the predator can no longer confidently use. To further the argument that normal people cannot accept that people turn to dark forces, why don't they think how absurd it is to sexually molest a child in the first place? Realizing how far that goes will enable you to understand that there are no limits to the absurdity of the child molesters' behavior and beliefs. Belief is the predator's strongest reason and driving force. The prime message I convey here to the believer in outside forces is that these believers end up in tragic failure in prison and degradation.

Creationist or Christian readers will note that this part of *Predator Down* is intermingled with evolution throughout the text, and Satan is assumed activity in a child molester's life. This is one hundred percent biblically supported. Thus, belief is injected into the text as most child molesters incorporate some sort of fantastic religion into their doings, usually, due to personal conviction or hope of grace. I also inject belief that if God is Christ reincarnate or any other religion, then Satan does exist. I leave both the creationist and evolutionist to bring forward and put the Predator Down, by any means or method of awareness. Awareness is the key to putting the predator out and the good guys in society at large. There is a good guy in you.

Mark was rewarded the trucking contract immediately after raping and killing Brandy. The demon found his love. In Mark's mind, the demon would protect him; he could not get caught. Now the work evolved to higher ground, in exchange for higher returns. The acid was brought by the demon, the blown head gasket on Eddie's truck brought the returns of the contract with Canami foods; Johnston giving away his prize rig, the money, all had come about since Mark deeded the demon by killing Brandy. The rewards would now be immense. The reason for getting caught by Shea through his daughter was that the demon was not present in his house. Now, the demon must be out. No one would ever know about Brandy, and he had his first contract. The demon was free of the old gothic ways and had entered into modern times. It came looking for his alliance, missing for years, and now it had ten barrels of acid. Now, Mark felt complete; the pain was gone; he has his luminary pathway.

To a truly enlightened counselor, Mark would be, by every definition, a fully evolved addict at the climax of the illness. The drug addict evolves from cigarettes to marijuana onto the opiates. Mark progressed from sexual mental deviation in his illness to molesting his own child, and then went on to serial rape killing. In his evolution, he had adapted to his environment; fooling his probation officer and the State of Oregon was natural, his treatment counselor just as well might be the same. The end result made no difference. The fact that Mark was treatable was evidence that he knew what he was doing and was not fooled himself. The demon was only a backdrop religious "belief" from childhood, of which almost all of mankind has fallen to at some point in life. This animal adapts to destroy our most prized and beautiful entity, women. He must take God's pinnacle of creation down. There is absolutely no alternative for the unforgiven but to continue his destiny.

Adaptive Radiation, such a scientific term

· · · · · · · · · · · · · · ·

What is radiation, anyway? Cars have radiators. Ever thought about what that means? The car motor has a radiator to help cool it. So it must be that the radiator radiates the heat away from the motor. We have a way to radiate the heat away from us too, especially when the heat overcooks us. What it actually means is that we ourselves radiate away from a situation to something we can adapt to, when the *heat* is too high. If you can adjust to the current environment, are you doing that with anger or stress that is just tolerable? The truth is that is the time

to radiate, since the likelihood of you overheating is very high. This high stress has proven to cause both potential offenders and victims to put themselves into positions of failure through deviation. Recall Brandy was under stress. That is why she left with Mark. Mark was under stress.

Captain, you can get away on your own to be alone, but don't be lonely. Release yourself from time to time, so you can see the puzzle by yourself. You were also engineered to disconnect and value the world momentarily with your own mind. Then you can go back and tell those others exactly what you figured out.

If you do not occasionally feel stress, then I'd say there is a significant problem with you. Why? It means that you most likely are not concerned and are already disconnected. You know that means deviant actions are certain to arise from you? So, value this section as a point where you are able to identify your position and recognize your capacity to offend. So the rules are these:

1) If you are under stress and feel it, that's normal and you can radiate it away.

2) If you have intolerable stress, stop, get away from it. You are capable of deviance. The mind is indecisive under significant stress. Even something as simple as your diet could cause this.

3) If you feel no stress in a social environment where others do feel significant stress, you need to check yourself as to why. Are you unconcerned for them and are content with yourself? If so, it would be wise to investigate your inventory. It couldn't hurt to seek help, even professional council that understands empathy. The stress-free personality contains the trait of a high-risk predatory offender.

Chapter 6

Predators Allowed

~∽○~

"Sign in, your probation officer will be with you in a minute. Fill out your report for this period."

"I already did, so I'll just grab the newspaper, that OK?"

"Whatever."

The most feared parole officer in Lane County stepped into the waiting room, overhearing the small talk. Her reputation for sending parolees back to prison was why she was assigned Mark's case. By system protocol, the sex offenders were carefully routed back to the big house regardless of reformation.

"Come on in here, Mark, you can read the paper at home. You got a home?"

"Why, yes, Belinda, I sure do, and a contract too. I've got a job like you told me I'd better get."

"Take a seat, Mark. So what have you done this last two weeks? No, first where is your new home address."

"3317 Videra Drive, right here in Eugene."

"Did I hear you right? Videra Drive?"

"That's the highest rent district in town, yes I know. Isn't that what you were thinking? But like I said, I gotta new job, your recommendation last time I saw you. Seems to me you said it would be stand-before-the-judge time again if I hadn't found work. Well, nothing wrong with seeing someone reform and make it back to the top, is there?"

"Shut up! Where did you get the money for that?"

"Canami foods, my new contract; ten th-th-th-thousand a month. I've even acquired a new office to include my new personal secretary, Sarah Michaels. She appreciates the good money I pay her."

"Speaking of money, do you have the child support for Shea?"

"What?"

"I received a call from her last week. She is very ill."

"She sure is."

"Godammit, Mark, shut the hell up. What's the idea calling her, talking about what's in her? Swallowing and something to do with mother's milk still being in her?"

"It's all right to talk now?"

"Yes! Tell me exactly what you meant, and I mean exactly."

"Well, you see, it's a scientific fact, so it will be exact. I studied science and a little biology in school. I know a little more than even you do being a probation officer and all. You actually have particles of everything you've ever eaten inside you someplace, maybe in your eye, tongue. Actually the particles are so small they spread throughout your body, like a film or layer. You know like annual growth rings in a tree."

"It's a small amount though, right?"

"Depends on how much you consumed of that particular substance, and notice that I said *particular*. Everything is made of particles right down to the hadrons."

"Hadrons?"

"Hadrons, you know, electrons that circle the nucleus of protons and neutrons! Hadrons!"

"So, what I've eaten has broken down to atoms of something different than what I swallowed, I mean ate."

"Not at all, if you could break food down to that level, you'd be rich. All digestion does is break what you ate down to a liquid, like dissolving it so you can totally absorb it."

"So you're telling me some of my mother's milk is in me somewhere, now?"

"That would be the least substance found in you now; it gets pushed out with time but not totally. Since then, whatever you swallowed is in you in proportionally greater quantities. It's like we become polluted from what we load into our bodies."

Belinda became nauseated. She was hypnotized by Mark's confidence. His confidence was the demon working on her. "So it's true, then, you are what you eat."

"Yeah, that's why people who ate acid, LSD type, sometimes have flashbacks, some of it left in there reactivated when it started to move out. The stuff you swallowed usually activates when it gets moved out. That's why we get sick sometimes for a day without reason, especially women."

"Why women?"

"Because they swallow things that are foreign to the feminine body."

Belinda drifted in the mentality of Mark's space.

"God. We do."

"So what other kind of exacting questions do you have for me, Belinda?"

Belinda took a five-minute break and left the session only to take a walk down the hallway. She returned flush and wanted to dismiss Mark as soon as possible.

"Oh, ahh, let's see. I have to tell you that there won't be a need for child support. Shea has put your daughter up for adoption. How do you feel about that?"

"Best thing she could do."

"So, you don't have any protests?"

"Wouldn't matter if I did. I'm a jack off, low-life sex offender, right? Without rights to live, right?"

"You won this case; you didn't even have to go to jail; it was your decision to flee to Mexico. Now you're free from an incredibly large child support judgment. All you have to do is see me once a month for three years. You've made your own rights the way I see it."

"I'm only going to see you once a month?"

"Yes, you've been classified as non-predatory. You're not a hostile offender. You're actions with your daughter are considered as a misdemeanor, such as indecency."

"So I'm not listed on the hot sheet for registered offenders?"

"No, not at all. It's like your crime never happened, especially if you complete your treatment and probation. I've never seen a case like this."

"What do you mean?"

"I mean you're fucking lucky, or God is looking directly over. . ."

"The demon."

"Pardon me?"

"I mean I'm lucky, huh?"

"Damn lucky."

"I need to travel with my new job, sometimes out of state. I need to go to California tonight."

"Your truck driving school paid off, graduated today and working tonight. I need the phone number of your contractor."

"All right there on my report."

"Yes, I heard you mention that to our not-so-congenial secretary. You're one of the few who does what they're supposed to. Let me see here, Canami foods, Eddie is the contact. OK, does he know you're on probation?"

"No, the company has no background checks, I did some favors for them, and they chose me for the job. If you contact him, I'll lose the contract for sure."

"That's not the way it works in your case. I just need to know where you're going beforehand. If you violate, we violate you back to prison. So if you're caught outside California or Oregon this next . . .I see here seven days, it's back to the hokie, understand?"

"I won't be going back to jail, I guarantee you this much."

"Good, Mark, I have to say I was wrong about you; you're going to work out. Make sure you don't miss a treatment session. That could hurt you; judge's judge. So I will see you next month on the twenty-fifth. Pay your fees on the way out."

"Already did that, see you."

"Mark, can I ask you a question about the hadrons?"

"What?"

"How long does it take for what a person swallowed, I mean ate, to break down to the hadrons?"

"That's radioactive decay, Belinda, you're talking about great spans of time, millions, even billions of years to the hadrons. If you drank acid, it would break all that down, but, you're stuck with exactly what you consumed."

"Oh."

Mark was on top of the world. Hearing Belinda mention he was going to work out was a dead giveaway that she was his weakling and pliable putty. Now, he had his way to see Angie Maria in Mexico with a legitimate ticket through California. He had all the papers worked up for transportation through Baja. The demon would provide prey on the way.

Chapter 7

Ostracized Defiance

Mark disconnects the odometer of his new truck at a rest stop in Redding, California. This truck would cater to his victims more than he ever could. He took every precaution, including paying for his diesel in cash so that it would be unrecorded. If asked where he was from or going, his answer would be Washington. He buried his cellular phone in a shallow grave with the antenna above ground. His demon required tedious knowledgeable preparation. With special programming, he set it to auto-call home in Eugene at the expected time of perpetration to check messages on his answering machine. Knowing he would not have any messages, the phone was set to hang up in fifteen seconds, exactly what a living human would do.

The FBI would never clue in on this thinking. Mark credited the dark forces for his deviant arrangements. His acid bath evolved to the bathtub with the fiberglass hose as the drain to reach a street-side storm drain. The barrel was mounted just a bit higher than the tub, but in the trailer, it would gravity feed also by the special hose into the sleeper's bath. The procedure was secondary in his consciousness of normalcy, but primary as need for success. Between the two lights, he would be employed for elevation. The rapist had now entered the battlefield in full dress with extreme wantonness for his God of ultimate desire. The field laced by the most-high God's law enforcement, he treaded without option. The zero option left no intent of retreat causing the effect of the most highly motivated destroyer. The first semi-planned sacrifice ensued.

Saturday 6:00 p.m., Los Angeles, St. Louis Boulevard

Very few can accept and comprehend the simple and antisocial behavior of the rapist. They find it surprisingly ridiculous how easily victims are captured. In

Brandy's case, the predator knew his victim. The rapist usually targets women he knows, since it is easier for the predator in every respect. The following is a case involving a young girl who was being abused daily by her father. Incorporating the previously abused into Mark's serial cases is to condense the material for full realization of sex abuse within the time frame of this text and to keep the potential predator from putting the book down with added excitement.

Mark did not know where he was going or whom he was going to pick; therefore, he applied his technique through experience, which was very simple and inventive, as he proceeded. These victims fell into this same trap by refusing to believe that someone so harmless acting and sounding could rape them. The victims contemplated that the person *could* be a rapist, but certainly not fear being raped due to superiority over calamity. The rapist's methods are ludicrous to the majority of people, but among those are his victims. Note that Mark would not yet surprise-attack his victim then rape and kill. He was not a lion predator. He was a thinking human predator who had molested children. We cannot confuse the two, although both types do exist in society. Mark's character was exponentially more of a problem than a lion predator. This was proven in the case of Ted Bundy and many more, such as Citizen X in Russia and the Green River killer, and going back in time to Jack the Ripper.

The simplicity of Mark's predatory lure was identical, yet exaggerated and accelerated in the case, to enhance the point of how easy it is to be misled in both the professional environment in which the capture takes place as well as on the scene. I am talking directly to potential predators, ahead of time, hopefully. All the hidden messages exist here, which will apply to the potential predator.

Think about how much evidence you would leave if you picked an unknown victim. Just because you don't know the family she came from, doesn't mean that she hasn't got a beautiful family. It's horrifying to have beauty hate you. You can become beauty beforehand by listening to the beautiful.

The pathetic real world of Mark and his victim Gaby ensues.

"*Buenas Noches,* Senorita."

"*Hola*, you don't need to speak Spanish. I am good with the English."

"Yes, you certainly are. Look, I'm lost. I've never been in California before, and I need to go to Pasadena."

"Pasadena! You are lost, that's thirty miles back up Interstate Five and then over to the One Thirty Four freeway to the Two Ten. You're in trouble."

"No, I don't have to be there till Monday."

"You're all right, mucho time to find it, hey."

"Yeah, I'm a little scared down here. This place is crazy. I don't even know where I'm going to park this thing tonight."

"It sure looks like a nice thing."

Mark shuts down the rig parked next to an old closed up hospital, a park opposite, the neighborhood is medium kept up.

"So, what do you do around here for fun? Looks like nothing but concrete and street lights to dance to."

"If you have money, this is the place. Get anything you want here."

"I've got money but need directions. Money ain't doing nothing for me now."

"Believe me, money will get you where you want to go around here."

"I don't know what I'm going to do about getting around. That freeway is crazy."

"It's easy, man. You just a puppy out of the litter box."

"Your parents around?"

"Why you need to know that?"

"I was going to pay your mom or dad if they could help me. Maybe somebody could, ahh, you know like, show me a place to park."

"You are a scared pup, aren't you?"

"Please, I'm really lost, and I might wind up getting rolled."

"I'll show you. My mom doesn't need the money, I do. I want a fifty for this."

"Is it far?"

"No, but once I show you, then you can give me a ride back here. I don't want my parents knowing."

"Won't they be expecting you to be on time?"

"Don't worry about it; they're at church choir practice."

"Get in, while we have time."

"Okay. Wow, this is killer in here! Wait, don't start it up."

"Why, you change your mind?"

"No, Hell no, I want to look at this: DVD, VCR, TV, computer, bathroom, eeww with tub too, and what is this here!?"

"Oh, my liquor cabinet. I have tequila."

"You think because I'm Mexican all I like is Tequila?"

"When I lived in Mexico the natives didn't drink my Jim Beam."

"Hm, mm, lived in Mexico, you're right, but not here. Anything works in this ghetto."

"You want to do some drinking with me?"

"Oh, I dunno. I want to but I'm a little afraid."

"I'm not going to do nothing."

"Ha! I'm not afraid of you; you're a lost pussycat. I can see you got more fear than me. I'm afraid of my dad; he's such an asshole."

"He's got the machismo?"

"Real bad; he was born and raised in Guadalajara. He even scares my mom and me when he drives. That's why I walked tonight."

"I thought you said your mom drove."

"I didn't even want to take the chance he might."

"Seems to me going to church and all he'd yield a little."

"Are you kidding? Everyone in that fuckin' place would run you over, even in this big bastard. Believe me, that church, like all of 'em, is just a club."

"Hey."

"Ha, sorry. You got religion, too! That's why you're afraid. So, you got a woman?"

"I did in La Paz, but she got into dope and cocaine real bad. She went berserk on me several times. I couldn't hang with that. Finally, the cops locked her up so I came back."

"You lived in La Paz?"

"For three years."

"I want to live there so bad."

"You been there?"

"My dad has church connections there."

"Is it a Baptist church?"

"Yes, they're the uppity type though."

"Is it the one in Campeche colony, Pastor Francisco?"

"Oh, wow, do you know those people?"

"A little. My Maria, well when she *was* mine, went there before she started the shit."

"I don't know any of the congregation. I went with my dad on business trips that dealt with money, only not the Sunday thing. But I love the Malecon in La Paz, and the beaches are so cool, and Cabo is my dream."

"I have a house in La Paz up on the hill above the Marina. You had to have driven by it on the way to the church. You know where you turn by the hotel Palmira."

"That's real fucking nice up there. The view of the whole city and the Sea of Cortez. God it must be nice."

"Yeah, I'm actually going there when I'm done with you."

"No you're not."

"What?"

"You're going there when you're done with your business in Pasadena."

"Isn't that what I said?"

"No, you said when you were done with me."

"I must be thinking about you. I mean I wouldn't. Well you know, but I was thinking about your company.

"You're a little weird but honest, anyway. Most guys would have made some excuse. Don't get me out of place, I wouldn't mind hanging with you. I mean you're from Cabo and all. But how much money do I get for showing you this place?"

"All I have are fifty-dollar bills, so I guess it's fifty. I don't want to stop and get change and take a chance at being seen with you in here."

"I know what you're saying. So start this bad boy up and roll. Get on the Five north."

"I'm not following you."

"That's what I mean. You wouldn't last a day down here by yourself. But, yeah, a white twenty-five-year-old with a Mexican sixteen-year-old don't look right."

"Hell yes, that's why I asked you to have your mom help me. But I'm glad you wanted to, I mean I relate to . . ."

"Kids?"

"Well, I was searching for the right words, since you're not a kid. I'll relate this to you. The truth is I asked you before the white kid. White kids are, well, you know, messed. Mexicans have culture, even if they never lived in Mexico."

"Man, you talk basic. But you did hit that on center. If half the white boys I know heard you say that, I wished I could see it. I lived in Mexico until I was eleven. I know why crazy white boys get killed down there. Boy, you better be careful too!"

"So, then grab that Tequila. We'll kill a few here."

"Hmm, shit. Fuck it. Why not? Can you drive on this?"

"Shit, like an angel."

"You know, I like the way you drive. You have a soft touch." Mmm this is Gold! Best stuff. So, are you rich or something? Here, have a shot. You have any salt?"

"Si Senorita, and some limes in the fridge, too."

"My name by the way, it's Gabriela. There's another thing that I really like about you."

"What? Your name?"

"The fact that we didn't have to introduce each other. We just talked about whatever. You've learned the Mexican way from living in La Paz."

"You're right. No one there ever asked my name. Living there did open up my narrow gringo mind. My name is Mark."

"You're no longer a gringo, Marko. Here, drink to your lonely higher status of being a born again, Paisano."

"God, that sounds like a sick Pinche Madre! Maybe you should drink the Beam instead. Go on and down it, beaner."

"Haa! I could love a base guy like you."

"I've heard that before."

"Who?"

"Girl named Brandy. She would have been eighteen today."

"You do hang around younger people, don't you? Wait, did you say *would have been* eighteen?"

"Oh, ah I mean, I wasn't there today to celebrate. She's eighteen. But I knew her since she was twelve or thirteen."

"Like how so?"

"She was my best friend's kid."

"What's the referencing to her as *was*, and *knew*, is she like, dead?"

"Oh no! I just don't hang around her anymore, well I mean she's never there at my friend Joe's house when I visit now."

"Oh I got you, she was just there when you were. But you thought of this young girl when I mentioned I could love you. She must've left an impression on you of some sort to relate it to that. Tell me the truth, base guy.

"Actually, I told her to just tell me what she wanted to do when she said could have. We talked around that for a bit. She told me she loved me in a major way."

"How old was she then?"

"Seventeen."

"You think she did?"

"I'm sure of it."

"So, how did you feel about her? Have another shot first."

"Pretty good."

"Damn you're so base, dude. What does 'pretty good' mean?"

"It means she was my best friend's kid."

"So, why did you lead her on, when you told her to just tell you what she wanted to do?"

"I wanted to play with her a bit. I didn't think it would hurt. I stopped, 'cause I knew Joe would cut me loose."

"If not kill you. Like I said, you're honest. So let's change the subject. You start."

"Let's see, yeah, when you grow up, never have a subconscious."

"Why?"

"For example, you have a place of your own but need some extra cash. So you rent out a room and you get a roommate. Even if you don't need the cash, you get a roomy for their company. Bad thing to do."

"What does that have to do with your subconscious?"

"Well, you know, in your subconscious that, when you're gone, they're going to pick their nose and flick boogers all over your pad, man. That's so bad for your subconscious. I mean, you know it before they move in way in the back of your head. You visualize it everyday, so like it's subconscious stress before and during. It's a mother fucker."

"Ha ha, stop!"

"You walk across your carpet bare foot to turn on the TV and you wonder. That's stress."

"I'd use the remote always. You're ridiculous. No, you are nuts, Marko!"

"Why, you don't think so? You don't think they're going to flick at least one on your couch or favorite chair? That's not all; they do all kinds of shit you do know about."

"Fuck, man, well I do that at Claudia's house! This is so funny! You think of shit no one does but everyone does it."

"Oh, they think about it, but you see that's the difference. They're too mainstream to counsel the roomy about no flicking and all the other uglies. You relating? Man, I tell a motherfucker directly and exactly. I call that problem solving; they call it problematic. Fuck them. That's why those types of people are so fucked up. They haven't got enough balls to relate, so they act all nice about it. Then again, they try to ignore it, putting up with it and causing major stress. Stepping in someone else's snot just ain't the same thing."

"Damn, I sure was wrong about you! Yeah, fuck overly nice people and the ignoring ones to. But I don't have balls, so I guess the best thing for me is not to have a roommate. Speaking of fucked up, this tequila…"

"Is it bad?"

"No, it's bad for me. Now I'm the one that's fucked up."

"You don't look fucked up."

"I feel like I am."

"That's not what I meant."

"I know what you meant."

She looked over at Mark with an exploring eye. She told him to take the exit and that the truck stop was to the right. They pulled in. He wondered if she was upset and wanted to go or her look is of interest. They stopped.

"Hey, Mark, I'm going to go use that pay phone over there."

"Is there something wrong?"

"No, Mark, it's just that I'm drunk. I have to call Claudia. No, I can't do that 'cause my mom will want to talk to me. I can't call mom because we have caller ID, making the pay phone number show up. I'm in deep shit."

"Gaby. . ."

"I like that. You call me Gaby. What Marko?"

"Look, so what if you're in deep shit. How often can you go out and really live what you want. Look at the situation. Drink your ass off and tell your dad no flicking."

She stood up and staggered to the bathroom.

"Oh my God, that made so much sense. Fuck it, you're right. I want to get high. I want to live. You are so fucking right about concrete and lights. This isn't La Paz; it's fucked up money town L Goddamn A. That's why I got in the truck with you. I wanted to go for it, and for the money. You just had the stuff to say so."

She came out of the bathroom. Mark was sitting on the bed, semi reclined, with one foot on the floor.

"We all want a place we can go and be."

"That was so beautiful, and be . . . and BE! I want to *be*. Can I sit down here on the bed? I want to drink just a little more tequila. Did you know I could read lips?"

"You didn't tell me. Here, it's all yours."

"Thank you. Gracias, bro!"

Mark watched her tip the bottle up, as if it were water.

"De nada."

"*Tu eres, muy bonito, Marko*. Thank you for your compliment. Yeah, I can read lips. It helps me understand people."

"I'm sure it does, you know what the fuck they're saying about you. What compliment? You just gave me the bonito compliment."

"You stole my punch line! I know what you meant when you said I didn't look fucked up."

"*Tu eres muy bonita, si y tu.*"

"You told me the truth about everything, so far. Tell me what your thinking now, seeing me here on your bed. Like when you told Brandy to say what she wanted to say."

"I think you'd be a bit scared if I told you."

"Why would I be scared? You want to rape me because I'm drunk?"

"I wouldn't seduce you, and just because you're drunk doesn't change anything."

"Then tell me, do you want to fuck me?"

"I'm actually thinking something else."

"What's the else are you thinking."

"You know that subconscious thing I told you about. . ."

"Ha Ha, you mean I can't be your roommate!?"

"No, actually you can flick boogers all over my pad."

"You are so funny in a weird way, ha. Please tell me the other thing you were thinking."

"It's something I really want to do, and I don't think it's so abnormal."

She stopped laughing but had a gentle look of reception. "You've been in Mexico, Mark. You should know the open way by now. You don't have to hold back your talk just have respect. What do you want to do?"

"You don't want to know what I want to do. But I want to tell you something."

"I'm getting bored with this. But I can't go home now. Change the subject."

"All right, Gaby, listen to me. Even in Mexico there's a bit of this American wishful thinking fantasy bullshit. I see you have a great deal of wishful thinking. You've lived in L.A. a long time, and this place has you seeing as you would like to see, since it taught you something called 'societal norms.' But I'm here to tell you that is your biggest error. It's a lie that led you here. I'm telling you now the greatest truth there is. It's how this world really works as opposed to how people here wished it worked and that truth is polarizing to society. But to me, truth is enlightenment, and frees me to use that awesome and polarizing-to-you truth to my advantage. I don't have one question for you, I have an answer for you. That's why you fucking got in this truck with a total stranger."

"Fuck, man, you're starting to make me wish I hadn't."

"Why the fuck would you get in a semi with a stranger?"

"The money, Okay!"

"You just risked your life to a stranger for a fifty. Bullshit. Why the hell would you do that?"

"Fuck, why not?"

"You got in, since you are in some kind of fucked up living environment, and that truth has you wishful. Family bullshit, huh?"

"My father."

"That bad, bad enough to blow it away?"

"I couldn't tell you what that motherfucker does."

"He does you, doesn't he."

"Every day. Fuck it. My life is shit. I got nothing. That is why I got in with you. I can see it in you too. Your father?"

"No. My stepmother. Ever think about killing him?"

"All the time. You kill your stepmother?"

"Brandy is dead. That's one."

"So all this was a planned out big lie?"

"Truth."

"Why?"

"My life was as bad as yours is. I'm getting the disease out of me."

You're over me. I can't fight. Nothing is fair here. How can you kill a victim like yourself?"

"You know what all this is about now. It's in you the same as me. You'd do it if you could being the same product as I am. Stop being superficial. For years and years, you've suffered unto a person like me that's also in you."

"Jesus, what is going to go down? I need to go, please, just let me get out, here. Please, you know my life is fucked as it is. Don't do it to the wrong person."

"I'm going to take you south of the border. Blue Spot, it ain't, but there is a level of respect. I know personalities down there that will love to have you. You ever fuck someone besides your father?"

She turned over to him, out of options. She had to give the enemy her shirt, as well as her coat to survive. Being as abused in her mental state, she looked to Mark for the place she had to be for survival. Helsinki syndrome unraveled again. The lines started to roll.

"Could I really love a man who killed? But I do know why. I haven't done it, but I want to. I want to hurt someone so bad. I can understand what you did. I want to kill. I want to kill my father, but I can never do that. I want to kill someone like you."

"That won't work, Gaby. I know what you're trying to do."

Mark took her. For the duration, Gabriela found pseudo-love in her derangement. In rape all that she knew was actually brought to climax by her first non-blood male sexual mate. Bred to be lost from fear, her encounter was enlightening for it's pathetic worth. Raped by someone other than her father for the first time

she semi-surrendered to Mark. In her abuse, she was a realist. She only wanted to wait until someone she could love would take her away. She would run from Mark at first sight. She knew what was, which provided the awareness of rehabilitation that Mark walked from. She knew other Mexican girls in her exact situation.

She did know there was a way out, but she had been trapped before she met Mark. Mark's trap only signified the destiny of those who were stuck in that trap.

For many with the inter-communication of their abuse, it was a temporary growing up of an assigned life. Waiting for their freedom, they found security love in one another. Claudia was one whom she not only confided but shared her body with, as well. Gaby and Claudia were by every definition lesbians, due to parental sexual abuse. Mark could not comprehend that the life Gabriela lived was not a total waste, with a chance for blossoming into something beautiful. To him, it was as stomping on dung as he was as Gabriela and for the same reason. He could not see that he could be a flower. He chose to be impure iron, worth nothing but killing. He understood in as dung, out as dung.

Mark began with the mental rape of Gabriela. "I want a cigarette."

"I haven't see you smoke for the last two hours, and you don't taste like smoke."

"I do when I'm experimenting." Mark lit a Tareyton and looked to his right. "See that thing up on the wall?"

"I was wondering what that was the whole time."

"It's a commercial paper cutter. Cuts through five reams of paper, just as fast as you can bat an eye."

"You're not taking me to Mexico. God, I could love you so good!"

"Could, Gabriela not do. And stop trying. You're going to a better place, and you knew all along that's what I meant."

"Why? Why do you have to do this?"

"You'll know why, soon. Plus, I have a zeal for experimentation. You're going to do something for me."

Mark overpowered her, duct-taped her hands behind her back, and immobilized her thighs, knees, and ankles, wrapping the tape around her.

"I always wanted to know something that made me think so hard about death. For just a moment I think the life is still there."

"Why can't you just think about the life for now. Just live!"

"'Cause death is coming, anyway. Did you know that the number one is just as far from infinity as is the number one million? I'm going to die someday. You know you're going to die tonight but not exactly when. It's just closer than before, like the same distance from eternity. But I will know from my

experiment exactly when you die. I'll hold that moment of your life alive for-ever. You remember all those French stories about the guillotines. You know the beheading thing? That paper cutter is your guillotine."

Gaby tried her only reasonable defense. She was unusually strong, but con-sidering the abuse she'd lived through, this was what she expected of herself.

"I know more about being tormented than you ever will."

"Wrong, Gabs. I've got a bit of a history lesson for you! Haven't you ever wondered why all those people being beheaded went so easily? Don't answer. I'm not in the mood to hear some pathetic save-my-ass line. It's like this. On the weekends in Europe, when people had nothin' to do, they looked for entertain-ment. The television networks were about five hundred years off yet, so they had to make live TV. But this isn't really about the guillotine or entertainment, Gaby; it's about *why*. The Guillotine was the welcome wagon to those offenders. Yes, they looked forward to it! One reason was that they were tormented beyond belief in open public humiliation before going to that bad ass head chopper."

"But the truth is, the real torment came from within, as change had just gotten started in society. They couldn't accept themselves! And guess what for? Mostly child molestation and rape! Yes that's the shit, girl. The prosecution would read aloud to thousands, the offense making the offender cringe to the bottom of indignity. The crowds would go wild hearing the smut! While the offender was bound, the victim was allowed to mock him and have all the time they wanted to verbally abuse this doomed individual. Next, the victim disrobed his rapist to total nudity and taunted him with a blade, telling him exactly what she was to do.

Of course, she castrated the offender but laughed at him They played catch with other spectators! Yes, they tossed the package around the yard. Then stuffed the offender. It gets much worse, but you get the idea. Oh, it was a spectacle, Gabriela. The guillotine was definitely the welcome wagon, believe me. Rape goes way back, Gaby. Goes way back to Moses' law. Did you know it says in the Bible that, if the woman did not cry out when she was being raped, she was to be stoned, also? Why? Because she must have enjoyed the perversion! Yes, Gaby, people were freaks back then, too! They loved being abused and then they loved abusing the abuser to death. Oh yeah, this carried over to the dark ages of the guillotine. They searched out their entertainment quite well by the law. They had the written holy word for excuse to torment and behead women.

You see, not only did you not cry out, but I have permission because you submitted to the temptation. So you see, I'm ahead of your game, Gaby, because if I let you go, hehehe, you'd have me castrated by the District Attorney. In this case, it's the offender's revenge upon God's own. I'm coming straight back at the

standard maker. For labeling me unforgiven and registered, I have no choice but to go all the way and fight back. I've been humiliated, labeled, and ostracized, so the only way for me is what the standard maker has set. This is the defiance, the guillotine, the permission you gave me, and the imperfect law you live by. But then, again, it is not defiance, because it's the only road I have left. The Geraldos and dignitaries refuse to forgive the big mistake, and I made that one big, societal, unforgiving mistake. They sustain, extend, and perpetuate the set system of unforgiveness. When there is nothing left for me, why should I conform to the righteous? You get to be part of my road travels, Gaby. You're going down."

"You will never get away with it. You're going to leave so much evidence. You know you can't get away with this!"

"Wrong again! You'll be in the bathtub. You'll just drain out into a sewer somewhere."

"The blood and hair will still be in the tanks. You won't get rid of my body. The FBI will find me. You'll be caught and spend seven years on death row. Who knows; by then, they may electrocute you or something worse."

"You know what, I was wrong."

"Yes you. . ."

"Yes. You won't be going down a sewer, you get to go to the ocean. You see, it will be you, too, not the hadrons. The acid just turns you to liquid. You'll still be you floating around out in there the Pacific. What a nice—"

"Acid?"

"You're going down, *muchacha*. Time for me to get macho on your pathetic waste."

"Please, Mark. . ."

"The crying won't work. I'm faced now. Getting real game-faced, but we got some science to do. You'll be contributing to biologists, doctors, especially neurologists, Gaby. This experiment will answer the age-old question of the guillotine. I plan on making something good come out of all that head chopping. You participate, and you'll be the contributor to science. What do you say?"

"What do you want me to do?"

"Well, can't really tell you, because if I do I know you won't do what I ask."

"I swear I will, tell me."

"First, I gotta put you in the bathtub. There you go."

"This is where you can kill me. Why would I do what you ask, here?"

"Oh it will be obvious, sort of like a quick-trick question."

Mark slipped the spring-loaded paper cutter over Gaby's head. The super-sharp blade sits four inches above her throat.

"You see, all I have to do is release this clasp and heads roll! But if you participate, you will be a major contributor to life."

"Just tell me what to do."

"I promise and give my word, if you do what I say, you'll live."

"I swear too, I will. I'll do whatever you want. Please don't kill me."

"I'm not killing you. I'm freeing you. The truth is, I can't wait to get there."

Mark stood at the end of the tub, holding Gaby's head by her hair with his left hand and the paper cutter's release with his right.

"OK. Just keep your eyes wide open looking in my eyes. When you hear me say "look down," look down, keeping your eyelids wide open. Then look back at my mouth. You can do that?"

"Anything, please, you promised."

"Look down! Good . . . You're leaving. Wow, I am actually seeing you go. I see your life leaving. Going, going, gone—now! Well, if you couldn't hear me, you definitely could read those lips. It was a big lie. It's not instant death. You were alive for a good five seconds. I even felt a partial flexing of your neck muscles when you looked down. You didn't even know, 'cause you obeyed me by looking back up. Fuck, I just proved a major mystery! Myth busters, ha ha. Well, off to Colorado Boulevard, then to my baby in La Paz, *Mehicoooe*!"

The end of Gabriela's life, ended by Mark, is an example used here of what was happening to her by being trapped with and by her father. The guillotine is used as an example of how the father was severing Gabriela's head (Mind) from her body. He does not see her mind, and she realizes it and, at the moment that her head becomes severed, the father sees her head die shortly thereafter.

Mark was just used, here as a physical example of how horrible it is to be trapped at home with a sexually abusing father. Ask any abused child, and they will agree. This story of Mark taking Gabriela out is used to realistically display the child's daily trauma, as a friend or family member rapes her constantly. It truly is no different, and it is happening as you read this. If you doubt this hard reality, everything you just read can be verified in Los Angeles county court records.

The Tipping Point

. . . .

Seducers use lure, they tempt. Every man who ever lived is a seducer by nature, especially if we were created. If we evolved, then this "animal" is less of a seducer and has a stronger tendency to *take*, which is now classified as *rape*.

Rapists absolutely do use lure, and are not seductive date rapists. Rapists scheme, are method makers, and they use forceful use of tools like darkness, drugs, alcohol, money, cars, and least of all, their personality. People of character need nothing else to assist them. The most used instrument of all is a combination of surprise and the victim's naive "elsewhere" mind. With that, the rapist is like a shark, attacking ailing prey. Gabriela was ailing and taught to be so; she was her parents' product.

It's been said, "You shall not be tempted beyond that which you are capable of resisting." The rapist does not use temptation as his primary tool. He is more than well aware that charm is his number one deficiency. If anything, he will use that handicap, so you see it clearly, to make you feel empathy for him. The rapist violates your environment to steal you. He uses an entirely different and more effective method when it comes to deceiving females into a corner. Misleading intent is how the rape victim is deceived. *Predator Down* is more for the male, so I won't detail deception here for the female. For reference sake, Ted Bundy was a master of deception. Read his case files to fully understand predator deception. The way to see into the mind of the rapist is to know other words, "Be wise as serpents, yet harmless as doves." "I come as a thief in the night, be wary." "Always, always be wary; that cannot harm anyone." "Insult is better than injury."

Mark, being compared to a grocery store robber, had much in common with them. Once the robber decided to go into the store he opened himself up to numerous and endless actions. The robber intended to just go in, rob the clerk, and leave, but what happened was that he also killed all the clerks and burned down the store. The point was made that Mark truly started out just to have sex, but in his condition, he also acted upon his deviance; so then he raped, and then he killed in bizarre fashion.

The tipping point of going that far *started* with the first action of talking to Gabriela alone. Once he had physically gone into his plan, it was almost impossible to back out and highly likely it would reach a horrible tipping point. Once you put armament or a gun in your hands, your hands by nature begin to tremble, since your instinctive brain knows an arm or gun is used in aggression, not peace. The old brain then automatically highly energizes the body and gains control by pure chemistry, beyond your cortical control, since you allowed it beforehand to do so. You gave it the okay, causing the tipping point. Keep the cortex up front, and you won't take the first physical step, which is so difficult to withdraw from.

If you feel fear, anger, indecisiveness or confusion, withdraw at first awareness, and connect to the intellect. Mark was afraid when he contacted Gabriela.

You should never be afraid or allow yourself to feel fear under any circumstance. When you do feel fear, change it immediately for *concern*, which is calm rationale. Now that's evolution, Baby, and you can do it.

What page are you on?

·················

An attentive female will understand right away what "insult is better than injury" means. Gaby had difficulty with that. She had been traumatized to the point that she went the way most females are unable to understand. Most females would insult Mark by a simple "get lost" from the get go. Gaby's mind was magnetized, her thought processes were aligned, but from the pulling and pushing she had been taught.

Gaby actually had a very difficult time saying "get lost" to Mark, as her alignment was actually to search for Mark. Notice, I said "saying" get lost, not telling Mark to get lost. She had no foundation to command her life or language. She seemed to have command by her anger, yelling, and defenses. There were many things she wouldn't do because she couldn't. She wouldn't associate with healthy females, which would further distance her from norms. This was a vicious downward spiral that only her father could stop. Gaby was on the street in her short walk home, since she was inadvertently looking for more of the way the world was to her. That was exactly what she had been taught by her father.

Young lesbian behavior, at the age of eleven in third-world countries, is unbelievably high and is attributed to parental sexual abuse. These females can only get help by extreme discovery like these same North American sisters. Their not-so-rare cases will never give their fathers up to the police. They would deny the charges if they were brought out. She would even deny them on the witness stand, if she had admitted to it beforehand. I am leaving the reasons out here to send the primary message to the fathers, the point of this chapter. Your daughter will most likely die by alcohol, drugs, or by the way she allowed Mark to take her life, some such method of risk, even suicide. Her life doesn't really get any better with age, which causes realization, so life loses value to her. Yes, you know she will not testify against you on the stand in court, but she will continually die. She may kill you, however, before she dies completely.

The only way to save her and get her on a healthy road to recovery is by admitting everything you have done. It is her only hope; she will be forced into admitting it herself, and then she can be directed to get help. She will also see

you have some love and dignity; she may actually be able to recognize you as a real father. When she first learns that you admitted it to an authority, she will get an initial self-disguised burst of joy, respect, and hope that will last her entire life. She will no longer have to live her life lying. You would then go to your grave with a certain level of respect. Regardless of what you believe, one who claimed to be God has said all manner of evil can be forgiven, except blasphemy of the spirit. Gaby has a spirit; so does your daughter.

Notice this page is unnumbered. Pause here a minute and contemplate that page in your life without a number that definitely will be counted when your number is up.

Chapter 8

Rejection

❧

"Eighteen months I don't see my baby. Embrace me, Mark. *Te amo siempre*. I wait so long now I cry. Crazy, no?"

"Not as crazy as I am for you, tropical woman. God, I feel so peaceful here. This is my life. Soon, Angie, I will stay here. Maybe a few months more."

"Really? Forever here in La Paz?"

"Oh yes. I would stay now if it weren't for the money. But I have a real good contract."

"What is *contract*?"

"It means I have a business going, Baby. Soon, we'll be together forever. I feel so damn safe down here."

"I always protect you here, my love. I promise."

"I know you will."

"Wow, that is a big truck! Is this the business?"

"Yes, I had a load to dump in Pasadena, so I drove it down here."

"So how long you stay with me?"

"I can stay until Friday afternoon. We've got lots of loving to do."

"I had to put in a new window in front, Mark. The cyclone come and it break the other window. Please don't be angry."

"I'm not, Hon. It wasn't your fault."

"No, but I have the man put in a special glass. Very big and cost mucho money. You must pay him. I tell him you come yesterday, but you didn't get here yet. He comes again today."

"It's okay, love. You did the right thing. The window is thick. Gee that must be one-inch plate! I want to talk to him about getting some of that to take back with me for my work."

"Yes, it's special for the hurricanes. It's very strong but very expensive."

"It's fine. I'm just happy to see you and that you are safe."

"Thank you so much. You always understand me. Mmmm, come in you house with me, Gringo!"

Maria and Mark took advantage of every moment. They indulged in each other and the tropical environment. In their fresh reuniting, there was not one moment of tension. They were two as one, in more ways than met the eye. Two characters sharing the same antisocial disease immediately made acceptable and agreeable their self-satisfaction. A few normal couples ventured into third parties, but the diseased had an entirely different position. Angie's inability to communicate her sexuality was but part of the off-line position. The plan followed.

La Paz was a semi-tourist town. The only true attraction was the world's best sport fishing and the tropical beaches. The people were as laid back as the town was a traditional place of rest and peace. Love was overdeveloped in the women, as the men had little to do, except love the numerous women: one man to every six women. There was very little work in La Paz for men. It was mostly an administrative city, the capitol of Baja south. As gay as San Francisco was the capital for homosexuals worldwide, La Paz was the capital for desirable women. Not wanting to be known as lesbian, the women competed for men, and they started at an early age, when they had their appeal. It was commonplace for fifteen-year-olds to marry.

The senorita's fifteenth birthday, known as the *Quinceñera* was the day she promenaded herself in a light blue or white dress, making herself available. She usually already was at her fourteenth birthday. Just as there was a time limit set for the fifteenth birthday, the limit was breached. Childbirth at age sixteen was highly acceptable and was sought. By custom, on Sunday and Thursday evenings, eligible men, including visitors, such as anglers, strolled leisurely clockwise around the plazas in pairs or groups. The anxious but proud women walked counterclockwise. The women's manners were highly refined as they walked, making a quick glance up and down, followed by a second one, for an understanding moment was the clue for the favored candidate. She made no verbal advances.

Only after the promenade was finished and the music started, did the men get up from their seats to cross the plaza for the affable female. He would ask her to dance, and if the chemistries mixed, they would sit out a couple of dances, together. After the ball was over, *quien sabe*? Gringos almost always were rejected here, if not given hints that this was not the place for them. But Mark knew how to be refined in the Mexican way. He loved the tradition and all could see the

serious mildness in his eyes. He always brought home a senorita for Maria. It was her adrenaline of life that Mark understood. And he did comprehend from her experience and his past. The hatred of fatherhood would never leave Angie. Mark made his move in the prom with an affable beauty.

"*Hola*."

"*Buenas tardes*."

"I don't speak so good Spanish."

"Is OK, I can talk a little English with you. My name is Rosabla. What's yours?"

"Carlos."

"You don't look like a Carlos. You're dark but you are not Mexican. What's you last name eh?"

"Mendez."

"You are silly. You're not Carlos Mendez. You don't speak so good Spanish, si?"

"You wanna dance with Sr. Mendez, *mi amor*?"

"Absolutely not, unless you tell me your real name."

"Okay, adios."

"Hey, hey, come back here, Carlos Mendez. You know the Can Can?"

"C'mon."

"Wow, you dance like a matador. I've seen you before in La Paz. Yes, I see you swimming when it is cold. Where are you from, the North Pole?"

"Close to it, but I got enough cool to equalize any temperature."

"I wonder why you come to me?"

"You gave me the signal."

"So did all the others."

"I didn't see that."

"Oh yes, you did."

"No, really, I think I was looking at you the entire time."

"Why at me?"

"You're tall like me, and you have big Spanish eyes. I was mesmerized by your confidence."

"That's enough reasons, Mr. Carlos. You want a drink?"

"Let's walk the Malecon, okay?"

"Hmmm, Okay. Your real name?"

"Karl."

"You think Karl translates to Carlos in Spanish?"

"Ha ha, you know I did when I first moved here. Kinda dumb, huh."

"Most gringos are real dumb, very stupid. But you know some things. I can tell. But how you can swim in waters so cold."

"You call seventy degrees cold?"

"I can never live in America, you know. I only see snow in the television. I need a warm place to live."

"When it's cold out, we have warmth. You never had a night like that when it's cold out and your man warms you all night?"

"How you know that, Senor Karl, or whatever?"

"Too hot here for that kind of romance. Let's get a taco and some beer."

"I'm very hungry but I don't eat tacos. Let's get a beer, though, and walk down to Carlos and Charlie's. I want pizza. I have money for you."

"You and me might not get along."

"Why you say so?"

"Our appetites are different. You want to go see an American movie afterwards."

"No. American movies are so stupid and shallow. They make so much *especial* effects but no sentiments. I wouldn't waste my money on them; besides, they have tacos at Charlie's."

"Your money, huh. Where do you work?"

"At Logical."

"What do they do, logical things like walk down the Malecon with gringos, who watch stupid American movies?"

"We sell computers and software, also some real estate. Carlos' wife sells the houses. I just do all the real work."

"I know what you mean."

"You think so?"

"Sure, I'll bet that when she sells a house, you do all the paper work, Carlos' wife just shakes the hands of the buyers and takes all the credit and the money."

"It's true. I only get two thousand pesos a month. That's two hundred dollars. She gets thousands of dollars every time a house sells. I'm nineteen years old. I should make so much money for what I know. So much money. You know prostitutes make better money."

"I didn't know. I would never go with a prostitute."

"Why? Because of the AIDS or the morality."

"The AIDS is the immorality."

"Hmm, I'm not so sure I understand you."

"If you know someone, and then find you like them, what is the reason to stop all the love from happening? You know after the prostitute gets her money,

and they are finished, they have feelings for what they have done. They don't think of the money so much in this moment. They do think of each other."

"If you can think like that, then maybe we can get along."

"Thanks, here's Charlie's. Let's get that pizza."

"You said you've been in La Paz for some time. Where do you live?"

"Up on the mountain, over by Pedregal, you know above the marina."

"That's very expensive there. How you can have this place? Only very rich people live there, mostly corrupt people."

"Yeah, I have a live-in housekeeper too. She is very beautiful."

"So you are rich. That doesn't mean anything. Mexican women are loyal to love unlike your flighty American women."

"That's why I am here."

"You think you can get a Mexican woman."

"If she gives me the time to find out who I am."

"Who are you?"

"Person looking for what you are."

"So, this woman living in your house, why you don't be with her?"

"Because it's not the thing to do. She is different, anyway."

"What do you mean?"

"I think but I don't know for sure. I mean she is very beautiful, but there's something about her. . ."

"Is she a lesbian?"

"I think so."

"There are many here. Does she work very hard when you come around her?"

"Yes, very hard."

"That is the message to men to leave them alone. Here in Mexico it is a way, you know."

"Mexican's must have developed telepathy or something. You have so many ways."

"If you have as many years as we do with real people culture, these things develop. A way of making us understand one another. You have nothing like that in America."

"I think I have something like that."

"I know what you are talking about, you know why?"

"'Cause you have culture. You think you can see I'd be a good lover."

"How about a good man?"

"A good lover is a good man."

"I think we should see each other again."

"I will be back in La Paz next month. Maybe I will stay then."

"You are leaving?"

"Yes, tomorrow afternoon."

"Oh, that's to bad."

"It is. I wish I could spend some time with you now."

"Remember what you said, something about stopping the love? Why stop the love you said."

"Come to my home. Let's just be like we are now and take our time. We should let our feelings have the way here in Mexico. I can give you a ride home if you'd like."

"I'd like."

"I must use the telephone. I want to call home to let Angie know I'm coming. She can make us something to eat better than here."

"I'd like that too."

"I won't be a minute. I'll use the pay phone outside." Mark dialed for Angie's approval.

"Bueno."

"It's me."

"Do you have one for me?"

"Very very beautiful one, nineteen, too."

"Is she tall?"

"Oh yes, she is so fine, Angie. You are going to have so much fun."

"Why?"

"She asked me if you are a lesbian."

"You tell her about me?"

"No, honey I'm staying with your plan. You are the housekeeper just like you asked. She is a little weird, though, Hon. She said something about if you worked real hard when I was around. Said that was some kind of signal that you were a lesbian. I know she's okay, just a little weird."

"No, that is a signal that she knows. It doesn't mean a woman is lesbian, only to leave her alone."

"Yeah, I guess."

"You will have *sexo* with her first?"

"Yes, everything like you said for me to do."

"*Te amo*, Mark. You are still okay. It's fine for you to do this?"

"Very much okay! We are coming now. Bye." Mark returned and sat with Rosabla.

"I love this town!"

"Why you love this town, Mr. Carlos?"

"Telephone service is great."

"You like the Mexican desire, I think."

"I like the one sitting here."

"Maybe I like the one here, too. Can we go now?" Mark and Rosabla took the short ride to his executive, yet classical, Mexican home. There they met Angie at the door. She had made herself up just short of a prostitute's appearance. Just another cultural way to signal Rosabla. At the door, Rosabla and Angie were taken aback when they saw each other. Mark felt what he saw was that they'd known each other from a prior intimacy, not having negative effect on him.

"Hola!"

"*Si Angelina, como esta?*"

"Very good, and you?"

"I am happy to see you. Karl told me you worked here for him."

"Yes. It is a nice hacienda, no?"

"Very beautiful in here. Big windows to see the ocean by day and the city lights at night. La Paz is getting so big. Look, I can see the Malecon. You are so lucky."

Mark feeling left out intruded.

"La Paz isn't that big. You two seem to have met."

"Oh, but we would not have. Maria came to the store to by an English CD and some other software."

"Really, Angie?"

"Oh, I'm sorry Angie. I didn't know."

"No. It's okay. She can use my computer for whatever she wants."

"Good, then maybe I can help her after you leave."

"Please, Mark, can she? It would really help."

"If that's what you guys wanna do."

"Good, I go and get the supper for you. Is that right word, supper?"

Rosabla lets her know it is correct and motions for her to leave with her eyes.

"Yes, that is *perfecto* Maria."

Angie retreats to the kitchen. Rosabla is suspicious of the setup and questions Mark. "She is a lesbian. Why she call you Mark?"

"It's just an informal name I have her call me. How do you know she's a lesbian?"

"Look at her! See the black skirt, her makeup. She did her hair. She did all this, after you called her. She's a lesbian believe me. I'm sure she wants me, but you are going to have to tell her to no way Jose."

"You are absolutely sure of this?"

"Yes, she is a lesbian. Go now and tell her I respect her, but I am straight. If you do it now, she will not be angry by making her wait."

"Okay, I'll go talk to her." In disappointment Mark meets Angie in the kitchen.

"Hi, Baby give me one kiss. Mmmm."

"Angie, I have to tell you something, but I don't know really how."

"I cannot have *sexo* with her, Mark. She works downtown. I want to keep things quiet in La Paz. You are my love and I don't want problems for you here. She would get angry in more time when she saw all that we are. She could make a problem for us."

"Then what the fuck do I do about her? She wants to fuck me! She just mentioned the sex thing with you! And you forget to call me Karl!"

"I forgot. I will watch you and her. Please, I want to see. Do it in our bed. I can see from the window above."

"You mean the skylight? You sure?"

"Si si. Go take good care of she, *rapido*! Take the *cervesa*."

"My god,, my gawd!"

"Here Rosabla, it's Pacifico, my favorite beer in the world. Fuck that Pabst Blue Ribbon shit."

"Did you tell Angie?"

"Everything's cool."

"She make the dinner for you always, too?"

"No, actually I like to cook. You know, tacos!"

"I am not *stupido* you know. I understand you the first time."

"Yes, sorry."

"I think it was funny. You are kind of funny. Mexican men don't eat pussy."

"Oh. . .really?"

"Now you think I am fucked up, as you say."

"Not at all, but you surprised the hell out of me."

"You think living here in Mexico I don't hear all kind of shit talk from the *muchachos*? Talk about everything to me when I walk in the street to get my lunch every day. Taco this, taco that. You know it's all bullshit. They don't eat taco and don't know how."

"How do you know?"

"I was married for three years, and other Mexican man all the same. I think American man is a good man. In America when there is divorce, the woman take his house and every money he make. She don't suck his dick but for a few times in the beginning of the relationship. In Mexico, the man don't eat pussy but one time. We get married, have a baby, and he throw us out his life. American man and Mexican woman is the best combination ever. Si, it's very true. You know that, don't you, Mark?"

"Ah… Angie seems to think Mexican woman and Mexican woman are the best combo."

"Ha ha! Don't tell her this, she will blow you house way up! You are so funny. I want to make a joke out of that."

"A joke is right."

Angie enters to serve the meal. "Here is dinner Mark, Rosabla. *Plato Mexicana tradicional,* as you like Rosabla?"

Mark began to gesture as Rosabla answered Angie.

"Oh yes, I love it, Angie. I never think someday you would cook for me. Gracias."

"What were you going to say, Mark?"

"Nothing, Rosabla, I forgot."

"Well then you must eat the taco first. It has the most protein so you don't forget."

"I always eat the taco first. It's like the appetizer, only it takes much longer to eat."

"You must be a real funny man with the American people."

"From what they know of me, I think they would shoot me if I were to say something like that up there. Angie, do you think Mexican man and American woman can have the good life?"

"I wouldn't want to be with an American woman if . . ." Mark and Rosabla break out in laughter.

"Why so funny, why?"

"Well, we hope you wouldn't, Angie."

"I was going to say if I was a man."

"Why?"

"'Cause she would take all my shit. But if I was Mexican man, I wouldn't have so much shit to take."

Mark again gestured to speak, but Rosabla cuts him off.

"Mmmm, this is so good. You have a real good cook in the house. Angie, why don't you come by the office. I'll sneak you a few computer programs. I told Mark how they don't do any real work and expect me to do it all."

"Yes, Rosabla, I want the Microsoft browser you told me about with the translation program. That way I can read the English on the Internet. You still have it?"

"Yes, many. I can get it for you tonight if you'd like. Why don't you ride with us when Mark takes me home. I have the keys to the office tonight. I closed up and just took a walk to the Malecon, being Thursday night, you know. I met Mark and here we are."

"*Muchas gracias,* Rosabla. That will help me more than anything to learn the English. But don't you worry that they know you steal it?"

"No, there is one man that they question for stealing and he opens up at seven. I'll make sure I go in after him. He will get the blame."

"I can pay for it," Mark said, getting his word in. "For you, Angie. It's cool. I can do that."

"That would make me look good, too, Mark. We can take it tonight, and I can leave a note in Carlos' desk that I bring the money in tomorrow. He will think I am honest this way, and I can get his confidence."

"Maybe more money, too."

"That's the idea, Mark."

"That was good supper, Angie. Thank you."

Rosabla had found her way out of this one.

"Yes, maybe we should go now, before the security people come around. I don't want the hassle."

"You want to go now, Rosabla?"

"I think it's a good idea, Mark. Before it gets too late. We can come back, yes?"

Mark was stunned. "Oh, sure we can. Well, let's blow this taco stand."

The three rod down to the store with Rosabla in the center of the single bench seat of Mark's pickup truck. Rosabla and Angie spoke Spanish beyond Mark's understanding the entire way. Rosabla got Angie the software and Mark gave Rosabla one of his fifty-dollar bills. They returned to the pickup truck. Rosabla made her escape, viewing Mark as a waste of time.

"You know something, Mark. I don't want you to drive all the way back up to your house then back here again. I must work in the morning. You understand, no?"

"Are you sure? It is no problem."

"Yes, I am sure."

"Well, I guess I can give you a ride home."

"No, no. I live upstairs here in the apartment. Gracias, goodnight!"

Mark was taken aback and absorbs the rejection. "Goodnight Rosabla."

"*Buenas noches*, Angelina!"

Rosabla walked off into the night, stomping her heals, which echoed off the pavement. Mark was stupefied.

"Wow, that didn't work out at all," Mark said.

"It's no big deal, Mark. Let's go home. Just you and me. She's a sophisticated bitch."

"Goddamn, your English is getting better!"

"That's Spanish, Mark. *Sophisticated* is mucho Spanish. So few men understand sophistication."

"You think I lack sophistication Angie?"

Angie gave Mark a blank stare in her disappointment with the way he handled the evening.

Rosabla, like so many aware people in third-world countries could see through Mark right away. Her intent then became to use him. She never had intended to be sexual with this fickle mind. It is those of us in the United States who lack this awareness, due to our proud disbelief. That arrogant pride gets us into legal trouble. The truth is we North Americans are far behind when it comes to love and sex, but not war and abuse. We simply don't see it through our thick lenses. So many people have been damaged and others thrown into prison for being incredibly naïve.

Maria, by herself, was by no means blind to Mark. She just couldn't accept that he was like her father. For the first time, he seemed like a boy to her, but he gave her what she wanted. He gave her that *something* she couldn't do on her own. She did live in small town La Paz. She didn't like to advertise sexual preferences. She could not let go of Mark. He filled the gap like no other man, because he really wasn't one. They give each other their every deviant want. This love they did have. He returned to Oregon. He would come and go many times. He had a channel to the addiction that could not be satisfied.

Chapter 9

Colorado's Red River

❧

"City of Pasadena, how may I direct your call?"

"A storm drain is broken, and—"

"That'll be public works. I'll transfer you."

"Public works, how can I help you?"

"Hi, this is John Bebe down on Colorado and Altadena. A kid got hurt out here this morning riding his bicycle. The metal grate to the storm drain is, well, missing. He rode his bike over it, or in it I should say. I guess he does this every day, but today, the grate looks sort of melted. If you don't want a series of lawsuits you better come out here and fix this."

"The kid didn't fall in did he?"

"Oh no. No, it's a small drain, but the bike tire went in and threw him off. He did break his elbow though. It's right out front close to my store. This could be really dangerous. You need to send someone right away."

"Okay, Mr. Bebe, we'll get right on it. Thank you for the call."

The call was sent out as routine but, upon inspection by a city work crew, they found what they thought to be an illegal dumping. This action alone was a very serious one in the Los Angeles area, requiring special attention. They called public works.

"Yeah, Dispatch, this is Keith down at 2536 East Colorado. We got some kinda perp here. The drain grate is melted away. Some kind of acid. We've checked out down below and this stuff ate through a half-inch of concrete and is pooled up in spots for a good hundred feet. Some kind of red acid. We have a definite illegal dumping site."

"Why would anyone dump on Colorado Boulevard? That sounds like a protest."

"I dunno, Chris. What do we do?"

footer page number

"Barricade it off and we'll get the proper clean up and investigation on this. Wait till a city cop gets there to split. They may want to talk at you."

"Good enough."

The city's agencies and news crews were on the spot, including Paul Harris from the Environmental Protection Agency.

"Mr. Harris?"

"Yes, I'm Paul."

"I'm detective Bill Worthy from special crimes unit, L.A. Have any idea what this is?"

"Some way to start a Monday. I don't know what to say at this point. We do know this acid does have a contaminant in it. There's no known corrosive with this much potency if you will, having this brown-red tint. It had to have been used in heavy industrial applications. Probably used for cleaning heavy iron parts. Then the user had to dump it, since it's very expensive to dispose of. Most of these chemicals are used and controlled by the feds. If it's what I think it is, the Navy is the only ones using it in any quantities."

"What do they use it for?"

"They use it in nuclear submarines as a safety valve if they're about to sink. This acid will dissolve the plutonium in the reactors, so that, when it mixes with seawater, it becomes semi-tolerable to the environment. Only in very deep waters, of course."

"We have a perp out here with nuke material?"

"I wouldn't worry, Bill. It's probably been in some warehouse for years when they couldn't afford to dispose of it. This stuff used to be common in the Sixties. You won't see it again. Actually, it was as safe a place as it gets to dump it. Unless it rains it's staying right below your feet. It didn't get in the ground at all, since there's far to much concrete."

"That's a relief. You know that we'd have had to dig this whole street up and replace the ground if it had gone through."

"That's right."

"You're going to test it then, right, Paul?"

"We will know next week exactly what it is. I'll let you know personally."

"Please!"

Mark had arrived in La Paz about the time the authorities had at his Pasadena mockery. As stymied as they were about the acid dumping Mark was unaware of his fame in Pasadena, as he drove through Southern California on his way back to Eugene. The serial rapist-killer was into himself. Gabriela never crossed his

mind. He had what satisfied the disease of the stepmother. The only molestation was Rosabla's refusal and the fifty-dollar bill. Mark could not accept the fact that he'd been had. In time, his sick mind understood that Rosabla had kept the fifty and knew she never left a note for Carlos. Her suave way began to crawl in him, leading to the prejudice that drove him. He would now be the master of his candidates. The power he sought would no longer be suppressed. He met with Eddie to take the trucking contract.

"Hi, Robert, come on in. I've got all your paperwork and application here. Wow, you really want this contract don't you!"

"I sure do."

"Yes, I see. No one ever has completed his or her interview papers before the actual interview!"

"I like to be efficient; besides, I thought we had our interview out on highway 395."

"Yes, yes. . .you know the strangest thing happened that night after you left."

"Oh. . .what?"

"Jean returned with the mechanics to work on the truck about nine p.m., and we thought ghosts were coming out of the desert!"

"Oh my God. What are you talking about?"

"We heard this most dire screaming. It was frantic. The whole place seemed like an amphitheater, you know, since it was a very calm night. The howling would not stop but faded off in the distance after about an hour. Really freaky! We could still hear it, but from what seemed like miles away. Jean and I did the regular run again on Friday, and you'd never guess what we read in the *Harney County News*."

"What, what?"

"Here, I have it. Heifer loses hoof on the hoof. A stray cow was found languishing at the Double S ranch, minus her front left hoof. Local veterinarian Dr. Walton had never seen anything like this one. He ruled out traps, since the wound did not bear the characteristics of severing. Dr. Walton thinks aliens mutilated the cow. The cow died of shock and was slaughtered on the ranch. Mr. Robinson, pharmacist for Valley Falls, lashed at Walton's unprofessional analysis, stating that this was a chemical burn. The cow must have wandered into something. . .out there. What you make of that?"

"Stay out of there is what I make of that!"

"I'll say. Damn rattlesnake scared the Jesus out of me. I can't imagine stepping into something that'd melt off my foot. Well, anyway. . .you got any question about the contract?"

"It's all straight up. I see that you need me this week. I'll be on time. You don't have to worry. This is a piece of cake for me. I like eastern Oregon and know it really well. Four runs a week is perfect for me."

"It's going to develop into a bunch more than that, Rob. We have out-of-state work coming up. It'll be yours to if you can prove it."

"I will. You can count on it."

"Good, by the way, I noticed on your paperwork that you used the name Mark."

"Yes, sorry Eddie, but I don't give my name out to strangers, especially on the road."

"The boss will like that about you. No sense in letting competition know what you're up to is there?"

"Damn straight on that. Okay I'll be in Portland on Friday."

"Bye, Mark, and good luck."

Mark definitely had ambition for the trucking business. The incentive was another alley he could not live without. He had no concern that the hokie Oregon newspaper could be connected to Pasadena or Jerica. Even if the police were shown the light, they would never come close enough for an indictment.

The trucking business would expand into an interstate affair. He landed several other contracts, believing this to be rewards for his deeds to the demon, even to the last step of Satan's throne. His new secretary Sarah was highly motivated and wanted to make something of her twenty-five years. Hired for amusement by Mark, her belief in Christianity was small-time flaunting. She was in fact an excellent marketer of the new business. Mark could not recognize anything she performed to accomplish the expansion. His belief in himself and his deeds to the demon were the rewards.

Mark stayed clear of Pasadena for a stretch. New York City, Denver, and Seattle were not so fortunate. In the next five months, he killed five times. Los Angeles Detective Worthy had no idea of the serious perp entering his domain. Paul Harris, a straight by-the-book character kept telephone contact with Worthy.

"Detective Worthy speaking."

"Hello, Bill. Paul Harris here. How are you today?"

"I'm busier than a cat in a litter box, Paul. How's the life of Riley with that kick-back G job."

"Ha. Well it is a living. I do have the lab reports for you on the illegal dumping over on Colorado."

"Oh, yeah. I'd nearly forgotten about that. It's been three weeks now."

"Sorry for the delay. The department took it as low ball. But it is as I suggested, nitric acid."

"So, nothing I need to follow up on, then?"

"Nah, the analysis of the contaminate was an iron base, probably used for cleaning heavy stuff. The technical part is vague, due to the potent nature of the acid. That attribute left us a bit foggy."

"How so?"

"It was almost as if it were a hemoglobin-type of iron, but we ruled that out. This stuff is extremely powerful, so it really breaks down the chemistry of the element in question."

"Hemoglobin-type iron?"

"Sorry, as in blood iron. But, like I said, it's something we'll probably never know, unless a company employee rats them off."

"How's the clean up going on that?"

"All done, they fixed it up like new."

"Good. I do need a copy of the lab reports for my file. If anything else comes up let us know, won't you?"

"Sure thing, I'll fax it over. Talk to you later."

"Thank you."

Mark had read the news report in the *Los Angeles Times*. Elated to see the report, he hoped for the grim news that should stun the Angelinos into fear. To his disappointment, a simple unrelated toxic dumping was all that had been reported. The same result in New York City three weeks later agitated him to step in. He attributed this to the stupidity of government overspending on toilet seats. He needed the anonymous fame for his genius. The idiots could never make the connection without Mark's intervention. The telephone was beckoning.

"Los Angeles special crimes unit."

"Yes. . .may I please speak to Detective Worthy, please?"

"I have to get your name, Sir. We can no longer accept direct calls to special crimes. You may call the general police business line if you don't wish to leave your name."

"Will I be put through to him if I do?"

"Yes, of course."

"This is detective Allen of the New York Metro Special Crimes Unit."

"Why didn't you say so? I'll put you right through."

"Detective Worthy. . ."

"Hi, Bill, detective Les Allen in New York. I don't think we've talked before."

"No, I don't think so either. What can I do for the Big Apple today?"

"Well, I was reading the *LA Times* last month about an illegal dumping in Pasadena. What do you guys make of that out there?"

"Nothing much, just what the paper wrote is all she wrote. What has your interest?"

"You hadn't heard, huh?"

"Don't tell me."

"Yes, same exact make. Storm drain, red corrosive acid on a hell of a busy downtown street. Just like Colorado Boulevard. Did you get a breakdown of the chemistry?"

"Yes, simple cleaning of iron works. I have to respect your alertness to this."

"I grew up in LA. I take *The Times* by subscription. I really didn't read the article, until it happened up here. I looked it up again, today, and saw your name in the article."

"You're sure it's a match?"

"Absolutely, yes. It is exactly the same type of acid and analysis. Get a copy of the Sunday *NY Times* two weeks ago Sunday."

"Fax me all you have. Give me your fax number, and I'll give you what we got. Hello, hello, hmm, disconnected. I'll ring up the switchboard."

"Shari speaking."

"Yeah, Shari, sorry to ring you, but did detective Allen leave a fax number when he checked in?"

"No, it was odd, though. He acted like he didn't know he had to give his name to be put through."

"Good cop. He was testing you, Shari."

"Good thing I'm doing my job. I sure wouldn't want to be arrested in a police station."

"You sure wouldn't. I need you to look up the fax number for New York special crimes."

"Yep, have it on the computer, ah 666-353-0918."

"Thanks, keep your guard up."

The real Detective Allen received the report the following morning in New York, due to the three-hour time delay. It was eight-thirty in New York but six-thirty p.m. in Denver where Mark made the call, and his current victim was about to be released into Sixth and Oak Street. Worthy did not mention in his fax that Allen had contacted him. He only sent the lab reports of the Pasadena incident and a copy of the Los Angeles news release.

"What the hell is dis?"

"I dunno, Allen. Some cop out in LA faxed it to you last night."

"What, no fucking courtesy letter, nothin'?"

"That's it, I don't know what to make of it. Something here about a lab report, dumping acid in a storm drain. What the fuck?"

"Hey, you remember, two weeks ago out by Central."

"Yeah, some prick didn't wanna pay a disposal fee, so big freaking deal. What's he doing wasting paper telling me this shit? LA cops; about as stuck up as Madonna. Don't think they gotta do a damn thing that requires moving their ass. You know I bought a goddamn California car once; never do that again."

"Why'd you buy a car from Cal?"

"They didn't have the model I wanted here. They did a locate and found one in Fag town. Damn car farted at me all the time."

Fag town?"

"San Francisco, you ignoramus. Fucking car would fart up through the car-buretor every time I stepped on it. So much smog control on it, I got a speeding ticket in the damn thing because I couldn't stand it farting all the time. Fucking smog. Hell, this arrogant shit head cop's got some smog coming. California arro-gance! Ah send him out a fax of our report. Be a real snob about it too. Send him an invitation to the fucking ball though nothin' else. Dumb ass California cop."

"Anything you say, Lester."

"Hey watch it or I'll transfer your ass to this guy, what's his name. . .Worthy. Shit, he ain't worthy. Fuck the invitation."

The fax sent back to Worthy was interpreted as simply completing their authentic communication, leaving the case without action for a duration of three more killings. No one in the country knew the most dangerous man alive was at work. Mark would feel no remorse for his deeds to his recompensing demon. He felt the emptiness of the equation. Calling on Angie alleviated the self-pity in these moments.

"I have a collect call from Mark in the United States. Do you accept the charges?"

"Si, please."

"Baby, I don't hear from you for two weeks. Why?"

"I'm really sorry, Angie. I want to save as much money as I can, and it costs so much to call Mexico. I want you to have the money. But I love you so much and I wish I could be there in this moment."

"I love you so much too. You don't have to speak the broken English for me to understand. I have the translator on the computer now. I work on it everyday. Everyone says I am talking very good now."

"You really are, but just to hear you is sufficient for me."

"Are you okay, Mark?"

"No. I want to come home, but I have to wait a little longer. I have so much to do."

"I wait day and night. But I'm coming to see you if you don't come next week."

"I'm going to come in two more weeks, Baby, I promise. I can stay for two weeks. I have people working for me now, and I won't have to see my probation officer."

"You are still driving the big truck?"

"Yes, we have three now, but they're rented. Still, the money is the best I've ever made. Thirty some thousand a month, Hon. It won't be long, and I'll be home forever for you."

"You sound happy now."

"Yeah, this is what I needed. Talking with my wife. Let's get married when I come, Baby. Do you think we can?"

"*Mi amor*, this is what I wait to hear for so long. I wonder why we didn't so long ago."

"You are such a good woman, Angie. I put the houses in your name. Now you want to marry me after the fact. You are the best of the best. Remember our first Christmas in the old house? Remember all the children and the party?"

"Yes that is when I put in the computer 'I love my gringo Mark.'"

"Did Rosabla ever help you with the computer after I left?"

"No, she never call me back."

"Don't worry, I'll find you better."

"This time? When you come this time?"

"I can't wait to do this for you."

"Is many lesbians in your town?"

"No, it's a small town; besides, you would not like an American woman. They think everything is funny. You would not have the love with her. I know Fabi wants to be with you, Angie."

"How do you know?"

"You promise you won't be angry?"

"I promise."

"I fucked her that Christmas. I didn't know you were lesbian, then, or I would have told you."

"Oh! I wish I can see that. What did she tell you?"

"She asked me if you would sleep with her. I said 'Hell no!' that you were straight. If you'd told me the truth, then you could've been with her now. She knew that your father raped you many times."

"Yes this is true. I told her before I know you. I wanted her to understand that I liked her, but she said nothing."

"Are you upset that we talk like this, Angie?"

"Oh no, no, not at all. I love this man who is so open to my life. I want this life so much. You think Fabi would be okay for you?"

"Yes, she was very clean. She took me seriously, too."

"Can you live with two women? You see us have the love so much and this no molest you, Mark?"

"I did it before with you and Cynthia close to six months, no?"

"Yes, but you are very angry when we go out and get drunk."

"I wasn't angry for that. I was angry because you got into trouble with the police. She was fifteen. You're lucky she lied for you."

"She loved me, Mark. It's different in Mexico. The woman will not talk to the police these things. Anyway, she would need evidence to prove I have sex with her. It's different here in Mexico, not like America, where the woman can say what she wants to and they believe her."

"Yes, but what about when I had sex with her? They can do evidence samples there. I saw that."

"Yes, that is how they put my papa in the prison. I remember the fucking doctor take his shit out my pussy. I want to kill these mother fuckers..."

"Angie, please, this is not what we need now."

"I'm so angry sometimes. Please forgive me."

"I promise, I'll bring Fabi home when I get down there. Actually, why don't you go to her house? She's only down the street half a kilometer."

"You think I can do that?"

"Yes, you must be strong for what you want."

"I wish I am strong like you, but I am afraid she will laugh at me."

"Angie, I promise this girl wants you. Go get her. Ask her to come to the house to help you clean or whatever."

"Yes, that is a good idea. Maybe she will tell me."

"No, she won't. I told her you were straight. Just come out and do what you want. She will go along with you, I promise. Just kiss her and think she is me. I'm telling you, just walk up to her and kiss her. You will be so happy you did."

"You are so strong. I wished I was a man. I want to do that to Fabi, but I have mucho nervous."

"The first time you take control, Angie, it will be so easy for you after that. You could have many women."

"I don't want many women. I just want one to love me."

"Really? You mean like forever?"

"Yes, don't you know that?"

"Yes. . . I did, I just wanted to hear you say so . . . Wow."

"I love you forever, Mark. You are my Messiah. You know what that mean?"

"Yes, I save you. I save your love, Maria. I'll see you in two weeks."

"Remember what you say, Mark, you take my love with you . . . and I yours."

"I do. I promise I do. Bye, my tropical woman."

The conversation took Mark's emptiness for the moment and filled it with an unwanted substitute he did not expect. It was the time for understanding that playmates were not the future, but rather possible competition. Could Angie love him for a retirement plan's length of time he planned on bringing to Mexico? If she loved a woman as much, the sharing might wind up Mexican woman and Mexican woman forcing Mark back to the USA and prison. The thought of seeing love between two women permanently in his home was not at all the same as spells of diversity. Maybe some men could have two lovers, but Mark was not a lover. He could not be identified by any name, except that of Rapist.

Chapter 10

Seattle Slew

As part of Mark's three-year probation program he was required to attend treatment with a qualified sex offense counselor. He sat down with his privately-paid psychologist, Peter. Due to the fact that social science lacked the hard definitive standard of proof that was the hallmark of the physical sciences, sex offenders have often been certified as *treated*.

"Mark, I like your progress. I believe you'll complete the program before your probation is up. Most offenders take five to seven years but, considering the non-violent nature of your crime and the realization of the impact on Heather, you should get through this. You've seen what the effects are on Maria; even after years have passed by."

"Do you think the damage her father left her with is permanent?"

"From what you tell me about her, she has a lifetime wound. She should be taken out of any environment that reflects her childhood. You told me about Maria wanting to have a full-time female lover and be married to you. This is classical of her type of abuse, especially from the father. She will look to women her entire life, if she continues in this frame of mind."

"You don't think it's possible she could naturally be a lesbian, you know, like from birth? I've seen some of these women and men on day TV, *Sally*, and such who say they've always been homosexual."

"The odds of that are slim, combined with her father's severe abuse and her desire for you and a woman points an entirely different direction. I have to consider your feelings concerning this in your progress; you understand that I'm sure."

"Yes, I do. I just care about her."

"You're going to have to concentrate on your daughter and yourself, Mark. For the next two and a-half years, you're being evaluated by the State of Oregon.

The fact that you came back from Mexico and knocked on the jailhouse door is what went in your favor. I also believe that no other offender I council has come to your level of understanding. But that does not mean you're totally treatable. What does make you treatable is, if you truly turn away from all the offenses, and walk it straight. How do you feel in your mind about your offenses and what you desired?"

"I have a pretty clear mind now. I feel horribly repulsed, when I think back about what I did. I'm sure this could never be me again."

"That's what most offenders say. Some are lying; some really believe this. But the only way we can be somewhat sure is years of treatment and a strict program. Also, you did have a misdemeanor charge against you ten years before, for masturbation in the presence of a five-year-old, Shari. You lied at the trial, even paid a witness, Joe, to testify on your behalf. You have been forthcoming with me about all this and admitted your guilt only to me. I do want you to know that I'm telling you this for you. You need the long-term observation and counseling. I'll do everything possible to convince parole you have completed the program in the two and a-half years left. You have proved yourself as a businessman. I'm a private counselor that you pay, and I stand behind my clients. Just make sure you can keep up your payments to me. The state's offender program is very hard, and many of the offenders wind back up in prison."

"Why do they go back in?"

"The state decides everything, Mark, everything. You're pretty safe here. But over there would be bad for you because of Shari. They know you're guilty. Vengeance is the State's; you savvy?"

"They didn't consider Shari at the time I came back. Why would they now?"

"Your lawyer didn't tell you?"

"What?"

"The D.A. who prosecuted that case buried the file to avoid his exposure for losing. Shari's mother brought it to light after the deal was cut for you. She couldn't believe you walked again. Everyone's keeping a lid on your case, but if they get you inside, you're gone, kid."

"Why didn't she come forward beforehand?"

"Mark, people don't even want publicity for this type of crime. Besides, she was sure you'd get serious time. A lot of people out there want a piece of you. I would recommend that you send a cashier's check to this woman for all the money she's spent on counseling for Shari."

"For the grief, also."

"Are you telling me this because you will?"

"Yes, I will."

"Now, that is a real indication of a turnaround. These are the things I look for in my clients."

"I'll show you I can turn this around."

"Okay, Mark, see you in three weeks. Do all your homework."

"See you, Peter."

Mark had found a way to manipulate the system through his privately-paid sex offense counselor. After the offender comes to realization of his new low life position, he will sacrifice anything to gain some stature. This is what the system does not realize, how low it is to be an acknowledged, labeled, roaming sex offender. A human in this position is more dangerous than a caged animal that's just escaped. Mark made sure that whatever turned Peter in his direction, he would do. He planned his treatment sessions and probation meetings on the same days, so he could go on the hunt in between. He found his way up to Husky stadium in Seattle. The Huskies had just defeated UCLA for a berth at the Rose bowl in Pasadena. The fans were elated, including Kelly, a twenty-six-year old rooter who loved her Huskies football team enough to hitchhike from Tacoma. She wouldn't root in Husky stadium again.

"Hi! I'm going south. How about you?"

"Yes, I'm off to Yakima."

"Good, I need a ride to Tacoma."

"Well, that's on the way. I'm Jim."

"Kelly, thanks. Did you hear about the game?"

"Yeah. Shit we're going again. Isn't that awesome?"

"You're a Huskies fan."

"Am I? I played here."

"You don't say? What year?"

"1978 and 79. Warren was our quarterback, remember?"

"Well, I was only six then. You don't look that old."

"Yep, all of forty-four."

"You really kept your youth, you know that?"

"I still get carded when I buy beer."

"God, I could use one of those right now."

"Got a case in the fridge. Help yourself."

"Oh. . . .why not. You're an ex-Husky."

"Hey, I am a Husky. I want a beer, too. The win is to be celebrated."

"Yes, you're a Husky. That's worth drinking to. Gawd, that is a nice sleeper you got back there! What's the glass cover for over the bathtub?

"Oh, a guy down in Mexico did that, he put these huge windows in my house down there for the cyclones. It keeps the water from splashing around, if I can't find a place to dump right away. See how he sealed that up like that?"

"Yes, seems like a lot of work to take it off when you want a bath. You drive nationally or just in Washington?"

"Just around here, I don't like the long haul you know, wife and kids."

"You're married?"

"Oh yeah, wouldn't have it any other way."

"Most guys wouldn't say so to a blonde on the road."

"Well, like I said, I'm forty-four, but I need to get off the road for a minute. This beer has gone right through me."

"I know the feeling. At least you have your own bathroom on the road."

Mark pulled off on an exit to a dark side street. He took an extended amount of time in the sleeper, hoping to lure Kelly in. He waited with a police night stick. There would be no seduction this time. She was Rosabla in his mind.

Kelly got up from the cab seat and peered into the sleeper.

"Hey, Jim, are you okay? Jim? What'd you do, fall in your bathtub? Oh God, nooo! Stop you bastard!"

Mark savagely beat Kelly with his police nightstick, driven by hatred of Rosabla and desire, revealing his utter insanity. "Three strikes and your out! Get you out of these stupid purple pants. I can't wait to see the look on your face when you wake up in there. No way you can imagine what your tied-up ass is going to go through. Hands behind the back, duct tape up the ankles, now hurry the fuck up and wake up."

A half hour passed as Mark drove back to Husky stadium. He parked the rig by a storm drain he had selected that thousands of people would walk over for the Sunday professional football game. Kelly was kicking at the glass-covered tub the deviant had manufactured for the easier deeds he performed for the demon. He had become wracked with the competition of having to seduce the prey. Now, it would be all force, which was much easier—and quicker.

"Hi there! Can you hear me in there? Yeah, that Mexican did a good job. Ceramic covered rubber seal all the way around. I can barely hear you; what did you say? Oh yeah, I couldn't wait to fuck you. You were out too long. It hurts huh, yeah I'll bet, both places too. Here, let me open the overflow. There, I can hear you much better now. What did you say?"

"What the fuck kind of animal are you? You fucking low life. I swear if you gave me AIDS. . . ."

"AIDS, is that the moment's concern?"

"What the hell are you planning to do?"

"Ahh . . .you're going to have to guess. Your hint is that your whole life is going down the drain. The method is one word, two syllables, starts with an A. Well it does depend on what type it is, but this is the best kind. What's the matter, don't wanna play?"

"You are one sick demented asshole."

"Oh, I was going to make it be a fast acid flow, but I think not. Now it's going to be a trickle."

"Acid?"

"You guessed! I like seeing you in there, so smart and all, naked, fucked-up cunt. I'll never pick up an old lady like you again. I had to fuck you up the ass, even that was a disappointment. Nothing over nineteen from here on out. Well, I got a real woman waiting in La Paz. Better get on with it!"

"You'll never get away with this!"

"Ah, I have five times. You're number six. Oh, the first couple were real difficult but you're by far the cleanest and easiest. I didn't mean you were clean, far from that. I was talking about the facilities here. You know, I decapitated three of them. The blood just skirts out the carotid arteries and for so long! The heart didn't stop pounding for almost five minutes. I had to prove a scientific thing. You know they say one experiment's results isn't sufficient evidence."

"What the hell is wrong with you?!"

"I wanted to know if people were still conscious immediately following the guillotine. You know, haven't you ever wondered about all those people who got their heads hacked? I had to know, fuck it, had to find out somehow. Seemed like the thing to do. Christ, I'm not going to feel guilty. They did it for fun. I did it for science's sake! I wondered if they saw themselves tumble down into the barrel. That had to be a trip feeling, seeing everything just bouncing and rolling by into the bucket. That must have been where the term 'kick the bucket' got born. I'm the first to prove that you do stay conscious, for an average of five seconds, clearly enough time to understand. Anyway, I can't waste time telling the dead. I need to get that published to the living! Shit, who knows . . . head transplants! Bye-bye, beeatch!"

"In God's name, what have I done to deserve this?"

"It's what I've done, Kelly. I've raped, and I know the power. I can take as I please. I'm the core of all rapists and the meaning of rape. I am like Satan in the flesh. I come to take the most desired of creation, the vagina and all that goes with her. What I do is the culmination of all men's desires that are inhibited by civilized law. I make my own place in the law. Can you imagine the immense satisfaction that brings to both flesh and spirit?"

"In the name of Jesus Christ, I command you to get out of him, Satan. I plead the blood of Jesus, the Blood of Jesus Christ!"

"I don't think you can do that. The written word says the prayers of a sinner in trouble is damnation to his own soul!"

"Oh fuck, oh fuck, Jesus, please come and take me away now."

"Nope, he ain't gonna listen. Remember all the times you missed church, didn't testify and witness, banged your boss, sucked the next-door neighbor off. Gotta be more wary; the rapist comes like a thief in the night, too, and he came first. Jesus was real about that kinda shit, Baby. He don't come in these times of need for people like you, especially like this. You belong to Lucifer, and he don't like what you just said, either. Matter a fact he hates it worse than Jehovah. Don't you know you shouldn't surrender to Charlie, then tell him he's a sloped-forehead commie? Oh I forgot, you wouldn't know about 'Nam. Now take me, for example, I'm fucking loyal right up to the goddamn end. Even Hitler knew what he was doing. That's why he and Eva did themselves. Yep, right up to glory day; faith, the thing hoped for. You're not going to have a leg in hell to stand on. Shit, I'm gonna have a whip. I'll be lookin' for you! Opening the floodgates, woe, look at you. Mother fucking Mary."

Chapter 11

All Things

~

"Angie?"

"Oh no, Señor, she come to the phone."

"Hi, Baby, you telephone me much more now. You coming Monday?"

"I think late Monday or Tuesday. Love you, Babe. Who was that?"

"Hee hee, it's Fabi. When we sleep together, she tell me everything about you. You did it more than you tell me."

"Yeah, I kinda did. Are you angry?"

"Why? I would never know Fabi if you didn't."

"So, does she live there, now?"

"Oh no! She wants more time and we need to ask you first."

"Baby, I wouldn't have fucked her in the first place if I didn't like her. She doesn't need to ask me. I can't wait to be with her again. God, she was fun. So, I take it you are with her; you are involved." Mark asked, wanting to know exactly what they were doing for his excitement sake, and Angie understood this.

"Not so much, she is slow with me, but she say I lick her pussy better than you do. But you are better to me on that. Her Momma wants to talk to you about her living here. She said she is happy Fabi is with me, because I cannot get her pregnant. She tell me this."

"Oh, shit, what a way to think. Ah, I'm sorry. *La Madre de Fabi es lesbiana,* Angie."

"*Yo se yo se,* I know that a long time ago. What are you sorry for? I don't understand."

"Never mind. So, if everything works out like you want, you think we can live together forever."

"Please don't say that, Mark. That scares me so much to think we would not be together. Nothing can stop this love. Remember, I love your heart. Your heart is more important to me than Fabi. Only you can stop this love."

"When I get there I want to sit down and talk with you and Fabi about all of this."

"With the Mother of Fabi, too, Mark, all of us."

"Ah, oh my, hmmm. I'll see you soon. I'm on my way now. Love you."

"Love you, Mark."

Mark drove from Seattle to stop in Eugene to talk with his counselor, Peter, a practicing Christian. The coming change in his life with Angie was of financial and longevity concerns to survive in La Paz till death does its part. He had a plan with the amount of money that would hold him over. He could not stay in Mexico if the plan failed. The consequences would be the five-year prison sentence without protective custody. His memories of Angie's description of her father's fate haunted him daily. Shea was now working as a stripper in a well-known nightclub. She had connections to inmates in the Oregon penal system. He knew she would not hesitate to expose him. He was a marked man if he failed. Mark telephoned Peter.

"Good evening."

"Hi, Peter, I'm sorry to bother you so late. This is Mark."

"Oh, Mark, feel free to call me anytime. It's what I'm here for. What's on your mind?"

"Well, I've spoken to Angie. She says she can live with me forever, and also with a lesbian lover who she actually wants me to also be involved with. The thing that's so hard for me is that it seems so natural for her and the girl to include the girl's mother's permission. I'm psyched."

"This is the Jake brake syndrome."

"You said what?"

"You know, like the Jake brake on your truck down in Mexico; those things are so loud it'll scare the pants off you. Up here we have Jake brakes, but you can't hear them because they're muffled."

"You are right about that, but the Jake brake I'm talking about really doesn't compare to trucks; we're talking about two women."

"This is our cultural difference from Mexico and most other parts of the world. In Japan, you will see billboard advertisements of body lotion picturing two beautiful young women kissing and in a complete embrace, French-style kissing mind you. You have just started to experience something out of your

accustomed domain of Oregon. But you need to withdraw from all of it now, Mark. Like I said, concentrate on yourself and your daughter."

"I definitely am, but I'm still interested in returning to Mexico when my probation is up. I just want to know if these things are normal."

"When you're rehabilitated, Mark. Then maybe this would be okay. The idea of something being normal is not in your identity, now. But yes, it would be a part of something pertaining to a norm, only because it is so commonplace. We just never hear of it as so blown up as the place your talking about. Mark, something you must consider if you get back together with Angie is your true history. She would be rocked, if she found out on her own that you violated your daughter. This would not only lead you to have to start your life all over again, but it would crush Angie's heart. She never could be rehabilitated. If she is a lesbian due to her father's abuse, she would remain so. Nothing could change that. You need to telephone that young lady. From what I know of you, you can be tactful. It's possible that she could see hope in a man if you were forthcoming with her. She could see true repentance; you know that. All people can grasp the truth in the right light. I honestly think God brought the two of you together so you could see the damage in Angie."

"Yeah, I thought that so many times. Angie's symptoms of abuse have shown me things that I feel real shitty about doing to my daughter."

"Speaking of your daughter, Mark, she loves you so much. You'll be able to see her very soon. The courts recognize your non-violent nature and have to let you see her. She has been writing letters to you and asks about you daily. She has absolutely nothing negative to say about you. I do need to tell you, though, some lifetime damage has been done."

"How so?"

"Well, Mark, we go by evidence. Heather was observed in dementia-type behavior."

"As what dementia?"

"This is not going to be easy for you, but you do have to know the facts of your daughter's case."

"I can handle it."

"She was observed letting and coercing the neighbor's dog into licking her vagina. This is the damage you caused. She also asked the foster parent's father to lick her privates. The boyfriend that Shea lived with is now being investigated for the same offense. She is constantly touching herself, in and out of company."

"I really did fuck her up didn't I?"

"You have to look ahead. No matter what mistakes we humans make, solving them and moving on is the answer. You already realize and confronted your actions; now it's time to move away from that and into rehabilitation. Are you with me, Mark?"

"I'm trying. What do you think will become of her behavior?"

"As she reaches puberty, the natural sexuality she shall develop will mask the underlying effect, giving her an outward sense of normal development. The childhood damages stay and are correctable, so that she can adjust to career living. The damage we will try to correct, but you have to understand she must want to correct this behavior. She must also see that you're correcting your deviant behavior. It's as difficult for the victim to recover from damage as it is for the offender to be treated for the illness. She will need years of treatment and positive, wholesome living. The nature of your offense is highly focused, too. It was not at all a physical torment for her. You woke up her innocence from developmental growth to sensuality to sexuality. By committing oral sodomy on her, you actually created a deviance stronger than normal father-daughter bonding. This leads to many avenues of deviance she would be capable of by her own intellect or imagination, such as the dog. Her adult life could turn out extremely deviant, if not criminal. We will discuss any other impacts, as your treatment plan of awareness."

"I have to tell you something I've never told anyone."

"Tell me now, Mark, while you feel like doing so, and don't twist it."

"All that stuff you just told me about the victim going down avenues according to their own imagination for what was shown them. It is very much me. What I did to my daughter so many times, my stepmother forced me to do to her. For years and years."

"Well, I'm happy you never told the courts that. You'd be locked up and forgotten about."

"Because I'd be considered messed up beyond repair, right?"

"The state is as primitive as apes, and they don't care to rehabilitate. But I care and we will get you the right treatment. Do not discuss your stepmother with your parole officer or anyone else in the system. Keep that between us for the period of your probation. I'm actually surprised you're in a state of acceptance and treatable, so soon. I'm pleased with you, Mark. You're going to make it."

"Good night, Peter."

"God bless you, Mark. See you in three weeks."

Mark conversed solo in his severe mental illness believing the demon hears him, and more so, God.

"All these things, this is who I am. Fuck it. God won't forgive me now. Peter is but one out of a million who would ever accept me. My fucking stepmother did me. I wouldn't have known any of this unless I got counseling. Like, Angie, the counselor showed her how fucked up she was. That's why she's fucked up. She realizes it now. I'm shaking Peter off. I am who I am. I am a rapist. My mother died and God replaced her with Karen, my rapist. She taught me who I am now. God will pay for this. The God that created this will pay. He didn't protect us. He didn't protect my Heather. He's not going to protect my prey." Mark proceeded.

Chapter 12

The Burn

❦

"Hi, Fabi, how are you?"

"I am very good, and you, Mark?"

"Whca . . . hmmm, that's a warm welcome."

"Yes, Angie, wants me to make you feel me."

"I sure do feel you. Goddamn, I might get to like this after all. My Angie!"

"Baby, *te quiero mucho*, Mark. Welcome home."

"I do love you. I have two women embracing me now. I do feel this love. I could not understand before but I do now."

"It's not play, Mark; it is reality."

"I spoke to a counselor about this in Oregon. He says this is normal in many parts of the world. I have to adjust to this, to love you both the right way."

"You do know how, Mark. You showed me. You showed Fabi. You brought us together. You gave us your home. You gave me my life back. You are my messiah. I pray for you so much, I feel sometimes in the night your pain. I feel so much pain in you sometimes. I don't have the love like this all my life and I think it's my turn to help you."

"This is a dream to me. I hear those words up here on a mountain, where no one can see us. The God I serve is the way."

"You don't bring your big truck. This is your car? It is so flashy."

"No, it's yours. I left the truck in San Ysidro. You will have to drive me back to Tijuana. Is that a deal or what?"

"Oh, *si si*! What kind of car is this?"

"Mustang HO convertible; best fucking car ever made."

"Come, Mark, in the house. We make the supper for you. We make the love for you. Soon you feel no more pain. You are in La Paz now. You are home."

The next two weeks were like a paradise so few Americans would ever experience. They worked, traveled, partied, lived like many people would dream about. In all this time, Mark was natural. He did not have to pretend he was convinced of Angie's words. He did know how because he showed them. They discussed everything with Fabi's mother. Mark's shroud had broken down to her knowledge and way. The enlightenment and time had brought to Mark's mind Peter's advice. He would talk to Angie about his history. The third day before leaving, he sat down with her, exposing all of himself.

"Baby, I need to talk to you about something very, very important; something that maybe will cause you do not to want to be with me any more if I tell you, but I have to."

"Nothing you can tell me would make me feel different, Mark. And you don't have to speak broken English with me, I learn so much on the computer."

"This is very serious, Angie."

"Okay, I sit down with you."

"I want Fabi to hear this, too. I want to tell you both."

"I hear you, Mark. I come too. I listen."

"You said you could feel my pain. I have a reason for this pain that only people like you and me understand. I know other people who never have what we experience can never understand. I want to tell you something no one else knows. I only told my counselor."

"You can have the confidence in us, Mark."

"I am taking a big risk in telling you, but I want you to know I want help and am getting it in America."

"What is the risk, Mark?"

"That you and Angie would hate me and never love me again."

"This is no possible, Mark. Angie and I love you. You don't believe that?"

"Yes, I do and that is why I must tell you. When I was a little boy my Mother died. My father remarried a woman who hated me. Many horrid things were done. In the beginning it was not so bad. Then she started making me lick her vagina. She would put my face in her legs and hold me, until I would pass out. She was a larger woman and very strong. At times, I would choke on my vomit because she had a bad odor. She would come in my room at night when my father slept and put herself on my face. I still hear her whispering, but commanding voice, saying lick the poison from my privy. Savor my poison, you maggot. My left shoulder became chronically dislocated from her knees on me. My sinuses where extremely tender. I bled and had constant infections. She would urinate in bed and blame it on me to my father. She would usually urinate when

she achieved orgasm by forcing my face on her vagina. I had long hair, so she could hold it and forcefully bring herself climax and urinate. She would always tell me to swallow but I spat it out. When I cut my hair very short with the razor, she knew why I did it and broke my left elbow. She made me tell my father I fell while running. He was very angry with me for months, because we didn't have insurance. We were poor and the doctor's bills hurt. I think what hurt the most was that I could never get my father's confidence, because I was so fucked up. I didn't have any identity. I fucked everything up. I could not compete. All the other children and my relatives shunned me, thinking I was a freak.

From that time on, she would beat me. She broke my molar teeth. I lived in so much pain for that. We did not have money for the dentist. I had to wait until I joined the Army at age seventeen to get my teeth fixed. I finished the last year of my high school in the Army, which was my only escape. I begged my father to sign an affidavit to let me join when I was seventeen. I would risk going to Viet Nam because of her. I could not tell my father; I knew she would kill me and herself. She would suck my penis, too; she put a kitchen knife under my scrotum and told me that, if I didn't come real fast, she would castrate me. She talked very graphically, like 'I will cut off your balls and dick with one stroke and put it in my mouth.' I have very small scars today where the knife broke the skin several times. She did many other things too, like cut the crotch out of my underwear to remind me what would happen if I told. In all the world, no one can understand how I feel for these things, unless it happened to them. To kill is always on my mind. There is so much more. I thought I could tell you everything, but I feel very sick now. I want to go and sleep. I want to smoke some of that shit.

I don't hurt from these things I have told you, though. I hurt from something I did. I tried to be my stepmother but could not come close. I was not forceful. The others don't matter. They are from a different avenue."

Mark got up and walked away, telling the pure truth. Fabi and Angie were frozen, with eyes locked on each other. Tears came from both of them, but Mark did not want that. He wanted to tell them about his daughter. But the truth of not telling wasn't the worry of his exposure, it was Heather's. He did not want them to feel her pain. The only true good part left in Mark was his born instinct for his daughter. He blamed his stepmother and envisioned that it was her who abused had Heather. The avenues of choice from intellect spoken of by Peter were also Mark's failure, in that he chose to use one of them to lie about rehabilitation. He would continue to kill with bloodthirsty vengeance.

Angie and Fabi went in to the TV room, the oversize windows captured the moon light reflection off the Bay of La Paz. "Mark?"

"Hi…hmmm…you come to me, always loving me."

"When my father is dead, I feel the vengeance. Then after time, I feel the love again, and I am so happy it is love for you. You see how beautiful the moon make the water tonight. I feel like that inside, but I burn for your stepmother."

"Then I will burn as I do, until my stepmother is dead. I don't have the moonlight or any light; I have pure black, and it's looking clear that she is the blackness."

"Where is your stepmother, Mark?"

"This is a good question. I've been burning to know that since I enlisted in the Army. She vanished the day I left twenty-seven years ago."

"It is easy to find anyone now."

"What do you mean, Fabi?"

"The computer! We can look anyone up. Sometimes you must pay but you have a visa card. Use the search on Microsoft."

"*Si*, Mark, lets try."

'How can I find her this way? I've asked the police and they don't know."

"Ha! They cannot find you when you are in Mexico with felony charges! You know why?"

"Why?"

"Because they really don't look. They wait for you to fuck up. It's the same in Mexico."

"Come, let's find the bitch."

"If you say so."

"Okay, put in her full name and date of birth if you have it."

"Are you kidding? I have everything on her. Karen Johnson…"

"What was her last known address?"

"Gee, Fabi, I didn't know you could do this. It was 2150 Laura Street, Springfield, Oregon."

"I learned how on the lesbian net. Okay, we go to the city's last known address from there. She changed her name to Wimber, Karen A. She put in a forwarding address to 89761 Highway 41, Kentucky. Go to Kentucky public records; see if she has any properties or employment records. She is listed with the state of Kentucky as Karen's Touch; it's a small business listing with the state-assumed business names. Her new address is 1130 N. Walnut, apartment 308,

Louisville. She has a heavy junk-mail listing with all the mail marketers. Looks like she enters contests. Too easy, Mark."

"She's not on the run like I was."

"She will be now, the bitch."

"I want to do her alone, Angie; only me."

"When my father is in the prison, we all go there to visit him. Well, not really to visit; we go there to tell everyone what he do to me and my sister. They make his life one hell, then they castrate him. For five years he have no dick and balls. They make him the woman. Then they kill him."

"Five years without a. . . . I cannot put Karen in prison now; you know that. Even you said evidence is needed in Mexico. It's a personal matter that I feel like celebrating! Let's go to Cabo!"

"Hoo! Maria, I love your Mark."

"I want to kick one sophisticated American bitch's ass in Cabo."

"Who, Angie?"

"I don't know, first one I see!"

"Goddamn, Baby, tame it."

"Can I drive the best fucking car ever made, Mark?"

"I know what you want, Maria, just keep an eye on the road . . . too. Ha Haaaa!"

"He is your Mark too, Fabi."

"Forever, Angie."

"*Si*, Mark."

"*Si, si, si, si,* Mark."

Mark returned to Oregon superficially believing that his pending sentence to be handed down to Karen would cure him. The killing he loved would stop, and his cleft in La Paz was knocking. He could sell the business and return with over a quarter million in cash, and the truck. A dream life waited, never to be replaced. He truly believed that his God was vindicating him for his deeds. To kill a seventy-year-old stepmother would raise him to the captain's rank in Hell. It was time to lay low and only go after Karen. Now he wished he hadn't called detective Worthy. The FBI would soon be on the case. He'd covered his tracks well, only paid cash, and was not logged to be in the places where he actually killed. When he was in New York, his log was San Francisco. He always drove safe and had time to take non-trucking routes, avoiding the scales and checkpoints. He could never be caught by forensics. He would pay seven thousand dollars to have his sleeper truck cleaned and completely remodeled inside. He disposed of

the old sleeper fixtures by himself, in fire. The glass top for the bathtub wound up on Juniper Mountain, stressing his subconscious he'd informed Gabriela of. The subconscious needed to think about it. He knew the FBI had super-tech forensics that intimidated NASA. He could only be caught in the act. Aware, he was all too cautious. But all this was to wait until he was finished with Karen. The remodeling would be done in Mexico, as would Karen.

Chapter 13

Wicked Recompense

❧

"Hi Mark. How was your vacation?"

"You wouldn't believe me, Sarah. I had so much fun. Business running smooth?"

"Yes, your truck is clean. I'm telling you, those guys jump when you talk about cleanliness."

"Nothing closer to Godliness, huh Sarah, ha ha."

"I swear I'm going to get you to come one Sunday."

"That's not such a holy day to come now."

"Ahhmm, you'll see the light. I've told everyone in the church about you at testimony time. You're on a prayer line."

"Testimony time? My office assistant has been praying for me in a church? Have mercy on YOUR SOUL!"

"You'll see. By the way, you have another new contract, actually two. One is an addition to Canami, for an out-of-country bid. It's a seasonal bid for tomatoes in Mexico."

"Mexico? Did you say fucking Mexico?"

"Mark, please."

"Oh, Baby, I'm sorry. I'll kiss the statue on the way out this Sunday. Mexico, Ho! Ho! Ho! Tell them we will take it at cost, no margins."

"Are you sure of that?"

"Oh it's a def. I'm driving it myself."

"I don't understand why you still drive, making all the money you do. Don't you want to run your business like an executive and go golfing?"

"The devil don't golf!"

"Very funny."

"So what does out-of-state scheduling look like this week?"

"We have the usual two runs to Vegas, one to Kansas City on Thursday, one to Chicago, and three to Redding. But Canami wants to start the run to Baja the following Friday. How are we going to do that with all the in-state scheduling we already have?

"Pay the guys overtime, Sarah. It's all about money. I'll take the Mexico ride. Where is it?"

"Just south of Ensenada, one hundred miles. They grow tomatoes there."

"Ain't that the proofs ticket? That is perfect for my need. Okay, I'll take the Kansas City run this week. That'll help the boys out a little. My God is sooo goood."

"I can never understand men. You want to drive to Kansas then the next week all the way to Mexico, for free. Men must be from Mars, because women are from that other world, Venus."

"Mars is livable, Sarah, Venus isn't."

"God must be a woman."

"Oh yea, then who was Jesus?"

"Can I tell you a secret?"

"I'm the master of secrets."

"I think I can show you God. I swear on a stack of Bibles I won't even tell a cop if you go with me one time."

"I tell you what. Make a deal with me. If you swear to something else. I'll go to church with you. As a matter of fact, you can tell the cops I went to church with you."

"Okay!"

"You can't tell anyone, even if it is a cop, a judge, or any living soul. You have to swear to God Almighty in the Holy Spirit."

"What do you want?"

"I want you to buy an airline ticket for me, for someone very special to me, but like it says in the Bible to do your alms in secret so your reward will be multiplied many times. So I don't want to tell anyone I'm doing this. I want you to pay cash for the ticket and use the name of the person I want to send it to."

"That is so nice. I'll do it!"

"Swear to Jesus and the Holy Spirit you and I never had anything to do with this and that you will never tell anyone or you blaspheme God."

"I swear to the Holy Spirit and Jesus Christ that I will never tell anyone that I bought a ticket for. . . who is the person?"

"Karen A. Wimber."

"For Karen A. Wimber and never say that Mark or I had anything to do with this, or I will be damned in Hell forever. So you're coming to church Sunday!"

"You're such a sucker!"

"Mark!"

"Just kidding, of course I am. Okay, it's to Cabo San Lucas for next Tuesday, not tomorrow, next Tuesday. Here's all of Karen's info."

"Wow. she's seventy years old. She's special. Doesn't she need a trip permit?"

"She'll get all that at the airport in Louisville, Kentucky, her departure point. Go first class, round trip all the way; hotel Los Arcos for seven days. You'll have to go to the airport in Portland for that. I'll pay you for the haul and overtime. Got all that?"

"Oh yeah!"

"Here's two thousand dollars, keep what's left over; the travel agency is in the airport for the hotel. Don't buy the ticket through them, they'll ask for ID. It's a private-company liability thing. Get her a rental car reservation with the agreement to be filled out in Cabo. If any one asks you anything what do you say?"

"I don't have to say anything, and I can't anyway."

"Good girl! Go!"

"Now?"

"Yes, I need to get the ticket to her!"

"Oh yeah!"

"Make sure my truck is ready for the Kansas run."

"Thank you, see you then!"

Mark watched Sarah drive off, wondering how God's people could be so vulnerable, but now he had to convince Karen. He walked down to the corner pay phone using a prepaid card.

"Hello, Karen's Touch."

"Hi Ms. Wimber, remember that contest you entered!"

"Oh my gosh, I enter so many. Did I win something?"

"Oh, yes Ma'am. You won a trip to Cabo San Lucas, Mexico, seven days, with rental car and a native female tourist guide. But don't say no yet; there is a cashier's check for twenty-five thousand dollars waiting for you there if you go. You want us to Fedex this ticket to you, or do you want to pass up the opportunity of a lifetime?"

"Oh my gosh, this is what I've been waiting for. Oh, please, don't tell me this is a joke!"

"No joke, you still on Walnut, number 308?"

"Yes, Sir, I am."

"You should get the ticket Wednesday, and you have to leave next Tuesday to qualify for the twenty-five grand. Is that a problem, Ms. Wimber?"

"Nnn no, no! It's just so sudden, and the trip so soon."

"Yes, that's the thing about winning. If you can't make it, we'll give it to the runner up."

"No, please, I'll take it."

"Okay, when you get there, hold up a sign that reads Wimber for Maria. She'll give you your lasting memory."

"Maria?"

"Yes, she'll be at your side the whole time. You have to go with her, so you can make an announcement at the Wabo that you have been reading our magazines for many profitable years. They will hand you the cashiers check there. Karen's Touch will be featured in a future issue."

"Oh, what magazine is this?"

"Life, Ms. Wimber, Life."

"Oh boy, I'll be waiting for the ticket."

"Real good, Ms. Wimber, real good. Bye Bye now and congratulations! Ha ha haaa!"

"God bless you, Son."

Mark hung up and then dialed for Maria.

"Goddamn, your ass. I've got to fact Angie!"

"*Bueno.*"

"Angie! Please listen very carefully."

Mark laid it on Angie, and the plan was accepted beyond his wildest dreams. Mexico was no place to be when you're in the caldron.

Brandy's disappearance had been handled by the Springfield police as a runaway case. She had a history of related run-ins to persuade the police that foul play was unlikely. Detective Rainey did the six-month follow up with her mother, Tammy. He had no idea of Mark's past associations with Tammy or Brandy. Rainy knocked on Tammy's door.

"Yes?"

"Hi, Tammy, I'm Detective Rainey with Eugene. I'm here to—"

"Have you found her? Is she alive?"

"We don't have any information; nothing. Tammy, let's go in and talk. Is that okay?"

"For whatever good it'll do! Why are you here? The Springfield cops had this. . . Ahh, come in."

"I work with follow-up, and this is the most crucial part of the investigation, being as late as it is now. I have looked over the case superficially. You were in Nevada. That's a given from all the evidence and personal testimony."

"I would never have hurt my Brandy."

"It's routine investigation. I need you to think really hard the next few days about all the male acquaintances Brandy ever had, no matter how long ago it was."

"I don't know if I could remember all of them. She was hard to control."

"Yes, I noticed she had some problems. They all seemed to start right around her thirteenth birthday."

"After we lost Joe."

"I didn't see anything about a Joe in the file. Who was he?"

"We lived together for ten years after my husband passed on from leukemia."

"What do you mean when you say 'we lost Joe?'"

"Joe fell off the waterfall in Oakridge a little over six years ago."

"Joe Mills? The Joe Mills?"

Rainey's mind was jolted, flooded with an overwhelming self-reprimand for his past incompetence in Mark's case. Joe was the false witness that Mark had brought in on Shari's sexual abuse case involving indecent masturbation. Joe's testimony acquitted Mark of endangering the welfare of a minor, including a one-year sentence and sex-offender classification. Thoughts convoluted his mind that he now had Mark in the kidnap felony of Brandy, but more so, how could he explain to Tammy why he had failed to make the connection of Mark to Joe. If the media got a hold of this, it was Rainey's career. Mark had been contacted in the Mills case by telephone by a different officer one month after Joe's disappearance. The reason for the contact was only to question Mark about Joe's hunting habits. Mark had been hunting with Joe on many occasions. He had informed the officer that Joe would keep on the hunt and would always wander farther than the group. In Joe's disappearance case, he was accompanied by three of his closest friends. Joe had even stopped by Mark's home to take him along, but he was not present. It had been a prior arrangement. They had thought Mark went on ahead without them, because they were an hour late.

They had called later that same evening to find out Mark had thrown a beer party; it was his thirty-third birthday. They had come over to let him know of Joe's disappearance. Mark was virtually unaffected. They said he had mentioned that Joe would turn up eventually, and then he had retreated with his beer and a Churchill high school girl to his room. Now, Rainey needed to save his job.

Rainy continued his conversation with Tammy. Tammy was disturbed over the incompetence.

"Yes, Joe Mills. He loved to hunt. You did not know he was with me. How is it possible you did not know that? His death made headline news."

Rainy had to invent a reason to save his career.

"Until yesterday, I was unaware of Brandy's case, Tammy. This is a Springfield case. I don't know what you know about a case that Joe testified in. But that's the real reason I'm here: Joe's connections with Mark Johnson relating to Brandy's disappearance."

"You're completely heading my daughter's case in a wrong direction. Mark hasn't even been around for years, and he and Joe were having troubles at the end. The relationship with Mark was on the rocks, but Brandy and him were nothing more than her being here."

"What was the trouble?"

"Joe was a bit upset over testifying for Mark. Joe did tell me that it was some ridiculous story Mark wanted him to say about a little girl walking into Mark's house when Joe was outside picking up a cleaning van."

"I'm well aware of Joe's testimony. I had never heard from anyone until now that Joe was coerced, but we believe Mark paid him."

"There was no bribery and Joe was not coerced. Joe did go and pick up the van. Mark just wanted to bring Joe in, so he could testify about that. Joe brought up the fact that he saw the little girl go into Mark's house at that time."

"Then what's ridiculous about it?"

"That's so stupid to take Joe out of his new day job to sit around for six hours to testify he picked up the van and saw her. He could have just written a statement."

"Did Joe ever tell you what that case was about?"

"No, Joe didn't know. Mark said he wanted to protect his family, and all Joe had to do was tell the court what he saw. I heard it was an initial misdemeanor charge. What was the case about?"

"I'm surprised you didn't know. That explains your continued relationship with Mark. But Joe knew full well what the case was about to the letter."

"Can you tell me what it was about now?"

"I could have told you then, but Mark won the case, and we feared lawsuits. So I backed out of the mire. He was charged with masturbating in this girl's presence. We had graphic testimony and detailed verbal content that a five-year-old child could not invent. Joe's testimony took away the element of 'beyond reasonable doubt.' His account supported Mark's claims that the child walked in on

him, supposedly surprising the both of them. The jury had no choice but to buy the letter of the law. Mark knew it, too. He was calm through the entire two-day trial. We also know that Joe was brought in falsely by Mark, due to his first trial date being canceled the very night before it was scheduled, in August of 1988. Joe was not on the witness docket then. But, suddenly, he appeared two weeks before on the rescheduled trial date, three months later in November."

"Okay, officer, at that time in August, Mark did not know where we were. We'd moved. Joe called Mark about going hunting in October. That's why Mark was so relieved to hear from Joe. His first question was if Joe remembered the last day he worked for him, about picking up the van. Joe said yes and they went out that night and had a few beers. Now I know why Mark was so nervous back then. God, getting caught having sex by your kids is one thing but jerking off in front of the neighbor's kid. Fuck, I wouldn't know what to do. That's fucked up."

"Tammy, in that phone conversation, did you hear Joe mention anything about the little girl?"

"No, just that Joe said yes to picking up the van on his last day of work."

"Did Joe have extra money at that time, Tammy?"

"He did. Yes he did, a lot. Shit."

"What were your daughter's feelings about Mark hanging around you guys back then?"

"Brandy was guy crazy. She really loved Mark. Now that I think about it, they spent as much, if not more, time in the house together than with Joe and me."

"What sort of conversation did they have?"

"Seemed like Mark went along with Brandy's interests, but mostly they horsed around, wrestled and stuff, you know."

"You let a thirty-two year old man wrestle with your daughter?"

"Well, no. It was more like we all did. Joe and I would get high all the time and roughhouse and Brandy was so fun to pick on. We laughed so hard at what Mark did once, we really cried."

"What could Mark do to make you laugh?"

"Mark was hilarious! I recall once, when he was wrestling with Brandy; she was actually getting the best of him when he got a bit rattled. He let it all out, but cool like. He held her down and gave her a mustache with a permanent black magic marker, then told her she was to take the mark of the beast. He put three big sixes on her forehead. It was hilarious to see Brandy manhandled like that, and when she looked in the mirror all hell broke loose. They just went off on each other. She looked so funny with crosses and 'Jesus saves at home federal,' written on her legs and arms. She did get the marker from him. He looked like

Frankenstein when it was over. They looked that way for days. Brandy stayed home, but he had to work. It was a gas. But they loved each other in kind of a special way. I never questioned Mark. I still have extreme difficulty with him jerking off to a kid. That's out of the arena."

"Did you ever have any relations with Mark?"

"None. He sold his business and left for Mexico."

"Tammy, you would be so surprised at what's in the mind of a rapist."

"Mark is not a rapist."

"Then why did he plead guilty to molesting his own daughter five and a-half years ago?"

"Oh, my God! So he didn't go to Mexico."

"Yes he did, before the indictment. For some reason, he came back and knocked on the door. He cut a deal because the original DA was out with a back injury. He was given three years probation, but then, he split to Mexico again. He spent eighteen months in prison after turning himself in a second time. Six months ago, he gets out, and five and a-half months ago Brandy disappears."

"What are you saying? Mark would not hurt Brandy. Wait a minute, if Mark only got probation, then he didn't physically rape Heather. He couldn't hurt anyone."

"Mark's abuse has traditionally been of a leading or seductive nature. Simple touching and oral cunillingus."

"What's that?"

"He admitted to licking her. We believe that he wants his victims to give him permission first, to satisfy his ego or acceptability. This is why the crimes are so extraordinary. He had a rough childhood. He lost his mother and was not well accepted by his stepmother. It's quite possible he was severely abused."

"Mark was lonely. He came over whenever he wasn't working. He would drop Heather off at Marilyn's house to babysit her. She was his age, but he didn't have any attraction to her. Now that I think of it, he related to so many young people and spent more time with Brandy than us."

"Do you know Paula and Jeremy?"

"No, Joe and I never met them. They were so young according to Brandy. She rode over to their house in his Ferrari with Lynn a few times. That's all I know of them. Do you know where Mark is now?"

"He's here in town. I'm not sure what he's doing or where he's living, but I will in the next hour. I want you to act as if he does not exist; do not contact him. If he calls and you know it's him from your caller ID, do not answer it. If he does call you, then you have to act like you never met me. Act as if I had told

you nothing here, today, but call me, if he attempts to make any form of contact with you; through friends or how ever, clear?"

"Very. Somehow I hope she did run off with him. You have read all the investigative reports, right?"

"Yes, but this is a recent case, and Mark is not mentioned in them."

"Then you know that there was an incoming call here from a pay phone the last night she was seen here."

"Yes, Tammy, that's why I want you to avoid him. If he called here, he knows your whereabouts. If you refuse to pick up the phone, it's quite possible he may decide to show up here. That would give us knowledge of him knowing your address. I noticed that your address is not listed in the directory. Please do everything I ask, even if I don't give you a reason."

"I understand now."

"Okay, I'll be in touch."

As Rainey left, he knew from Mark's abilities that, if he were Brandy's abductor, it would remain an unsolved case. The pay phone call alone and the fact that no one saw Brandy leave the house her last time, were just simple leads. He knew Mark had a talent for evasion far beyond that. What he respected about Mark was his steel frame of withstanding everything. He saw Mark adjust to his police-trained tactics, as if it were second nature. This led Rainey to telephone his probation officer, Linda Hamilton.

"Parole and Probation, this is Linda."

"Hi, Linda, Detective Rainy here, I hear you're on Mark Johnson's case now."

"Yes, fascinating guy, considering his offenses."

"How's he doing?"

"Very well! He's gotten a truck transport business totally up and running in six months, with numerous contracts. He does all his required work and is in professional treatment."

"Sounds too good. Can I get his address?"

"Yes. It's 3317 Videra Drive, in Eugene."

"God, the guy has more of a life than a. . ."

"Ah, ah, ah, Detective, we're all about corrections here, right?"

"Correct me if I'm wrong, is it working?"

"In his case, I believe so, yes. I've spoken with his doctor, his father, and the child. He's totally forthcoming. He even paid his first victim's would-be damages and counseling fees, as if he had lost the case. How can you dispute that?"

"Give me the work address."

Rainey got the information he needed from Linda. He felt he needed to contact Jeremy and Paula, placing trust with them was questionable, but he didn't have anywhere else to go. He first contacted Lee Self, about giving Paula the acid.

"Mr. Self?"

"Yes, I am Self."

"Do you know a Jeremy and Paula Kurtis?"

"I do, how are they? Haven't seen them in forever."

"Well, their daughter is not doing so well."

"God damnit, I told them to keep Mark away from there."

"How would you have known this is about Mark?"

"Hell, every time a kid gets molested in that circle, I've been called in to it."

"Who has called you in?"

"Well, way back, Mark tried to get me to witness in a case he won. After that, seems like about five or six years back, he asked me again, when it was about his daughter. He's got problems."

"Mr. Self, I need a sworn statement of what you just said on that, okay?"

"I suppose."

"Do you ever recall giving Paula a small quantity of cleaning acid from your business supply?"

"Yes, I gave her a quart of descaler acid for rusty toilets."

"You did then."

"What does that have to do with the kid?"

"She accidentally got in to it and lost her fingers."

"What!?"

"Yes, Sir, she lost all four fingers."

"Looky here, Mr. Investigator, you'd have to boil it and soak in it for the day to lose a hangnail."

"This is the acid you gave Paula? It was not industrial cleaning acid?"

"Ahh, everything's industrial, but there ain't no acid that will do what you just said, especially if it's a quick accident where you can clean up after yourself."

"How do you explain Jerica's hand, then?"

"Hey, come on back here."

Lee escorted detective Rainy to the back of his shoddy old home to a run-down washroom. The sink was lime-ridden and rusty.

"I've always got some here. Look, one point seven percent hydrochloric acid. Watch this, I'll pour a little here on the sink. See that take up the lime?"

"Yeah."

"Okay, watch this. Get it all over my hand and see that, nothing. Let that set for a few minutes. You see, it reacts to mineral deposits and rust; stuff that oxides up in the acid. Satisfied? Can I wash this off now?'

"That's unbelievable. So, where would a guy get all these acids and cleaners."

"There in the phone book under janitorial supply. There are about five or so suppliers in town."

"Thank you, Mr. Self. You better wash that off now."

"You sure are welcome. By the way, you ever watch Inspector *Clodumbo?*"

"That's *Colombo.* Yes I do, quite frequently"

"You sure act an awful lot like him."

Rainey could only feel beaten. He had fallen for Mark's diversion by not contacting Lee when he should have during Jerica's agony. Mark would be behind bars now, if he had followed protocol. He began to hope it wasn't Mark who had abducted Brandy, for his own sake. Now it was Rainey who contemplated looking for a life south of the border. He had to convince Paula to give Mark up. Jeremy and Paula had taken Jerica to a specialist in southern California, and took vacation. For that, Mark was given valuable time. Rainey felt he was getting close to the kill. Even though he knew his incompetence would be exposed, he proceeded.

Mark checked in with his office before crossing the border.

"Hi, Sarah!"

"Hey boss where you at?"

"San Diego, anything I need to know before I cross the border?"

"No, only some detective came around, a detective Rainey. He couldn't believe you went to church with me. I told him you got on your knees and prayed!"

"I wasn't praying. I was hiding my face and devilish laughter!"

"I know, but I got you there, didn't I?"

"What did he want?"

"Oh, nothing special, just what you did here and the like. He wanted to know where you were."

"Did you tell him?"

"Not at all, just that you were on a route and that you would be back in five days."

"What else?"

"Also, Lee's kid called right before that; said Rainey had talked to Lee the day before about some kind of acid and Paula's kid. Said Lee had the wrong kind

of acid to hurt Jerica. I don't know what he was trying to tell me. Isn't Lee's kid one of our competitors?"

"Yes. Did you mention any of that to Rainey; that Lee's kid called?"

"No, I thought it better just to listen. You don't do acid, like LSD, do you? God can help you with drugs better than anyone, Mark."

"Ha ha, you're a case, Sarah. No, it's okay, girl. Anything else?"

"That's it. Please be careful down there. You're three days early. I know you want to have fun but that place is, you know, Mexico."

"Pray, Sarah, that my hangover won't be too bad."

"Bye, Mark."

After crossing into Mexico and making his arrangements, Mark made his phone call to Angie.

"Hi, Baby!"

"Yes, everything is like you say!"

"Ha ha, she made it."

"Oh yes."

"She didn't get a chance to check in the hotel. I mean you took her straight to the house, right?"

"She's in the cyclone shelter inside the house. I have the police handcuffs on her and the chain to the big drain. She's fucked up, one big pussy. You're so smart, Mark. How you did this is too much for me to understand. I love you for to be so smart, too."

"Smart or not, it'll take me five hours to fly there. I used the ID you gave me for the ticket. I can only stay for the day, so please wait for me. I'll get a ride to the house. Don't leave there. I left the truck at the RV Park on the beach in Ensenada."

"I already do some thing's, Mark."

"Ehh, I can live with that. She know why?"

"She have no idea. I cannot wait to see the look on her face when she see you. It is her. I see the pictures you have of your family. It is her."

"My God, I'm finally going to get this. Love you, I come now."

"Bye, I wait only five hours!"

The trail started to gel in Pasadena. Paul Harris had been humbled. He called Worthy.

"Detective Worthy, I have some rather ugly news for you."

"I suppose your referring to your statement of not seeing this sort of thing again."

"Yes, I came across the quarterly serious-violations reports for Washington this week. A major dumping in Seattle. Several fans of the Seahawks football team were treated for severe burns. He didn't dump it close enough to the drain, it pooled up along the curb. Many of the people were wearing light footwear, such as sandals. We have determined this to be the same exact batch of acid as was dumped on Colorado Boulevard. We're re-analyzing the stuff now, using our best tests and are including the Seattle samples."

"Well, what about the dumping in New York City? How about the make up of the acid there?"

"New York?"

"Yes, a Detective telephoned me, said it happened a few months back."

"Oh, Jesus. I'll get the reports on that."

"I have a copy of those if you want."

"Sure, how did you come across them?"

"The detective sent them by fax. I can't recall his name. Said he used to live out here and read the *L.A. Times*, daily."

"Can you look up his name now? I need to call him before it gets too late, him being on the East Coast and all."

"Yeah, here it is, Les Allen, Metro special."

"I find it difficult to attribute three occasions of the same batch of acid in the furthest reaches of the States to anything but one mind with something very big on that mind."

"Call Les, see what he knows."

"Right."

Harris telephoned Allen at the New York Metro station.

"Detective Allen speaking."

"Hello Mr. Allen, this is Paul Harris, director of environmental safety in Southern California. Do you have a moment to discuss the illegal acid dumping you had up there a few months back?"

"Well, at least somebody out your way is courteous. Sure, for that I'll oblige you. Worst mess we had to clean up out here. Like the one in Boston last month. It was the same stuff."

"Oh, God, that makes four of these dumps now. I was just alerted to your call to detective Worthy after your incident. He told me about it just minutes ago."

"I didn't call the dead beat. He sent me a blind fax as if I'm supposed to read his fucking mind or something."

"You did not call LA?"

"No way. No one here knew what to make of it, until one of the street cops remembered. You got four of these?"

"Yes. Seattle was the one I came across."

"You got your hands full of stuff I don't deal with, Harris. Better call Boston Metro too."

"All right. I'm going to need samples."

"Yeah, we got about a pint in evidence, I'll courtesy you the whole damn thing. Tell that asshole out there to follow fax guidelines too."

"Thanks, I'll be in touch. Send it to EPA, Los Angeles. We'll pay the express postage."

Harris phoned Worthy.

"Detective Worthy speaking."

"Bill, it's Paul. I'm sorry to bug you, again, but Allen says there's been a forth dumping in Boston, same stuff."

"What the hell could be going on?"

"I don't know but it gets weirder. He says he's never talked to you, says the asshole just sent him this blind fax so he obliged you and sent a blind one back."

"Naw, he spoke to me. It was a short conversation. He probably forgot."

"Bill, I think you better call him. He remembers the fax well and told me tell the asshole to follow fax guidelines."

"No kidding? I'll call. Get back to work, Life of Riley."

Detective Worthy, a well-mannered and methodical cop didn't hesitate to call Allen.

"Detective Allen speaking."

"Yes, this is the asshole out in LA that needs lessons on faxing."

"Hey, this is a police telephone line. You need lessons on that too, dick."

"What's this about you never calling me and saying you used to live out here and in reading the *L.A. Times* like a super cop where you read about our illegal dumping? They let dick head, absent-minded cops…"

"Wait a fucking minute. I never lived in that stink hole, and if I did, I'd burn it from my memory, beach boy."

"Okay, then who called me?"

"The perp!"

"Damn, what the fuck is going on with this?"

"Well, surfer boy, you better track down the caller."

"Can't say it was nice talking to you."

"Make damn sure you let me know where that cock bite called you from. I want a charge his ass for impersonating me alone."

"I Will get the number to you in a bit."

Worthy sat back in his modest office kicking his feet up on the desk, not to blow off this seemingly lesser travail. Worthy had not gotten this special crimes unit position for being a non-thinker. He was, by all definitions, a good street cop where his career was born. There was something evil in one working mind that Worthy's gut sensed, more than felt. Maybe he thought the sickness he felt was coming by reason of the telephone call by who is now realizes was the "perp" himself. In Worthy's subconscious he was aware of the possibility. That one possibility was the most horrid killer he had ever imagined, one that, he realized, he had to defeat. Worthy started a simple ground-level systematic approach. It was set in his mind that if this was what it could be, this fellow would have to rear his ugly head again, maybe more than once, before he could catch him. He first followed up with the New York case by calling Shari, his secretary, a graduate in criminology.

"Shari, I need you to get the date off the fax sent to me from New York Metro, about four months ago. Get the computer records of all incoming calls the day before. I need this now."

"I'm on it. I remember him, Bill. He's the one who didn't ID himself. He was no cop. You have a call from Paul Harris again. That's three times he's called today."

"Put him through."

"Hi Paul, have I got news for you!"

"No, I have some horrifying news for the country, Bill. Remember I mentioned hemoglobin?"

"I do."

"It's an entire body, Bill. We can't tell if it's male or female but definitely an entire human body washed down Colorado. Someone out there has found the perfect way to dispose of any kind of body, or potential witness."

"Mother of God. It wasn't Allen that called. It was the perp. He wasn't getting the attention he wanted. He had to bring it to us. This is the AIDS of serial killers. Can we track down this batch of acid?"

"Unless we find one of the containers, this mega perp is free to roam. As a chemist, I'm telling you that this is the perfect crime. We have to go to the national news, Bill, on what we got. We can't wait for the details."

"Alert the proper departments in your chain, Paul. You call Detective Allen back in New York and give him all you have. That'll wake him up. Get Seattle informed of what were dealing with, then tell me everything I need to know. I'm contacting the FBI and the Mayor to get him to notify the governor. Jesus Christ, an original sinner, the career goes to light speed."

The secretary called Worthy. "Bill, I have the number. It came from Denver, a pay phone on Oak and Tenth Street."

"Good, Shari, please get me the Chief of Police in Denver, now. Stay on the line with me, Paul. Might as well get the poop here and now."

"God, I just hope it's where he lives."

"Wishful thinking. Nothing this hideous comes out of Colorado."

Shari connected the call from Denver.

"Captain Kovati is on conference line two, Bill."

"Hello, Captain. Detective Worthy and Paul Harris with environmental protection, we need to come straight to the issue. Have you had any type of illegal acid storm drain dumpings in Denver?"

"Three months ago, not really a drain but on Oak street. We would never have noticed it due to the rain, but it ate at the base of a bolted-metal power pole. Fell on a cab driver, electrocuting her. We didn't know it was acid, until the lab report came back last month. It was raining heavily that morning. Luckily no one else was hurt."

Chapter 14

Language of the Mad

❧

"Hi, tropical accomplices. Have you been naughty?"

"Papacito! How you get here?"

"I walked up the other side of the mountain. Don't need anyone knowing I'm here this particular week. Where is she?"

"Give me your embrace first, Mark."

"I'm sorry, Baby. I've only been thinking of her."

"You must always think of me first."

"If you only knew how much I think of you. You too, Fabi; come here!"

"I feel the love for you too, Mark. You are happy what we do for you?"

"Oh, hell yes. Now where's the witch?"

Angie took Mark to the dank, gray concrete shelter, a place of less than prison-like appearance. The single light bulb hanging in the center amplified the torment chamber-like surroundings. She was naked and chained by her right ankle to the home's main drainpipe.

"Come, quiet, she sleep now. . . See, it is her, no?"

"Mmhuh, that's my *madness* come to me. What's that blue stuff all over her....ha ha, crotch?"

"It is candle wax."

"What was the reason for ah that?"

"We have to keep her alive for you."

"What do you mean keep her alive?"

"So she don't losing all her bloody."

"Maria, did you cut something off?"

"Si, she was a real bitch, talking all kind of shit to me and Fabi. I almost killing her but I know you want to torment her first. I save the trophy for you. There in the jar. You are angry?"

"My fucking God. Fabi, would you please go get Canella?"

"Si."

"I'll wait until you come back. No Angie, I'm not angry. It's that I don't feel like I thought I would."

"What do you feel?"

"Like I'm not really satisfied. She seems to mean nothing to me seeing her there."

"She will when she wakes up. She is one fucker."

"Here is Canella, Mark."

"Thank you, Fabi. Let's wake up this bitch, this old memory. Oh boy, is it going to come back hard, too."

Mark sat down next to Karen and put his left arm around her neck. Angie and Fabi stood over them with their dog, Canella, a Doberman Pincer.

"Lick the poison. Lick the poison, you maggot!"

"Karen opened her eyes, and hearing the years of mad language, her entire body cringed. It had to be one of the nightmares. Seeing Mark could only be a nightmare."

"No! God no, it can't be..."

"Ha, the poison! So nice to see you again. Some contest, huh? But we aren't here for contests now, are we? More like a sex offender's sentencing. They say sex offender's cringe in court when their actions of madness are read aloud to the room filled with the righteous. What do you think is worse, the reading that you licked the poison from your stepson's privates in the presence of the whole world and your family, or to be physically tormented, alone? Ha ha!"

"This can't be! This can't be!" Karen looked down at herself, once again questioning if she was in some horrid nightmare she would wake from.

"Yes, you're abbreviated, it's gone all right! I see what you were hoping for. But it's all too real. It's now nightmare time, Baby, the real nightmare of pay back. And the pay is public humiliation and slow death. First, we start with public humiliation. Let me introduce you to your audience! On your right, Maria! Whom you invited to the party and my lover! On your left, my other lover! And she's a good lover, too. In the middle is the dog who gets it all clarified. Will she or won't she? The show is about to begin. Nice ass, Mom, in a jar, ha ha. Give me the jar, Fabi. Come here, Canella. Good puppy. Smell this, oh yes, get it, uh huh that's it. Man, did you see that, Mom? Dogs eat poison, too! In one big gulp. Actually, I didn't think the mutt would eat the nasty thing. Get rid of this animal tomorrow, Baby, if it doesn't die first. We need a thoroughbred, not a fucking stoop."

"I bury Canella tomorrow with this other animal."

"Don't cry now, that part's just a ways off yet. Remember what you said about Mexican people? That they're all dirty and stupid, remember that?"

"I did not. I did not. God help me. I'm old. That was a long time ago."

Mark hits her with his closed fist, bloodying her nose. "Time? Nothing like the present memories, Mom! Remember the two dollars you'd always give me to shut up?"

"Lord God, I'm sorry! I've got money. My credit cards all have the same pin numbers of 1685. There's thousands of dollars there. There's so much more in my apartment. Please let me go."

"You wanna live without your box? God, I wouldn't. Did you know Angie's dad lived without his for five fucking years? But thank you, Angie and Fabi appreciate the credit. They will be sure to empty the accounts. It's so hard to earn a living in Mexico."

"You are so smart, Mark. I love you so much."

"Fabi, you are incredible, too. When this is over, I'm going to give you what you want."

"Jesus, please let me go. I won't say anything."

"What's with this new name? Karen Wimper, wimpering are we? Satan's on the throne now, Mom. Fabi, can you get naked? Can you remember my torment?"

"Si, this bitch going to lick my poison. I bring the pliers. I pull her teeth first."

"First, I need a little quality time."

Mark horrifyingly tortured his stepmother to within inches of death, Fabi and Angie fed her the same punishment she had inflicted on Mark, until she choked to death on her vomit. Mark gave the final orders.

"Don't kill the dog, Angie. I always want to remember that moment every time I give Canella love. Why don't you two shower? I don't want any of the witch on me. I'm taking the demon down to Tecalote beach in the boat. The sharks will finish her off. This was satisfaction!"

"The demon is dead in you, Mark?"

"Yes Fabi, very much so. I love you, too."

"Papi Chulo, you are the smartest man I ever know."

"You are the most woman I've ever known, Angie. I am the *Chulo, Papi, Papi Chulo*!"

During these moments of madness, the media in the States was having a heyday with the most publicized serial killing case in history. "This is *World News Tonight* with Peter Jennings."

"Good evening and welcome. I'm Peter Jennings. The most profound criminal case in America, dubbed the 'Acid Rapist,'" has police coast to coast in the frenzy of the twentieth century. On the loose, a serial killer who has discovered the perfect method of disposing of evidence, taunted police in Los Angeles. So far, a total of five victims have been dissolved in a powerful, federally-controlled nitric acid and dumped on city streets in Pasadena, New York, Denver, Seattle, and, most recently, Boston. It is said that the Navy uses the acid to dissolve plutonium in their nuclear submarines in the event of a sinking. The killer taunted Los Angeles special crimes unit detective Bill Worthy three months ago, telephoning him from the site in Denver, Colorado. There, the killer carefully drained the acid over the base of a power pole, which later toppled onto a taxi driver, killing her by electrocution. The first site, discovered nearly six months ago on Route Sixty Six, or Colorado Boulevard in Pasadena, had police baffled. It was deemed an illegal dumping of an acid, which has high fees to dispose of, nearly two hundred dollars per gallon. The caller posed as New York police sergeant Les Allen, asking Detective Worthy about the acid dump on Colorado, stating that he'd read it in the papers. He then told Worthy of the dumping in New York. It's not clear why the perpetrator made the call, but what is clear is that he knew both Allen and Worthy. The call was mishandled by Worthy as he did not properly follow up on the perp's call. He sent a blind fax of the dumping report on Colorado to Allen. Allen disregarded the report as routine reporting. In the three following months, the killer struck three more times, in Denver, Seattle, and Boston. These are only preliminary reports, as the case was brought to light only this morning by Paul Harris, an inspector for the EPA who tested the contents of the dumped acid, showing large amounts of hemoglobin, the iron in human blood, in the samples. We have Mr. Harris live from Pasadena. Connie?"

"Hi Peter, I'm standing on the spot where a young man, Kevin Lyons, inadvertently discovered the first known acid-dumping site. As he was riding his bicycle, the front tire crashed into the storm drain, flipping him off the bike and breaking his elbow. The acid dissolved the metal grate that normally covers the drain. From that point, Paul Harris discovered it to be highly potent nitric acid. Here's Paul. Just what kind of acid is this, Mr. Harris?"

While Harris earned his unwarranted fame, the rapist was in his Blue Spot of desire and satisfaction. He was laughing at the authorities, even though he was unaware of his national fame. Being in his tropical paradise was total escape. No one would ever catch him here. It was euphoria; his stepmother never knew Mark had to return to Oregon, picking up his newly remodeled truck in Ensenada, evidence free. His subconscious only aware, without effort suppressed the evil

he had done. The conscious Mark only cared about himself. He took the glass bathtub cover back to Juniper Mountain on his way to delivering his tomatoes to Lakeview. Sarah's comments about Lee's son mentioning detective Rainy and the acid prompted Mark to take countermeasures. He returned to Brandy's acid grave, to make sure it would not be found. Down the road a-half mile was a state department highway gravel pit. They left a small backhoe there to move the gravel. Mark borrowed it to move the acid grave and cover it with new, uncontaminated desert soil. He was very careful not to disturb nature, and he brushed off the tire tracks. Mark returned to his office.

"Did you enjoy Mexico?"

"There are so many things I wished I could tell people that I enjoy. Giving signals is kind of a good way to let people know what you think. You ever play around like that, Sarah?"

"Are you trying to send me signals, boss?"

"What if I were?"

"Hmmm. . .well, are you coming to church again Sunday?"

"I think I will. It's time for a reformation in my life. I feel so good about my trip to Mexico that I want to brag about it in church. I have killed the demon."

"That is the power of prayer, thank you, Jesus."

"Ha ha, you are so serious, Sarah."

'What's serious is the cop who's been coming around here."

"Been back, huh."

"Every day he parks across the street for a little while, mostly early when I first get here. Matter a fact, that's him rolling now. Looks like he's coming in. I sure hope we haven't violated any laws."

"Okay, show him in to my damn office."

Mark took his seat, knowing that, by telling Sarah to show Rainey in, that this would put her mentally on alert and defensive for him.

"Good morning, Sarah. I see Mark's truck is here."

"Yes, Mark's truck is here."

"Well, is he here?"

"Yeah, he is. Would you like to see him, Detective?"

"Yes. Thank you."

"Mark, Detective . . . ? I forget your name."

"Rainey."

"Detective Rainey is here to see you."

"Show him in."

Rainey stood in the doorway of Mark's office, certain he would jump on the moment and come out due to his fears. Mark was not in Jeremy's Camaro, attempting to avoid the law, now. He was with the master of crimes, confident, inviting the detective. It was now the glory of the challenge. Mark with his master knew Rainey could not defeat him.

"Please, sit down. I just have to finish this real quick like, for Sarah, transportation reports you know, especially when you're going in and out so much."

"Still going down south, too?"

"Yes, Detective, very nice this time of year. What do you need?"

"I know you really well, you fucking bastard. I won't waste much of your pretentious business time, but I know about Jerica, and Brandy. If you want to fight me, go for it, but I'll get the necessary warrants. I goddamn guarantee that you are going down either way."

"You don't need a single warrant. I'll sign whatever you like to further your investigation. Search it all; *Mi casa es su casa*. By the way, you mentioned Brandy?"

"I have to hand it to you, good response on Brandy. Let's get started."

The usual fight was gone in Mark, surprising Rainey. Mark had always kept his mouth shut and fought the system tooth and nail. Whether it was the IRS or a traffic cop, Mark would never bend. Rainey was certain he had him on forensic evidence, alone, and was granted permission to use department resources to include the local FBI's crime lab. Everything from bed sheets to telephone records were dissected. Rainey investigated his contract with Canami foods through Eddie, after he found out the nature of the contract from Mark himself. Rainey met with Eddie. Everything from allowing Eddie to use the truck to the cow losing it's hoof was discussed. Rainey met with the prosecuting attorney and the Chief of Police.

"This guy's bad luck for you, Rainey."

"I'm sure he's our man."

"I think you're sure you got beat by your man. You tore up his place, ransacked his business, excavated half of eastern Oregon. C'mon, what you got? A cow with a fucked up hoof and a kid with acid burns that the mother and father have sworn was their responsibility. As the D.A. of Lane County, I'd be laughed out of court for even trying to accuse him, much less go for an indictment."

"The parents are still on vacation, but I think I can get them to talk, if you're willing to offer them complete immunity for coming forward about Johnson."

"I can do that, but Children's Services is another story. Paula and Jeremy will have to be informed that they could lose their child to the State, by allowing a

known sex offender on parole to be in the kid's presence. If there is a connection to the accident and Mark Johnson, they will remove the kid, forever, in light of Paula's history. She lost two of her kids already. Do you think she'll let herself down again? I cannot stop Children's Services, nor could we get a state injunction to circumvent their authority. I'll make the deal, but your going to lose. You do lose this and I'm recommending a transfer. Mark's a small time jack off, and he's making us look like the jackees through your costly revenge."

"How about a wiretap on Jeremy's phone."

"That's easy enough, just add it to the authorizations for Johnson's taps."

"Chief, the guy is clever as hell and will go far out of his way to cover his tracks. For Christ's sakes, he had a completely new interior put in his truck. It was better before, according to the previous owner. He would only have done that to hide forensic evidence."

"What are you saying that would convince a jury, much less our system of procedure to get a bust?"

"I'm saying look in the mind of a rapist who knows what he's doing and lives not only his entire life for it but makes it his career. It's a fun thing for him, an arousal. With that, he'll do all he can to escape us. Yes, he is a jack off. This jack off is not a burglar; he is an addict who needs satisfaction. I've studied his cases. The graphic wording his kid and Shari testified to tell me this man is seriously perverted. He believes in something. He has some hidden motivation."

"He has never displayed or shown any type of hostility. Even in prison, he backed down. Rainey, I will give you one last shot, and then you will walk away, got it?"

"Yes, thank you."

Rainey had his plan worked out, and it was a plan Mark was used to using with success.

Mark knew he had to act. He started with one of his stepping stones, Sarah.

"Sarah!"

"Yes, Master."

"Come into my office, please."

"I want you to call this number and ask this lady for her daughter's cellular number. They're scheduled to come home today and I have a great surprise for them. This is a friend of mine's mother. Just say you're an old acquaintance. You are because you know me and I have known them. Go for it."

"What if she asks which daughter?"

"She only has the one and she never questions women."

Sarah, having blind faith in Mark due to his pretentious repentance and her weakness for him, did his deed by getting the number. Mark called Paula from a pay phone five miles out of town.

"Hello."

"Paula, please don't hang up. I want to help Jerica. I feel so bad. I've raised eleven thousand dollars. I really want you guys to have it, please."

Paula's sentimental side was her weakness. She didn't care about the money, but when she heard that Mark wanted to give the large amount, it convinced her he was extremely remorseful.

"I don't know what to do, Mark. We can't meet you. Children's Services warned us after the accident."

"You know it was an accident and I feel so shitty. I'll have someone bring you the money. When will you be home?"

"In about two hours."

"I'll send Sarah over, a friend of mine from church."

"Oh, okay. I'll see her, I guess. Okay."

"Bye, Paula, and I am sorry."

"Goodbye, Mark."

Mark knew the initial connection with Paula and Jeremy would be his undoing. The unintentional events that happen before a crime is planned are the connections to convictions. These thoughts were foremost in Mark's mind. If he had known of the acid's potential as disposal for his rape victims, he'd never have used it to clean Paula's bathroom. This was his only downfall, and he needed to pay the high cash price, or it would be death row as the alternate. Since Paula and Jeremy had been on vacation, they were probably not aware of Peter Jennings' news of the acid killer. Sarah got the money to Paula an hour before Detective Rainey visited Jeremy. Jeremy and Paula took his visit as a routine follow-up, as he said he would do, but they hadn't, since he was waiting for Mark to slip up, which he actually did by using the acid again. But there had to be the initial connection.

"Jeremy, let's kinda talk, off the record. I give you my word, no prosecution will come to you or Paula."

"I had been confident that Paula and I wouldn't be in direct trouble with the criminal system."

"I hear what you're saying very clearly, but do we have to tell anyone else if it's off the record? Let's say someone was never actually in the presence of your daughter, say he left beforehand, or he had come here when Jerica was playing outside and handed you the acid. You can't be held responsible for that."

"You're suggesting that if this someone were here, we'd lie about it?"

"They lie. Sometimes, we use the same ammunition, especially when we know. No one gets hurt and the bad guy goes down, like he should."

"I need you to understand something even clearer."

"I'm still on track with you."

"Go explain that to Paula. Tell her I sent you in. I'll wait out here, you know, so no one gets hurt. Three's a crowd when using this kind of ammunition. Testimonial crowding."

"All right, Jeremy."

"Whatever she says."

"I hear you."

After making the plan clear to Paula, she had an inkling about giving Mark up. Paula didn't know what to think of the money, now, but a flash of reality hit home with her. She spoke with Rainey.

"If I did make such a statement, wouldn't Mark have the chance to face me in the courtroom to challenge all this? Face-to-face testimony, right?"

"Ah . . . yes, you would have to testify."

"Either way it's a lie. I know you just want to fuck him because he's a sex offender."

"Goodbye, Paula. You just cost me."

"Self preservation, this is mine. Go get a real job or keep the robbers out of my ass!"

"Everything okay in here, Paula."

"Fine Jer, let's go make a baby."

"See you detective. Good luck."

Mark had won. He'd lay low for a month, then it was time to get the glass cover. He loved the desert so. Sarah mentioned that business was slumping.

"Mark, it's not looking good!"

"Yeah, things have been a bit uneventful lately."

"Our drivers aren't getting delivery on time, and we haven't gotten any new contracts in over a month. Canami says if we don't string a tighter bail, were going to lose their contract."

"I better go back to work then."

"How can that help? You'd just be one driver, and you'd miss going to church with me. We just need good people."

"I'll prove it to you. I'll drive for two weeks and business will take off."

"Well, okay, but I want to run an advertisement for experienced drivers. You're paying these apprentices high wages."

"Whatever, Sarah. I'll take the Kansas run, scheduled to leave tomorrow. It's a pick up run, so I'll leave now to be on time. Reschedule in the drivers who are on time. Terminate the screw-up."

"Screw-ups, Mark. Four of our drivers are smoking crack. I know that much. I don't understand your methods."

"You'll see in a few days…Sister Sarah! Goodbye."

"Yeah. Probably got a girl in Kansas."

As Mark left he muttered to himself, "No, but I'll get one."

Rainey was dead on about Mark. This man could not curb the desire, by ridding himself of Karen. Mark had opened up wide to Peter, and Mark hated this counselor, now, for showing him his true self. In doing so, the hobby was intensified deep within. Pressing the denial of this, he went after his desire in the darkness of self-camouflage. So few people could understand this addiction, even from the curative point of view. The main reason why rape has never been understood. From a woman's point of view, being physically weaker, it makes sense a rapist would do it for the power over her, especially since women have been overpowered for many years, proving you don't have to sexually rape. Such a desire to construct a scheme of elaborate detail for the satisfaction of raping, would lead one to believe in a much-elevated motivation. To kill? Self preserva-tion for sure, combined with the caution of an intelligence spy makes for some weighty religion when operating at this level. The reason a man rapes a woman in the free world? She is the jewel, coveted, and worshipped, a God some can-not "experience." She cannot share herself with every worshipper. She is the Goddess as the fully aware Lucifer ascended to the throne of the Almighty only to be thrown into the rape farm of Satan's Hell. In the intellect Lucifer had in knowing he'd fail and suffer for, he found the beauty for the moment. Satan raped God, and it was worth it by reason of experiencing what he never would have in eternity. And in eternity, Satan will always have refuge in this beautiful, to him, memory of experiencing her. She will suffer the symptoms. The lesser human male, seeing the Goddess, must know her in his moment. But to rape a woman is not an overthrow. No. It is a thief stealing her love. The human male needs fulfillment. If he isn't satisfied, he will pursue the calling at any cost. The victim has not been overthrown, she has not been put out, she has been robbed, has been reduced. The victim's subsequent symptoms of loss of dignity and being controlled are the side effects, not the reasons she was raped. She and her God have long since laid the set standard and payback for rape.

Mark, having his reason, would be the defiant evolved male Praying Mantis and have moment after moment, giving his God the life for stealing the love that neither could otherwise experience. He knew full well the set standard of payback and suffering. He waited for it, so all he was responsible for was to reminisce and live his actions of pleasure for eternity. There was nothing more enjoyable to him or his cast-out God. The real reason for rape was to occupy once more the place the fallen angel once had, but now he has no place, no euphoria left. Mark knew he must steal lost paradise to experience it time after time through the flesh.

Chapter 15

Jeffery D. and the Human

Mark set out on his hunt, exploring a new possibility of any persuasion. His innermost identity had to be exposed, even to himself. A soul for the Bright Star was all that he needed, but Mark wanted self-satisfaction more than his delusion for dark redemption. His perfect woman had remained primary prey. He had slipped far into eternity, past the line most fear to cross, he inevitably discovered a myriad of information, including information that led to further questions. The one question was who he really was, and he absolutely had to answer this himself, because he wouldn't allow anyone else to. The only honest solution was to test himself. That by itself revealed that he was, in fact, highly cognitive and an opponent not to be underestimated, that he should be considered at any capacity, even as an above-average contributor, if he could be persuaded to be good or a man on trial for double homicide of his wife and wife's lover. But his destiny was without question. Now he needed to know his intricate and specific identity to secure himself. At this stage, he was more dangerous than his had been or would be in the future, as he found a temporary means to disguise himself within society, as an innocent to be overlooked by the decision makers. This was the one factor that allowed his serial murder cases to become extended into a world series, baffling police. Citizen X of Russia was actually captured and released, because of this very same deception. Citizen X had fifty-two confirmed rapes and killings. He would never have been convicted if a solder had not seen him leave his last crime scene, which was an eight-year-old by the name of Natasha, the soldier's niece. The authorities had to later invent a ridiculous excuse of rare semen and blood typing, which they originally and correctly had on Citizen X. What's being demonstrated here is this serial killer had to be literally caught on site, rather than to be identified through forensics. He fit perfectly in society and that allowed him to kill at least ten more times. What complicates matters is that

the predator knows by awareness this is one of his defense weapons. He knows how to do this, use this, and fit in very well. Does the name Orange Juice, ahh, mean anything innocent? Lets move on.

Mark's eighteen wheeler found Jeffery D., a young twist, hitchhiking on highway 41A in Kentucky. Predators cannot betray each other. It is the highest code of conduct to their rewarding belief master. The master would severely punish any hindering of individual assignments. In this sense, they avoid each other, when they discover each other. Only they truly know how alone they are. No one knows how lonely an S.O. is except another S.O.

Mark picked up this hitchhiker, his kind. "Hey, thanks man, long haul to Memphis. Supposed to be there tonight."

"Not going that far, but I'll get you within fifty miles. I'm O. Mark J. Who might you be?"

"Jeffery D. Fifty miles will be perfect. I got a ride from there. Say, this is a damn nice sleeper. Goddamn bathtub, too."

"Yeah, it is the ticket, ain't it?"

"Cruising all about the country in this is totally off the hook."

"Off the hook?"

"Means it's getting away with murder or something, too good to be true, O. Mark J."

"Ha ha, that's some fresh smack, Jeffery D. Give me the connect."

Mark extended his fist and Jeffery D. gave it the butt with his, signifying the connection of the moment.

"Truck is nice, Mark, but a knowing person like myself is acutely sharp to one hidden subtly."

"Oh, yeah, what's that?"

"What do you use the acid for?"

Mark was taken and he gave it away. "How, I mean, what...?"

"I can smell traces of it. It's a different mix, but all acids have that battery smell. I was wondering what could be so spiked for a moment, but then I realized being a trucker you probably get into the industrial stuff."

Mark did his best to invent. "Yes, we pack around just about anything."

"So, what do you use it for?"

"Cleaning, and getting rid of things."

"I use it for control."

"Control?"

"Yep, I use muriatic acid. Doesn't do too much damage, but it gets to the core of my objective."

"Dangerous stuff to use, Jeffery?"

"Not so bad. I use a plastic turkey baster to apply it. It works just enough to get the desired results."

"Well Mr. D., I use it to get rid of the results. I guess my results are controlled beforehand. Yeah, I do have total control when I use this stuff, but I do it for my satisfaction."

"I get rid of mine, too, but in a different way. I feel the consumption. You like what you do?"

"I enjoy what I do. I feel like I'm racing, but winning big, not worried anymore about what's behind me. It doesn't matter anymore. All I have to live for is right here in that odor's results."

"Being a trucker and making good money has been good to you, Mark. But there's a life for a few of us who take it down a different highway."

"Believe me, I know. The route I've chosen has left me with the strongest ambition to get as much done as I can for the little time I have left to face the music or be the orchestration."

"Quotas, they're everywhere. If I didn't have to concern myself with that, it would be a free ride."

"My results go down the drain."

"Sorry to hear that. I eventually eat mine."

"Don't we all, and doesn't that go down the drain?"

"Not like I do, Mark."

"Methods don't matter. Getting there does. I do whatever it takes. In the end, I will be rewarded."

"You sure about that?"

"If I succeed, there is no alternative for me but to go all the way with it. As it is, I'm fucked."

"You aren't that much different than me, really. Driving this big truck around, making the dollars, getting down the highway."

"Hmmm, it's all a highway to hell. In the end, he who did the most hell gets the handle of the whip."

"And those who lose?"

"They're fucked forever. It's like being living shit."

"You think you're going to win, Mark, driving this route?"

"Win my portion. What I do so few have compared. My reward awaits since I am aware."

"You don't want any control do you?

"It isn't in application here. I just found out that I'm truly focused. You don't sound like you'd be any fun anyway, Jeffery. I sit here and look at you. You got your feet all tucked back under the seat like you're all inhibited. See me? Mine are set out in front of me, like I got some where to go, something to do, direction, and most of all, I'm not all pushed back into a place others have tried to put me in. Hell, I bust out on that. So you like to be in control. Well, someone has already started on you. Get your feet out where you can control yourself; as it is others will take note and you'll be eaten alive."

"You noticed that."

"I have to. Like when I go out to eat and see very few people doing that, their feet are tucked back up under their seat. Then I think, how I am unable to do that, but I blow off their reasons, as I see no reason in them."

"You think about shit like that? That's self control."

"I'm into total control, but you're not the type of person I would try. We are like cousins in the arena. Our opponents wouldn't even understand us in contention. The Devil is a rich son of a bitch, you know that?"

"Ha ha, you are off the hook, Mark J. You're right about the rewards, it's what we live for. Let me out anywhere you like."

"What about Memphis?"

"Ah, to hell with Memphis. Like I said, you're off the hook, and we have no reason to be talking."

"You're right. Hey look, there's a bus stop. Check out the lovely waiting for my ride."

"She is a hottie, isn't she? Yeah, ok she's yours. This will be a good place. Thanks for the ride, Mark."

Mark pulled the rig into a grocery store parking lot where his next prey waited at the city of Hopkinsville bus stop. D got out.

"Okay, see you around, O. Mark J."

"Right, hey tuck back. What's the D.?"

"Dahmer, take care you murdering acid rapist."

"They, like you, always get tough afterwards, once you're in the clear."

"You misunderstand. I told you to take care."

Jeffery Dahmer was shanked to death in prison. He really did use a turkey baster filled with acid on his victims.

Mark was relieved to know he would not rape a member of the darkness but the fact that Jeffery did not have courage for the challenge embarrassed and exposed Mark as being a member of the weak. The truth was, Jeffery D. knew and revealed to Mark he was fearful, in the same league. Jeffery would have lost

terribly badly if he had tried, leaving Mark with no satisfaction, anyway. There must be some siding, some belief that the lukewarm are spit. To Mark there was not a lukewarm woman in existence. She either burned or turned to ice by nature and Hell had not the fury. He wanted a fight with the penetrating fury to defeat her.

Mark laid the trap at the bus stop. She was a black teen with extraordinary street smarts. He again accelerated the conversation to focus and avoid mental loss of subject material.

"Hey Mister, you dropped your wallet."

"Well thank you there, youngster. I see you're waiting for the bus. Where about you going?"

"I ain't so young. I'm a teenager."

"Yes, you are, aren't you. Well, that's young for an old man like me who can't keep track of his money. Look at that. You could have run off with over three thousand dollars!"

"Oh, shit, you had all that in there?"

"Still do because of you. How can I repay you?"

"It's all right. Where are you going with all that money?"

"I was looking for a birthday card for my wife, but I'm new here. I wished I could find a place. I have to get it in the mail today or she won't get it on time."

"Ha, that's going to be a very nice birthday card! Anyway, I know a place about five miles up in Hopkinsville."

"Is it easy to find?"

"Well, I was going there, but I'm taking the bus."

"Are you from Kentucky?"

"Yes, my dad is in the Army here at Fort Campbell. I hate it in there on the base. I walk out here to catch the bus when my friend is busy with her guitar lessons."

"If you want, I can save you the bus fare. I'll give you a little reward when I get change, too."

"I don't know, the acid rapist is still out there."

"What did you say?"

"The acid rapist. You know the one who dumps all his victims in the drains."

"Really, how did you hear of such a thing?"

"It was all over the news last month. My dad says they haven't caught him yet."

"I was out of country in Mexico then. Hmmm. I'd like to know more about that myself. That sounds freaky, hmmm, acid rapist."

"Yeah, they say he probably is a rapist. It's not his objective to kill, but he has to get rid of the evidence. The FBI is real worried; they say they will never find him, unless they trace down the acid and connect him to it or catch him in the act. The acid completely dissolves the corpses. It's the big scare now."

"Jesus, I guess so. Is he really that big of an item now? That's gruesome. Has he raped anybody around here?"

"Wow! All these questions. Yes, he's a big item. He hasn't struck here but just about everywhere else. They think he's a trucker like you."

"Oh, no, no, no. That isn't any good. Well, I suppose you better take the bus then, but if you want I'm on my way."

"I don't know. What's your name?"

"O.J. or O Johnny. Ring a bell?"

"That's too redneck to be a rapist. I'm Anna. You don't talk like no rapist. Besides, you need to get your wife her birthday card. I suppose it will be alright."

"Okay, I'll help you in. It's a big step up."

"That's okay, I can jump. You never seen me in the long jump. I have the state record at twenty-one feet, three inches."

"That 's incredible. I only went twenty feet, and I'm a guy! No white girl I know can go fifteen feet."

"You think black women are more competitive than white women?"

"I know so. The facts prove it. I'll bet there isn't a white woman in your school who can run as fast as the slowest black woman."

"Your right, and I like that you said *woman*. Says you respect blacks, too."

"I respect all women with a Godly reverence. But did you know it says in the Bible that women were to shut up in church and, if they want to know something, they are to hold their peace until they get home to ask their husbands in private? I think that's a bunch of shit."

"Damn, that's the thing I keep say'n, and in church, too. Oh, I do some talking in church, let me tell you. You know we make the babies. If it weren't for us, they would be nobody. We've gotta be worth our weight in gold for what we can do."

"I think we evolved, and I think women are higher on the evolutionary scale than men, with the exception of physical strength. Women would make the world a better place if they were in charge, like all of 'em were presidents and governors. There wouldn't be any Hitlers and war. Women got the touch. I mean look at yourself, for example; see how slender your fingers are, perfect for touch, and you don't have hair growing on your back!"

"Ha ha, you're patronizing but clever. But that's a way I never saw it, funny as it is. The truth of it is, we don't ever talk about things like that. That's so weird. You know, there are a lot of men in jail like the acid rapist should be. Women don't do things so much as that. I mean they do things, but not near as much."

"Hormones."

"Yeah, I had a class in biology. The teacher talked all about testosterone. Must be hard being a man controlling all that fight from evolution. But I don't know. It's hard to say. My dad is a sergeant. He has a lot of fight in him. My mom died four years ago, and he can't seem to keep a woman now. He's always looking for a woman. My friend's mama says there isn't a man who isn't looking, even if he were married."

"You think that's true?"

"I don't know if he looks so much. Maybe it's an opportunity thing. But I understand if he does. I am a female, a young female, and I do have urges, but we females have been taught to control our urges. Therefore, I'm smart enough to know that a man must have some serious urges that I just might not be able to control. I want to ask you that. You're married. Can you be honest with a stranger?"

"I can be honest with my wife."

"What do you mean?"

"My wife lives in Mexico. She's Mexican, but that doesn't mean her preferences stereotype all Mexicans."

"What are her preferences?"

"I wonder if I should talk about these things to you. Your dad might be pissed."

"You ain't never going to see my dad, and I wouldn't tell him."

"You know, I'd really like to tell you, because it would open up the close-minded ways you get educated in the United States. But I see you're not closed-minded. You've been able somehow to see more than most for your age. Anyway, in most other countries, there aren't problems with things like that acid rapist. Most of the world has a traditional culture of open sexuality. Here, we close ourselves up and make sex a closet thing. After being deprived from it for so long, some people feast on it, and sometimes abuse it because they never got it. Most foreigners grow up with sex openly, as a part of everyday life. You ever seen a foreigner someplace talking, and the subject of sex comes up? Seems like he or, even more so, she makes herself an idiot for talking so bluntly about her husband's penis in public."

"Damn you sure can bring things out in the open."

"Oh, I can be really open about my wife."

"You can't tell me though, right?"

"I could if you really wanted to know."

"I have to tell you the truth. After hearing this much, I do want to."

"This might not be easy for you. First of all, we're not perverts. We're what the world is most. Deviance is not some dark, horrible evil. Think of two ships leaving some cold country in the far north. Both have to go more than halfway around the world. The first ship leaves, taking the cold north route. The second ship, who is captained by a person, who wants warmth to enjoy himself, takes a more southern sunny route. That is a deviant route from the first. That's deviance from the norm. It's just a different way. The Americans are actually different making us the deviant.

"I always respected the black way of thinking about sex, more so than the white. White people get psychotic. I've never seen that type of behavior in black people. But I have seen rape in black people, as well as whites. I see a great deal of respect in black family sexuality. In Mexico, it goes as far as it does anywhere, with a great deal of respect. I love my Maria so much for who she is and the fact that she can openly come to me and tell me she wants to be with a woman, as well as with me, forever."

"She's bisexual then."

"I guess that's what it would be, if you had to label it. But, how do you label someone? Is a code name like *bisexual* a replacement for Anna? Can you visualize that people there do not look at her as deviant or psycho, but as simply Maria?"

"God, I wished I could see everything. Being schooled here really stinks. You really love her as much, as if she was straight?"

"I think she has opened up things that I'd never known, which allows me to love her more than I ever could have not knowing what I do now. Even scriptwriters and movie producers in Hollywood can't put it down right. You know that *Boys Don't Cry* thing, the flick. All they were trying to say was lesbians make the most unique and fantastic love. If you ever saw two real lesbians get it on, you'd know what I'm talking about. I mean they smile at each other for twenty mothers when they make it. Angie never smiles at me like that, when I'm down on her doing my very best. After I saw her make love to another woman, I knew I was missing out on the best thing I could never have. She was so fucking happy. I was more than jealous at first, but now I love to see her happy like that. Those experiences did teach me how to make love right, making it more than right. That's what *Boys Don't Cry* was all about. But they showed a cool scene and her positive side effects on the bitch. I got the message, but that's because I already knew about woman on woman. Angie ain't all closed up on the lesbian route,

either. There's a lot to her. If I make love with someone else, it's no offense to her, but an enlightenment, knowing that I'm being myself and happy."

"If you have sex with someone else up here, would you tell her about it?"

"I would make it a point to."

"Have you ever done that?'

"No, I had a hard time crossing the line. I've only been married to her six months, but I've known her for three years. You asked me a personal question, now I want to ask you one. Have you ever had sex and wanted more from someone else?"

"Why you asking?"

"For you, for you to understand your own sexuality and preferences."

"You're right. I really never wanted to confront that since I think I'm a bit young."

"Just think about it, if you don't want to answer me."

"I have and I think you're asking me for your reasons, too."

"It's true, every man is a seducer in his own way. I can admit it, but like I said before, I don't cross the line unless given permission."

"So you can tell me. You'd like to squirm with me."

"Yes, goddammit, I would, and that's the American way you been taught. I showed you respect. I would never have disrespected an honest, open mind."

"Man, you're right. This is true. I'm sorry, man. I know every man wants to fuck. Why would I say that squirm shit?"

"American way, Anna."

"So, you like to make it with a black girl, huh?"

"It's not that I'd put a label on it like "make it." I'd like to take my time and experience each other, some real good living, some real love. And yes, because you're black, I do believe you have characteristics white women don't have which would, in fact, be very pleasing to me."

"Hmmm, I believe you. I don't think you're patronizing me. You think people could come to the point of having sex like it's a handshake?"

"Never. I think each moment we can really live and each moment we do what we desire to do, unless we are afraid. The hell thing you know. The thing is, we don't really keep sex a sacred thing. We want to keep it an exciting thing. A handshake is not exciting, and we don't want to dull sex. But why withhold ourselves from what we want to do, when it means so much to us. The logic of walking away empty is flouting our emotions to do self-damage. How does it make sense to avoid enjoying life, unless you were trained to be stupid? The

objective to life is enjoying it. Surviving is beneath that. Surviving also entails having sex, so no matter what point of view you take, sex is in."

"So, you would make love to a total stranger?"

"It really does not take time to become acquainted. The stranger is eliminated much faster by the sixth sense than extended communication. If it were all coming together right, sex would be our next step. But sex would not be the last step. We aren't worms or cattle. We are spirit-filled human beings. We got spirit and feelings. Why not feel for the right moment?"

"What about this moment?"

"I just want to feel beautiful. I want to make the moment beautiful for both of us. Let's find a swimming hole. I don't have to be back up in Kansas until tomorrow. They got swimming holes in Kentucky, don't they?"

"Damn, I thought you'd want to stop and go back there to the sleeper! Yes, we got swimming holes all over. Let's go."

"Mark and Anna spent the entire afternoon together. She had found a friend and Mark had found his sex Goddess. They stayed in the sleeper for the night. Anna gave way to enjoying Mark, accepting her father's punishment as worth it. He got what he wanted, his Goddess this time without the resistance and offense. The predator did not fit the mold that the narrow-minded put him into. He was extremely capable when opportunity came. He took extreme advantage of those moments to support and defend himself in society, as he was aware of what society expected. He realized the possibility of being captured; therefore, he used those moments of obedience and happenstance to strengthen his inner self. Believing in that, he praised himself to others concerning his rare successes. These rare successes had acquitted guilty sex offenders in court. This encounter with Anna would later clear and free Mark of any suspicions.

Dahmer was insane, yang is yin, and man is Human, and ah, O was J bird! Ya know what I mean!

Anna only saw this side of the predator for now, so she explored him further. "I'd like to meet Maria someday O. Johnny, and know your real name."

"You will meet her, if you understood making your destiny that I told Brandy about. I gave you Maria's address. Remember the Blue Spot I told you about, girl? There is a blue spot we'll all find one day. Go home before your dad gets himself in trouble. I'll call on you someday very soon, girl."

"Oh J. you better. That was the ride of my young life. I never had no man do what you do. You're better than damn!

Chapter 16

No Second Chances

❦

"My my, Ms. Sarah, you are lookin' good today. You expected me back today, ha ha?"

"You're in good spirits, Mark. I suppose you should be. Canami gave you the Idaho contract."

"No shit. Well I told you. Just got to get out there and do ha hew it!"

"Speaking of doing it in Idaho, that acid rape guy stuck somebody in Boise yesterday."

"You see that on the news?"

"Are you kidding? It's been everywhere the last half an hour—radio and the TV."

"So it just came out now, then?"

"Yes, this guy is a real extremist. You know this makes six now, and they're happening all over. It makes me wonder if he isn't a trucker. Lucky for you, if they thought it was you, that your route in was from Nevada."

"You think they'd suspect me."

"Oh no. I was just saying as an example."

"I hadn't even heard about it, until a black girl in Kentucky told me about it three days ago."

"That's since you were in Meh hee choe when the big news flash came out; sort of died down for awhile. What were you doing in Kentucky?"

"I was too early, so I went down there to fart around. Went swimming with a real nice black girl."

"You like black folks, Mark?"

"Yes I do. I think they got some real culture and they aren't afraid to let it show. I like solid people. I believe black people could go along way if they had

the total freedom whites do. Name was Anna William's, father was in the Army there at Campbell."

"She must have been young."

"Oh, I didn't pay any attention to that. Anyway, I'll take the Las Vegas run tomorrow. Going to go home now."

Detective Rainey had also heard the news of the Boise case. It was obvious only to Rainey that Mark took the north route to Idaho, then turned east to Oregon. There were no truck scales on Highway 95 into Oregon; however, he would take the chance. He took it upon himself to inform the FBI of Mark's background, without permission from the Chief of Police. Rainey knew he would never be competent, unless he used unorthodox and non-policy procedures to bring the case to its true light. Rainey informed the Feds of Jerica and the recovered cow hoof, which had been cleaned.

The FBI's interest peaked, believing Rainey had submitted an authorized report. The case was given the go ahead, and FBI agents discovered Mark's stepmother had been reported missing when doing a family background check. The ticket had been purchased in Oregon, and Mark's past requests to locate her through the police sealed the bid for his nation-wide, all-points bulletin. But three more victims too late. The Vegas run was carnage. Three prostitutes would find gambling with Mark had lesser odds than the strip. They all found their way to Tucson, Arizona, in what they assumed would be a fun run to Mexico. Mark returned to Juniper to dispose of the two barrels and the bathtub. It was beginning to look like a junkyard on the desolate mountain. Even if it were discovered, the connection to Mark was impossible. The evidence was only circumstantial. He cleaned it as well as he would his truck. He found his business under obvious and open surveillance.

"Mr. Johnson."

"Yes."

"I'm agent Ryan with the FBI. You're wanted for questioning in the disappearance of your stepmother, Karen Wimber."

"Well, she disappeared when I enlisted in the army over twenty-five years ago. How is it she suddenly now pops up *missing*."

"We think you know the answer to that. Airline ticket purchased one hundred miles from here, two thousand mile run from her. What do you make of that?"

"Find out why and who I guess. Where did she go?"

Detective Rainey was standing by, beginning to feel vindicated, knowing the FBI would smash Mark to powder.

"That's just it, and we are going to find out why and who, right here, today. We're going to search the entire premises for crime lab analysis, forensic evidence in other words."

"That's fine. I need to see your warrant, first, though."

"Ryan looked at Rainey in disappointment and hopefulness."

"I didn't see the warrant, Rainey. You did get that, right?"

"I was sure. . .he'd let us. . ."

"Oh well, guys, you should be going now. Have fun talking to the judge. You find it may be difficult. I demand to be notified of the hearing request for warrant, Mr. Ryan, since I've been informed of my constitutional right to object without reasonable cause. If you do get the warrant, be sure and find something; you'll all be poor if you don't. Don't you know?"

"We won't be poor. Let's go in now. It's a walk-in request. Care to join us?"

"No, I'll be there with my lawyer in an hour, my time limit."

Mark met with his well-informed council, Dan Gordon, a ruthless trial lawyer who had fourteen child sex-abuse acquittals under his belt. Judge Mattison was open-minded, accepting the request in his chamber. He commanded Rainey to show cause.

"Okay, Detective Rainey, let's see your stuff." The judge shuffled through some papers. "This is a bit odd. I don't see anything here but your personal notes to the FBI. Agent Ryan, do you have Eugene Police's official request for your involvement in a local missing persons case and a domestic accident involving a child, ah Jerica?"

"Well, no we assumed Rainey had . . ."

"No matter. I have all the other info here for a general warrant. Mr. Gordon, just what objections does your client have?"

"Your honor, my client has given his full cooperation. He is in total compliance with his conditions of probation. He is back in the top ten percent financially. His business contributes far in excess of expectations. Last month, in the first search by Eugene Police officers, my client suffered one full lost week of business due to the trucks being held up by forensics investigators. That was a total loss of seventeen thousand dollars in earned income. I also have here estimates of damages done to the properties in excess of six thousand dollars during the man-handled search.

"Actually, we are considering this police harassment of a convicted sex offender, who is, in fact, doing all he can to reform with treatment. Mark has a glowing report from his probation officer and treatment counselor. Lawsuits are not out of the question here, especially if this warrant fails to produce evidence

of any connectable crime, then the incalculability of getting a conviction, which will cost my client at least one hundred thousand more. I'd say the damages would net a cool three to four million."

"I was not made aware of a prior search," the judge answered fairly. Rainey, what exactly are you up to? You don't get departmental authorization for the Federal Bureau of Investigation! You think you're the god of operations, here? Now, I hear that this man has already been searched within a month!"

'Your honor, Mr. Johnson submitted to our search request—"

"Your damn straight he did. He turned himself in at the jail, too, something you're going to do! Give me your goddamn gun and badge. You are held without bail in contempt of my court and the court of . . . whoever prosecuted Mr. Johnson for violation of basic human rights. As for you, Ryan, send Rainey the bill. We and the city of Eugene did not request your assistance! Get the hell out of here!"

Mark openly flaunted his victory with the court. He thanked his lawyer. "Way to go, Danny Baby!"

"That's nothing. I have to get back to some real work. Take care."

Agent Ryan's experience negated any intimidation from Mark. He went straight for the bluff, knowing it was the criminal's folly.

"Mr. Johnson?"

"Yes, Agent Ryan."

"I want to apologize for all of this. I'd ask that you please keep me out of this. I'm going up for my ten year and I don't need any . . ."

Mark knew this was Ryan's only available attempt to get close. He'd give him more than expected. 'Don't sweat it, Ryan. Hey, my secretary Sarah, what did you think of her?'

'Well, she was a looker. I saw her Christian literature all over the office."

"Are you a church-goer, Ryan?"

"Yes, very much so. How about you?"

"Nah, I go with Darwin. But Sarah is available. Why don't you ask her out? She'd love it."

"Okay, I will. She was a very congenial person."

"You been working in Eugene long?"

"No, I just transferred here. I'm originally from De Moines."

"Well, if you're ever on the radio and you hear call sign Johnny Bell, that'd be me on the road again."

"Okay, Johnny Bell. I'm going to give Sarah that call."

Ryan knew all too well the challenge of the guilty, but this was all too much. This was Mark wanting more attention by someone in addition to Rainey. The challenge was always acceptable and nothing new to any official.

Ryan could not wait for Mark to return to Sarah, making the decision to hopefully surprise Mark psychologically by immediately making the call from the FBI office across the street. He had his assistant, Morgan, record the call.

"Ultra Trucking, this is Sarah."

"Hi, Sarah, this is Harold Ryan. I met you this afternoon."

"Oh, is everything okay? Do I still have my job?"

"Oh yes, yes of course. I'm calling to apologize, actually. Rainey is in jail for harassing Mark, as well as contempt of court. Mark's in the clear. He should be there any moment."

"I'm so relieved. I need this job so bad."

"Mark also mentioned you are a real church going Christian, too."

"He did? He told you that?"

"Yes, I was wondering if I could ask you out, maybe even come to church?"

"You mean go out with an FBI guy?"

"Mark thought it a good idea. He said you were for real."

"He actually set us up?"

"I take that as a yes?"

"Well, I go to the Church of the Nazarene on Mohawk. You can show up Wednesday evening at seven. I'll introduce you to the church at testimony time."

"Thank you, I...testimony time?"

"Oh, you'll love it. Everyone is so free. It's the best part of service."

"Okay...I'll be there then. Thank you."

"Bye, Harold."

"My God, a rapist can get a babe in his highway to hell eighteen wheeler but won't trust an officer of the highest Justice Department on the planet outside of a goddamn church."

"Credit is like sex, Harold. Some get it, some don't."

"Morgan, we better get some credit for this or Johnson walks."

"Who walks through the valley? Huh, who?"

"The fearless mother fucker that I am."

"I want this freak."

"All right, now let's get department approval for all of it or mine enemy shall eat in our presence."

"Done deal, I'm on this all the way and totally covert from the public. I'll get internal wiretaps, the whole nine yards."

Ryan's secretary alerted him to the latest case. "Agent Ryan, we have an update on the acid rapist, three separate sites in Tucson, Arizona, yesterday morning!"

"Fuck me, Johnson was just in Vegas yesterday! He's our man, no doubt about it. Without a warrant, how can we get surveillance?"

"We take vacations. Innocent bystanders reveal acid boy while off duty. That'll make us famous."

"I have nine days coming, Harold. But I'll bet they give me thirty when we shackle this dupe."

"And a medal. Mr. Johnson, you have a shadow."

Chapter 17

Testimony Time!

❧

"Wasn't that some good singing? It's always a joy to sing to Jesus, is it not?"

"Amen!"

"Just one announcement tonight, Julie wants all us faithful Wednesday niters to know that it's singles night for Jesus at her place Friday instead of Gillian's. I guess it's working out for the singles group. Gillian got married . . . let's see here, last week in ah . . . Reno. Well, it is time to hear from you. I'm sure Jesus has brought us some wonderful testimonies and with that, blessing our church. Sarah, I see you have brought another gentleman with Mark this week. You are just multiplying our flock, praise Jesus."

"Yes Pastor Ming, this is Harold from the FBI! He's a wonderful man. My job was in serious jeopardy when Harold stepped in and vindicated my boss, Mark. I just know that it was Jesus and this testimony that God does work when you think it's all over. Bam, he knocks old Satan right back in his place. Just like the song we were singing. Jesus is the answer."

"Harold, thank you so much for coming. Please stand and give us a word of faith!"

"It's a pleasure to be in such real company. I have never seen such enthusiasm. I will never again discount small churches. I'm honored."

"Mark, how has Jesus been to you this week?"

"Brother Ming, I'm drawing closer. I have to say that, if these are the end times, then this is a really sincere church. Agent Ryan has touched on to something that would be important if Jesus is the Messiah. I mean, you really talk Jesus enthusiastically here. I've never heard the name of Jesus so much. I have visited the Mormons and the Presbyterians and just so many others, and they don't talk about Jesus or the Way. They always talk about their domestic problems, such as child molestation, polygamy, the government, and status. I read

in the Holy Bible that, in the end times, come all kinds of preaching, but if they don't preach Jesus then it's just a bunch of ahh, huh, well, not God! I feel like God could be in the midst."

"God bless you, Mark, and we thank you for your candid honesty. Keep the search, Mark, and you shall find!"

Agent Ryan's molestation was sufficient before Mark made his facetious intimidation of Harold's false delight in the church. It would be an hour before he could get Sarah alone at the nearby Katy's coffee shop.

"Sarah, do you really think a man educated like Mark could get up and talk like that? Do you really think he is for real?"

"Why, Harold, judge not! That's just what being a real Christian is about, not to doubt. Ha! I made a rhyme. I'm going to use that in bible study. How could I use that?"

"Are you sure Mark isn't using you?"

"Now how could he do that?"

"We know that a young lady purchased an airline ticket for his stepmother, Ms. Wimber, in Portland. She received the ticket in the mail and used it. She never returned from Mexico. I'm going to be blunt with you. Did you buy that ticket for Mark?"

"I couldn't tell you a thing about that, Harold."

"Are you sure?"

"Absolutely, I swore to God."

"Well okay, I just don't know what to make of this."

"I said I swore to God! Don't you get it?"

"It's okay, Sarah, calm down. Is there anything else you can help me with?"

"He said he went out with a black girl in Kentucky, Anna Williams; her father was in the army at a place called Campbell."

"Really?!"

"Yes, said he went swimming with her."

"Thank you so much, Sarah. I really should be going, I'll call you tomorrow. Is that okay?"

"Please!"

Harold got to the radio in his undercover sedan. "Morgan!"

"Yep."

"Get on this ASAP. A solder in Kentucky at what I believe is Fort Campbell, a Williams. His daughter is an Anna Williams. Sarah gave him up. Said he went swimming with the kid. Get on it!"

"Done."

"Directory service, Fort Campbell. Name please."

"Williams, but I don't have a first name, operator. This is special agent Morgan Styles with the FBI. I need a search. The daughter's name is Anna Williams."

"This may take some time, sir. No, it's listed as Anna and Rodney Williams. I'll connect you."

"Hello."

"Mr. Williams?"

"This is Sergeant Williams."

"Yes, Sergeant Williams, this is Agent Styles of the FBI in Eugene Oregon. Do you have a daughter by the name of Anna?"

"Yes, she's out right now."

"When was the last time you saw her, Sir?"

"Fifteen minutes ago. She's spending the night at her girlfriend's house."

"She is okay then?"

"Yes, may I ask what this is about?"

"A certain Mark Johnson, who goes by a call sign of Johnny Bell, supposedly made contact with her. Are you aware of this?"

"You damn straight I am, and I'd like to hang that pervert."

"Okay, Sergeant Williams, I'll send a local agent over tomorrow to get an official statement from her. I'll arrange for a conference call with Special Agent Kurt Lewis. He's our top man out here; take your time with him. The call will be recorded, so get your facts straight, no wishy-washy testimony will do."

"Kurt Lewis, got it. That'll be easy. Got him, huh."

"This time we have, yes."

Morgan called Harold back.

"Yeah!"

"Oh yes, we have the bastard. I talked to the father. He wants to hang Johnson."

"Good, get over here fast. He's rigging up to leave now. We'll tail him. You get your leave papers authorized?"

"Nine days paid vacation. Everything is coming together. We have our man! I'll be there in ten."

Morgan and Harold observed Mark loading his gear on the truck and trailer. They attached a tracking radio on the trailer when Mark fueled up. Mark was unaware as he left on his route. They tailed him through the night and the morning, into northern California and, presently, at the Interstate Five junction bypassing San Francisco.

"Jesus, does this guy know what sleep is, much less a rest stop?"

"Didn't you ask Sarah what his route was?"

"She was getting pissed, swearing to God and so forth. I didn't want to push her. Hell, how was I going to know the moron was staying out so late? After church, he went on a route! This guy could fool my mama."

"He's only stopped once on the side of the road to piss in the ditch. Why doesn't the dick use his toilet?"

"Morgan, I think you hit something."

"He doesn't have a sewer drain."

"Fuck, he's doing the acid shit inside the sleeper, in that fucking bathtub the other owner told us about."

"Goddamn, that's why he replaced the tub. It was probably etched up so bad from the acid he considered it evidence."

"All we have to do is wait, now, either way, before or after."

"Fuck man, you just want this guy don't you. I mean, like who gives a shit about the person going down the etched bathtub drain? Right?"

"Right? You think I give a shit? The three bitches in Tucson were supposedly streetwalkers in Vegas. Hell, the guy is doing us a favor. I'm just doing my J. O. B. Etched or not. Fuck it. I'm sleeping. Wake me when you get tired and stay back five hundred yards. When he turns off, we'll reacquire him with the signal finder."

Ten hours later in Southern California, Harold and Morgan were anxious for news from Fort Campbell. Both had lost the charge in their cellular phone batteries and couldn't use the car's radio, since it was tuned to the special frequency in Eugene. They had not anticipated Mark leaving the area that soon. They hoped to get a stop from Mark, to use a pay phone. However, the rapist was well disciplined in his dire occupation.

"Morgan, this guy is up to some serious shit. There are only two exits left to the Mexican Border."

"He can't go in there, even if he does, we have jurisdiction fourteen miles in. If he crosses, we bust him."

"Oh ho ho, this guy would have been good except one premature slip up."

"What?"

"That's why he wanted me to go out with Sarah. He knew by telling her about Anna that she'd tell me. He wanted me to know before making his escape last night. This fucker has balls. Well, shit head, you didn't expect me to be on your ass!"

"Fuck, one more exit. He is going for it. He did plan it out!"

"He has to cross the line before I can stop him. Soon as he rings the bell, it's Morgan and Harold all over the big channel. We're famous already, partner! Worth the vacation?"

"Shit, Peter Jennings talked about this guy. We're going to be on top from here on out, buddy."

"Biggest rape serial killer bust to date. Yup, that was the last exit. Ha, maybe it was church. You should have heard the bitch. I saved her job by God's strange ways. Oh, she was all jacked up."

"Okay, get up there alongside him. Let him see us, just as he rings the bell."

"Shit, this is great. Okay, he's in; blow the horn once! Yeah, he sees us, Haa Haaaa! Look at his face!"

"What the fuck? They're waving him on. He's got permits. Go for it. Hit the siren!"

"Hey, stop that truck! Yes, he's illegal. Stop him now, *rapido!*"

"*Rapido*, what kind of shit is that? Look at these guys take him down. I'll bet Johnson just had a turtle."

The entire Border patrol and the Mexican federal police cut Mark off and had him at gunpoint. They wrestled him from the cab and cuff him on the Mexican cobblestone crossing. The leader approached the FBI agents. "I'm Captain Ramirez, señor, what do we have here?"

"This is Mark Johnson, suspected serial killer and rapist. We were waiting for him to cross the border to make the bust."

"You must come with me. We go to the detention center first, *si?*"

"Fine, we understand. Lead the way."

"How you doing, church boy? Find Jesus yet?"

"I once was lost but now am found."

"There will be plenty of finding lost time to think about that, before the rope comes to your end."

"Take a seat, Agent Ryan, Styles. Mr. Johnson does have legal papers here, so you must show me your warrant and extradition request."

"No problem. The locals will have it here within the hour. Just give us a phone."

"Okay, but you must leave your credit card to pay with your signature on the slip. Here you go. This is standard procedure."

"I know."

"Make the call, Morgan."

"Hello, Kurt!"

"Yes, Morgan?"

"Yeah, what's up?"

"Where did you guys go?"

"Little vacation. Ran into Johnson on our way down Interstate Five. Decided to follow him into Mexico! Can you believe that?"

"No, I wouldn't waste my vacation time like that."

"Kurt, we got him. He's busted. The Mexican *Federalis* are holding him right now."

"For what?"

"Knock it off, Kurt. What kind of a statement did we get from the Williams kid?"

"She's a nineteen-year-old, recently professed lesbian who worships Johnson for being the best gentleman she has ever witnessed. Her father is about to disown her since her recent inkling for women has robbed him of one of his own dates. He hasn't got a statement. Never met Johnson. It's a total bogy. Now, what's that you were saying about Mark?"

"Oh Jesus. Does shit like this really happen? I mean does it really fucking happen?"

"I'm afraid it has, Morgan. What the hell are you guys doing?"

"Well, we got him for crossing the border. That's a probation violation right there."

"Didn't you know?"

"Know what?"

"He has court approval. He pays a heavy fee to do business down there."

"Oh Christ, Oh Christ."

"You are in some shit, Morgan. Is Harold with you?"

"Yes!"

"Goddamn. That's three hundred thousand dollars. The bureau is going to relieve you guys."

"What are you talking about?"

"You're going to find out soon enough about Mexican national law. Good bye, Morgan."

Captain Ramirez returned to the interrogation room with the local FBI representative. "Senor Morgan Styles, Harold Ryan, this is Charlie Glass with the FBI out of Tijuana."

."You guys got your papers?" Agent Glass inquires of Morgan.

"I'm afraid not."

"What are you saying, Morgan?"

"Shut up. It was your idea!"

"We don't have a bust?"

"We are the bust, asshole!"

"Looks like you gentlemen are in some deep doo doo."

"Yes, Charles. Just get us out of here."

"I'm afraid I can't do that. Johnson has dual citizenship by marriage. He has all his papers. He wants to press charges of false arrest on you two. I'm afraid the Mexican police will have to oblige him, because they don't want the charges to come down on them. You just caused a seriously incomprehensible act among the Mexican Feds. They have a right to fine the U.S. government and hold you until the bill is paid. You just committed an act of war, by crossing the border illegally, brandishing firearms on a citizen. You two ever see the inside of a Mexican jail?"

"Jesus no."

"The fuckin' guy is married?"

"Yes, Harold, to a Mexican National."

"What in the hell? A Mexican jail? Johnson's a fucking Mexican citizen?"

"Well, I dread saying this, but when you do get out, they're going to send you back up to Oregon, where you will catch career hell. But after being in a Mexican jail, the federal pen will be like a Holiday Inn. You need the Mexican federal statute titles on that, or should I call for some council?"

As ridiculous as this all sounds, actual cases just like this are documented and researchable. American bounty hunters have also died in Mexican jails, since going down there only with the intent of looking for fugitives is a federal crime against the country of Mexico itself. Crossing the border with a firearm is an automatic five-year federal sentence, whether you are a law officer or not. Many American grandmothers have spent years in Mexican jails for having an unloaded gun in the trunk, which was forgotten there by family members. Many others have been jailed, who just plain didn't know that guns were illegal in Mexico. An American official who brandishes a firearm in Mexico is considered to have committed an act of war. Guns are illegal in Mexico!

This was not in Mark's plan; by bringing up Anna to Sarah, he only wanted to place doubt or innocence in any one capable of being a threat. He knew in her flighty character she'd give that much of him up. He had hoped someone would find out about Anna. Now, the FBI fully understood. He was well aware that, eventually, the feds would know him to be the rapist. Catching him was not a concern. He just wanted them to also know he could love when it was his

way, complete submission. Without realizing that, he knew they could never catch him, because they could never see him. The proof was there in the bungled G-men case at the border. Anna's army father knew the only way to catch a gorilla was to use guerilla warfare. Mark was deep in the jungle. The FBI, standing ineptly on the street corner thinking they had the view, were the viewed. No one, absolutely no one, could see him now. As they got this close they dared not look inside him now. They might see what was in them, only with less competence. All of this could have been solved before Mark had contacted Brandy, but our law enforcement system has something called politics of the stiff-necked suit bearers, or too smart for themselves. A child caught Mark. It took humility, not naïve and ignorant arrogance.

Chapter 18

Can it be?

❧

"Hi, Tropical Woman."

"Mark, I don't expect you. I'm so happy to see you. Give me you love."

"I am very happy now, my Maria. Many things have changed."

"No between us though, no?"

"Never. My love can never change for you. You have shown me the only peace I've ever known. My lawyer and I have worked a deal with the Judge in America. I paid all my fines in advance. He cut short my probation, I'm free."

"You can stay now, forever?"

"Yes, Baby, forever. I want to stay for one month, paint the house, put in a Jacuzzi, fix up the swimming pool, and make love the rest of the time."

"We can make one baby Mark, please. You promised me before when you get liberated."

"We will try, then."

"I cannot tell you what this mean to me. I live for this moment, when I can have your child. This day I put your child in your arms I will feel like a Queen."

"Let's walk to the beach, Angie, just you and me."

"Si, Fabi sleep now anyway. She work in the night."

"What does she do?"

"She take a computer class at La Paz University in the evening then she work on the Malecon in one disco for to make the drinks. The Americans come here so much now and spend the money. She is very tired always now."

"I can see you haven't been studying your English so much."

"*Si*, I look at all the shit in America on the computer. How you say in English? It sucks. I think America sucks now. I want you to speak Spanish. Why not? We live in Mexico now. I like to hear you say *Te Amo Mi Amor*. It sounds so much more the way I feel."

"I like to say *te amo, te amo, te amo*, Angie."

"You know I wish to hear this every day?"

"I'll learn the Spanish. I want to be your best friend in all things."

"I do not understand. What means best friend."

"In everything I want to be the one for you. I want to be able to talk to you about everything."

"In Spanish too or we have much problems to be best friends."

"I promise I will learn. Is it okay we walk all the way to the beach? You feel you can?"

"It's easy. I have been walking. No, how you say when you go walking?"

"Jogging."

"*Si*, jogging. My English will come back to me now you are here."

"This is what I want to talk to you about. Some things always come back to me."

"You talk about your stepmother again."

"No, but I talk about me. What she did to me? Do you think what she did to me messed me up? I'm not normal, am I Angie?"

"I remember when we fight a long time ago, when I am angry for no reason you think. I get very angry in those times, remember?"

"It is why I left for the prison in Oregon."

"Remember what you said to me before you go one time?"

"I'm sorry, no."

"You said I need to kill the bug that is up in my ass."

"You did."

"I did and only you can do that if you want to. Do you want to or do you want to feed the bug?"

"My God, Angie, you do know me."

"You must choose, *mi amor*. It is only a decision of your passion now. I know by killing the bug that I have chosen the clean and good. I have peace now and don't make pain for others. I did not know you have this problem with Karen, and I love you. You hide your problem very well. If you can put out the bug and you have peace, think how much more the life we can have in peace."

"If I'm sick or want something bad, but now I really changed for the good, can I tell you something I did and you still love me?"

"Mark, I can forgive anything. I don't care what it is. Especially if you feel it's something you feel so bad about. Now, I know you do something. I remember when you talk about your stepmother. It is I who is bad because I don't listen to you. I think you only want to kill her."

"I really did not care to kill her. It's something she did to me that I did to someone else, and I feel like an animal because of it. But when I did it, I felt like it was right."

"You hurt someone?"

"Not a physical pain, but I showed them something that woke them up very early. It is very difficult for me to tell you, and I risk your love by telling you. But I love you so much I must not hide this any longer. I want to be a good person with you, all my life with you with a good mind."

"The person you do this to is okay now, is alive?"

"Oh yes, and very happy too. I am surprised how happy."

"Mark, it is time."

Mark gave his confession to Maria, preparing her for the most probable future day of true exposure. This confession would serve as his still available good self.

"When my Heather was four years old, I kissed her, there, no more than that. She loved me for this."

"This all you do, only lick her genital?"

"This is the most difficult moment of my life right now, Angie. I'm more than humiliated. I feel like a worm. But I swear, nothing more in any other way."

"This is a natural sign of affection when the children are very little. In countries like Guatemala, this is considered wholesomeness in the family. You are worried all this time for this?"

"In America, it is called sodomy. A sick and highly punishable offense."

"Yes, if the act is desirous for her sexuality and is abusive. Don't you love your Heather?"

"God, so much. I wish I could be her father."

"This is what all we have tried to teach you, Fabi, her Mama, and me. You cannot see these things, Mark? You cannot let go of the simple Gringo way?"

"I do. Something of power has put a doubt in me."

"This is the way of your stupid country, America. Your police and fucked up people think their Jesus is the only Jesus."

"People here do what I did?"

"It is something that happen sometimes but is not an intention to hurt or perversion. It is no illegal. But you promise me you never fucking your Heather!"

"I swear and give you my word. I would never have told you anything if not to tell you this."

"I can see in you and I can see that you cannot be the man my father was. Why you do this to Heather?"

"I don't really know. I think it did come naturally to me. I actually told her I couldn't do it anymore, as she was older and that Jesus could not come into my heart for doing that. I was sorry about it. I lost it in her presence. I cried right in front of her. She saw my self-dejection and felt sorry for me. I think this prompted her to tell Shea, since Heather felt remorse for me. After this, several other false accusations came out against me."

"Mark, this was the problem of not knowing how to be a father because of your laws that come into your family. All you had to do was say no to her and be a father. She would want to grow up and get her man when the time was right. But by showing her you were sorry did something she could not understand. She only wanted to ask her mother why you were sorry, not accuse you of hurting her. She was curious to know what could possibly be wrong. From there, the police fuck everything up."

"I am okay?"

"You must kill the bug that is up your ass. I must say to you I feel this a long time ago. I don't know what it was then but I do now. I love you even now, because it bother your conscience. The fact you tell me is like confession of wanting to be straight. The fact that you are here with me tell me you love me, and that is a good thing, from a good heart. So I say again, kill that bug which you told me about."

"I'll try and work on that. Hey…I found a girl in Kentucky, Anna. She's nice!"

"Really?"

"I told her a little about us. I had so much fun after I told her about you. We went swimming. I have her telephone number. Here, take it. She said that she really hoped to talk to you someday. I told her when we get to the Blue Spot we would all know each other."

"Mmm, I love your story of the Blue Spot. Did you tell her the story?"

"I told her about what you let me do and that it makes you feel sexual for me. Like your Blue Spot."

"You have me for your Blue Spot forever. She make the love good for you?"

"She did, but it was not so good for me, because I have a hard time thinking it is okay for me to do that when you are my woman. I still need time to be able to give my love to someone else. It is easy for me with Fabi, because you are here, and Fabi also thinks in this way. But Anna was new to this way of thinking. I told her I loved her because I felt it, in the way she allowed me in. I think I would

have more satisfaction sometimes if I take the love from someone, like it were mine to take."

"You must be very careful with that, Mark. You mean you feel like rape?"

"Maria, I feel like I want to take you and go crazy! That is what I mean."

"Then you must catch me. Come, let's go diving, *pinche gordo gringo*!"

"What did you call me?!?"

"Ha ha, fat white boy. You need to drop that *pansota*! Come get me, *gordo chulo*!"

"Ho, yeah sassy! You are not so easy to catch."

"Kiss me like you did Rosabla."

"You saw me? You were spying."

"*Si*, I want so much to see that. But I don't think you really want to and I wait for you to take off his panties!"

"What the Jesus?"

"Si, hee hee, Rosabla is one pervert. How it feels to kiss one pervert man?!? Haa Gringo!!"

"You're shitting me."

"No shitting allowed. I tell Fabi. She laugh too much she choking. We think you are very *stupido* in this moment."

"You would have let me!"

"Si, I think it so funny this night but I think you can tell this person is a man. I am so surprised. I never forget this! But that's why he don't fuck you, because he know me."

"I think you found out Rosabla was a man the hard way!"

"You are ridiculous. He could not get hard! Ha ha!"

"Fuck meee! Where is all this going?"

"You need to be careful, Gringo. I see that your eye isn't really wide open yet. This is serious, Mark. I see a problem with you that you overlooked. But who cares where it goes? Come here. Forget the crazy things in the world. We have each other now, and I want only you. I change for the good life. We put Fabi out, just you and me, okay?"

"That makes me feel like I'm home. We make the change, we can."

"You are *mi amor*. You must get your honor back. I know what is your pain now. You think you are one low animal for what the police in Oregon make you feel. You are a man. Be up now, Mark. Forget what is the past. It is you now. You have done what you had to. It is finished. Now, I want you to be more careful and listen to me and learn from me, Chulo. You can do this?"

"I never thought these things could come to be. I thought I would always have to live my life hiding this from you. I am so impressed with you. Can it be, Mary of the Angels?"

"Let's be a couple of devils. Remember the first time you make the love to me in Balandra? *Tu eres un Manta Raya!*"

"*Te amo mi bonita, te amo.*"

Chapter 19

Into the Never

❦

"Detective Worthy speaking."

"Hi Bill, Paul Harris here. I have what could be *the* break in the Acid Rapist case. The acid is all from the same batch. It was actually a fairly recent manufacture for a new submarine in Bremerton, Washington. The company keeps samples of all the batches to record the recipe of each required specification. The batch of nearly six hundred gallons never made it there. It was a successful hijacking of a nuclear reactor transport truck. I've alerted the FBI about the batch. They had assumed the acid was stolen with the reactor. I have all the info here for you."

"Jesus, Paul, this is the crack. Fax it all now! You know we have nine direct murders, plus the cab driver in Denver, right?"

"Yes, but I was reading it may be at least one higher. You know that Johnson guy the feds bungled up over a month ago at the border?"

"Idiots."

"A detective Rainey has a missing person's case highly connectable to Johnson."

"I don't know. I looked that over. What you going to say about Oregon cops? He did thirty days for contempt in the case."

"Yes, but if you put that aside and look at it geographically: Seattle, Boise, and Pasadena. Then we see that Johnson does, in fact, frequent Mexico. The nuclear reactor transport truck was found abandoned in Eugene, Oregon. He was in Vegas the night before the three dumps in Tucson. Three prostitutes come up missing in Vegas puts Johnson as the pivot man in this circle jerk, Bill."

"Goddamn. I'm going to request a special assignment. The first case was here."

"You shouldn't have a problem with that. I'll send this over now."

"Right."

Worthy obtained his request to include Mark's entire file. The file contained everything on Johnson, including birth and military records. He noted the disappearance of Brandy and his stepmother. It was clear to Worthy that Mark could have driven to the acid sites from the scheduled truck routes. He had to discount the extended routes, due to the lack of a credit card trail. The odometer was surely disconnected when going farther than the routes specified. The personal record searches didn't produce any prejudiced police notes or deviant incidents. He knew his only hope of a bust was personal identification of Johnson on the way to and from his crime scenes. He began his cross-country adventure with nothing more than pictures of Mark. He would visit more than three hundred fueling stations and other likely stops. His first stop on Colorado Boulevard was his best find.

"Hello, may I help you?"

"Yes, Mr. Bebe, I don't know if you remember me back when you reported the drain grate to the city."

"Yes, yes, you're the L.A. cop that came here. I read all about this and saw it on national TV. Kinda made my place famous here in Pasadena."

"What do you do here?"

"We sell wallpaper and specialty paint for the more upscale homes in the area. I also have an eight-unit apartment upstairs. I was home with my mother during entire timeframe that this happened."

"I'm sure, John. I have a photograph here. This is it. Maybe you seen this guy around here the night this all took place."

"No, I haven't seen him in over two years. That's Mark Johnson. Asshole stole my air conditioner when he moved out."

"Wait a minute. You know him?"

"Sure, a wonderful tenant for about four months. Stayed in his room all the time. Said he was having problems with his Mexican girlfriend, so he needed a place to hang. He was real proud of his daughter; showed us pictures of her that he put up in his apartment. Was real honest, until he left with my air."

"Did he say anything specific that was not in the norm of things?"

"Well, no, at the end, he said it didn't work out with his girl in Mexico. He telephoned her frequently. Said that he had to return to Oregon. Yes, it was strange, said that he had to go knock on the door, no more out to the edge of forever, into the never, had no place else to go. I always wondered what that meant."

"I can tell you what it meant if you keep this all to yourself."

"I don't want to talk about this stuff if he's connected to this acid thing."

"Mr. Bebe, he went to Oregon to turn himself in for sodomy of his daughter. He was hiding here. He probably had a falling out with his woman in Mexico. He couldn't manage down there, alone, and certainly could not take a job here, or he'd get arrested. He had no option."

"I'm not announcing that. Oh, that would kill my business and my mother. She works here most the time. She liked Mark until he left. I had just bought that air conditioner, too."

"He probably needed some quick cash. Anything else you can remember?"

"Yes, said that he was working on a book and that he found a publisher. He was always typing, especially very late into the morning."

"This guy, a writer, ha. John. I'll have to check around. Please get the rental records, while I check around outside. I'll just follow up, as if it were the air conditioner thing. Save the grief and keep it quiet."

"That would be perfect, huh. I'm glad he took the thing now. The only other person I know he associated with is old man Susuki at the liquor store, two doors down."

"Okay, Mr. Bebe, I'll be in and out. Next time someone steals something, report it. We would have had a database on Johnson months ago if you had filed a report."

"Well, I'll have you know I did. They said this was a civil matter, and I'd have to take it upon myself in small claims."

"Yeah, things aren't what they used to be. I'll go talk to Susuki, now, if you'd get the rental agreement out for Johnson."

Worthy took the short stroll down to Susuki's liquor store.

"Mr. Susuki?"

"Yea, that's me."

"Detective Worthy, LAPD. John Bebe told me that you had occasional contact with Mark Johnson. Recognize him?"

"Yeah, kid came in once in awhile, liked Jim Beam. He almost got me hooked on it."

"Drank excessively?"

"Oh no, maybe a fifth once a week."

"What can you tell me about him?"

"Well, he hated John. Of course most of us round here don't care much for him, either."

"What was his dislike for John?"

"Said he was a fag. Always snooping around and getting too close. Acted like he had no balls. Into never-never land, talk like that. Said he would give him a

wake up. One of the few guys around here that'd make me laugh. He cut me a deal on an air conditioner. Ten bottles of beam. Couldn't beat that."

"I take it you and John don't talk much."

"Actually, I think he *is* a fruitcake. He never comes down here."

"The air conditioner came from John's place."

"Oh, hmmm, I suppose you need that then."

"Let's forget it. What else can you tell me about Johnson?"

"He said he was trying to start a new cleaning service and wanted to know if I needed any cleaning. I said the two bathrooms were real shitty, and if he could do something with them then I'd pay him."

"Did he?"

"Oh, he was real good about that. The fixtures all came out new looking. I thought I was going to have to replace them beforehand. I did eventually, though, because it didn't last. The plumber said that when you use acid, it etches the glaze opening up the porcelain to be stained. But I had to replace the stuff anyway, so no biggy."

"You said he used acid to clean the bathroom?"

"On the toilets. They were old and rusty, real bad. He got them looking so good, even I'd take one in there. But, yeah, I ordered the acid for him through National."

"And when was all this?"

"Oh boy, probably two years or so back."

"Thank you, Mr. Susuki."

"What about the air conditioner?"

"Don't tell John!"

"Then what the hell was this about?"

"The air."

Worthy now realized that Mark had been through much more difficult times than he'd let on. These events with Bebe had taken place two years before, revealing that this predator was struggling just to make ends meet concerning his social life. The struggle was evolving negatively into someone other than the outward put-on image. The image eventually fell to the historic forceful reptile.

Mark had money, but what he did not have was a connection with the world that brought him his riches. This was Mark's deepest annoyance and fear, since he could not even buy his way in. His solution was to completely steal his way totally out. Mark came back two years later to steal a life and dump her down the drain, right in front of those who refused to see who he really was. Mark accepted Bebe. Bebe had a mindset. Bebe was gay, Mark was not. Bebe saw Bebe

in Mark. Mark wanted Bebe to see Mark, but the majority was blind to this character. The Predator was difficult to recognize, except by oneself, only when he read about himself, right now. Awareness was unfolding in the minds of many. The help needed then is yours and easily found.

Worthy followed up with John. "Here's the rental agreement Mark signed."

"Strange, he used his correct name and social security number, even his address in Eugene."

"Maybe he wanted to be caught, but I never run a credit check when a person had the money he did. Plus he was real cool with me."

"He had money?"

"Hell yes, over sixty thousand dollars. Said he sold his house in Mexico. He was always so sad about that."

"Didn't you ever suspect him of something, having all that money on him?"

"That's the way things get done in Mexico. I've had property there. Few people write checks, especially in Baja."

"He confided all this in you?"

"In the beginning, but then he withdrew. Banged on that old typewriter for hours."

"John, I give you my word, this is crucial to the investigation. Did you make any kind of advances on Mark?"

"Well…"

"That's good enough, Mr. Bebe. I'd like you to write down everything you recall about this man. Have it ready for me next week. I'll be seeing you."

Worthy had it clear in his head that he could not catch Mark from forensic evidence now. Mark had only wanted to place fear in Bebe for the acid dumping. The predator made the non-prey aware he was susceptible as desirable prey. He couldn't punish John any other way, without getting busted. Worthy now knew he had to get into the mind of this rapist. The rapist was suffering. Worthy took the suffering trail back to his daughter in Oregon. He arranged for a legal interview in the early evening with Mark's eleven-year-old daughter, Heather, at the Child Advocacy Center.

"Hi, Heather, what do you have there?"

"It's a stone my dad gave to me in the desert."

"Oh? Where in the desert? Can you remember?"

"There are two places. One is the *Oh wah hee*, and the other is Juniper."

"I know that place. It's called the Owhyee River Canyon."

"That's what I said."

"What did you guys do there?"

"My daddy took me there and showed me how beautiful it was. He said look at all that big and beautiful country. But he said I was bigger inside and that nothing was more beautiful than what's in me."

"Is that where you got the stone?"

"No. That was on Juniper. We picked flowers there. That is where he showed me what was in me, that beautiful place he talked about. A rattlesnake came out of the pretty blue flowers. My daddy threw this stone and hit it so hard in the head it went away. My dad saved me."

"So your dad put the hole in it and made a necklace for you?"

"No, after he went away, I asked my grandpa to do it. It's a little big and too heavy to wear for a necklace, but I carry it around with me everywhere. It goes everywhere I go. I can't seem to get rid of it. I talk on the phone with it and other things that are easy when I can change hands you know. But it's really hard to take a shower with it. When I take a shower, it really gets in the way. I thought it would wear out or get smaller, but it stayed the same, after all I've done with it. Someday, I want to show it to my daddy to remind him of the snake. But only Jesus the biggest rock of all can save my dad. He doesn't think so though."

"Why doesn't he think so?"

"Because when we were in bed one night, he was sorry for what he did to me and said that Jesus would never come in his heart again. He told me Jesus said something about a millstone and being better if he were never born for offending a little one of his. He cried and said he was sorry. After that night, he was gone. No, the police took me first, after I told my mom that Jesus could never come in daddy's heart, then he went away after some more time. They said he went to Mexico, but they weren't sure."

"Would you like to see your daddy again, Heather?"

"I want to go to Mexico. I want to be with my dad."

"Detective Worthy, you have an urgent call from Pasadena," the secretary said.

"Okay, Heather, I'll talk to you again. Bye bye."

"Worthy speaking."

"Shari here, Bill. I have an urgent message from the FBI. Another site came up this morning, in De Moines, Iowa. It's more than taunting. The site is in the FBI's office back parking lot. They have no surveillance, nothing. He pulled it off again, no witnesses, nothing. He didn't use a drain, half the agencies cars have melted tires. It's a fifty-gallon pool located at the parking lot entrance. He didn't stay long. The body is in the lot, or what's left of it. They say he dumped a fair

quantity of the acid first, then pushed a conscious but gagged and tied female approximately twenty-five years in. She struggled to the near corner, as if she were trying to assault him; then she died of shock. The report goes on to say it looks as though he took more acid to her by a hosing method. The acid then gravity-flowed to the low point in the lot, which is the entrance."

"Oh Jesus, no!"

"There's more. The forensics technician did not go home last night, nor did she report for work this morning. Her car is still in the lot parked nearby. They believe it's her, Bill."

"I'm talking to Johnson's kid right now. You'd never believe it if you were a jury member. Fax it all here to Eugene. I'm catching the next flight to De Moines."

"On it's way now. They ruled Johnson out. He made a call to his residence, checking his answering machine from his cellular in Reno, Nevada. The call was made at approximately the same time of the incident. They just tracked him down at six p.m. Mountain Time a few moments ago. They're observing him in Reno as we speak. He's been in the same place all night through this afternoon. This is exactly the same place from where he made the call. They sent in an undercover agent asking for directions. Johnson said he was sick and could not drive. He was concerned about leaving his truck there. It can't be him, Bill. He was there all night."

"If he was there all night. He could have driven from De Moines, starting at nine, and got there this afternoon in Reno. That's twenty-one hours. He could have done that easily."

"They don't see it that way. Bill, he used his phone at nine last night. No links, no forwarding, direct from his current position."

"God, I'd hope to believe that from his kid, but I know it's him. I haven't told the FBI yet, Shari, but he used to live at 2536 E. Colorado. He lived in the fucking apartment that Bebe owns, right smack in front of the first acid dumping. John made an advance on him. He used his real name. Bebe didn't check him out. When Johnson left, he wanted to give a signal to the cops he'd hid there before turning himself in up in Eugene by stealing Bebe's air conditioner. Pasadena refused Bebe's report about the air conditioner. He then comes back years later and dumps acid right on Bebe's front door. I can imagine all of this has made Johnson feel invincible. He's coming right at us to get attention. It seems like he's crying or wanting someone, anyone at all, to see his insides. But all he gets is zero notice. So he tries harder to be noticed. This is as surreal as it gets, but it's the truth."

"This is the most intense and bizarre individual I've ever heard of. That's enough for me. He's highly motivated."

Shari's exaggerated remarks of being the most intense and bizarre individual were knowingly invented and far from the truth. This was the shame and denial from human pride and arrogance. Mark was living out who he had decided to become. That was true. But he was not rare and he was not bizarre, when compared to human imagination. Actually, Mark had started out quite typical. Do not be misled or try to convince yourself that humans are of a level or position of wishful normal behavioral thinking on your part. Rather, stop and think how far the human mind can go in either direction, and I will show you how short you came up. There is no end, no limit; it goes forever in the cycle of life. I will show you insanity. Show the world your sanity. Show it to yourself first.

"I think he has a Satanic fall back or surrender," Worthy replied to Shari's remarks. "Like he has given up, he is going to do whatever comes to mind if it feeds him and defies us. He wants most of all for us to know his *message* more than he wants us to know it's him doing it. Like it's us that caused his personality. That's why there's some caution in his actions; he doesn't want to be caught, just yet. He needs some time or some attention to prove himself. Heather said he mentioned he was unforgiven and unforgivable. She has held on to a very graphic image of him. He's going after who and what has hurt him in every element of his imagination."

"Aren't you going to tell the Feds?"

"I don't legally have to. Believe me, Shari, Mark J. has strategically and ingeniously sidestepped the FBI. They can't even be convinced now. I'm going to New York to snoop around the site there. When all the smoke clears in De Moines, I'll check it out. Don't worry about the fax for now. I don't think there's a relevant thing in it except his message about the forensics. It's not the way to catch him, and he's being more than clear about it. He wants everyone to know him personally. This is at the heart of a rapist's message, why he rapes. He's trying to show us it's his disease for an excuse to go the distance. We have ignored him because of our own fear and denial. The Tech is a simple message, but the core of it is deep in there."

"Well, I do agree with you. He certainly would not have randomly dumped in Pasadena. That definitely is a message."

"I'll call you from New York."

Sad but true, not one of these government employed lawmen connected Agent Ryan's prior work place in De Moines or his comment to Mark about

forensic evidence to his direct attack on the forensic lab technician. If they had known of his motivation of rewards for deeding the dark spirit or reptilian beginning, they'd know he'd believe his reward would be of the highest order to date. And Mark did believe. Agents Harold Ryan and Morgan Styles had both been killed in the Tijuana prison. Harold gave away that they were agents for the FBI, by talking about the incident in De Moines. The official report was that they had escaped. Mark was tearing them up and he knew it. He knew he eventually would fall but, in the meantime, he was educating those who refused to listen. People like Worthy learned too late, but had he and others wanted to know beforehand, they could have helped Mark long ago. That was the beauty of total awareness of the ugly. Partial awareness of our enemy is obviously dangerous to us. For Mark, it was also too late. Now he knew it to be the Bright Star's guidance and received worship. He now had rank in both worlds.

Worthy visited his buddy in New York City.

Chapter 20

No Change

❧

"Detective Allen?"

"Yes, who's asking?"

"I'm not sure how you feel about me being here. I'm Bill Worthy, LAPD."

"Oh Jesus, didn't you make me famous. All three major net works, virtually every small town down to the hick radio station out there in Oregon. Ahh, what the hell? Feds screwed up too. But this thing out in fucking De Moines, Christ, this guy is the walking flesh of Satan. Lake of fire, mother of God."

"Pardon me?"

"What?"

"You said lake of fire."

"Yeah, like in the Book of Revelations. All whose names that are not found written in the book of life shall be cast into the lake of fire. The fucking message he put in the parking lot with the hose and the acid. *Capice*, Bill?"

"I didn't get that report."

"You are a buck short and a day late, ain't you! What the hell are you doing here?"

"I wanted to check around the neighborhood where he dumped."

"Fuck it, five hundred block and Thirty-Fourth. Go on. Three streets down and right on Thirty-Fourth, got it. Ya!"

Worthy walked the area, not finding any significance to the dumpsite, no living arrangements, only a business sector. He stopped in a convenience store on Thirty-Sixth. A rustic man in his late sixties sat on a stool behind the counter of the modest older store.

"Watch out for that door, it'll slap you right on the cheeks, soon as you let go."

"Thanks for the warning."

"You're a new face. Rare around here to see a new face. Where do you work at?"

"Los Angeles Police Department."

"Oh yeah? What did he do now?"

"Who, Sir?"

"My kid, damn fool been in and out of Chino more time than I got years."

"Well, I don't think he's a problem. I was wondering if I could ask you to ID someone. Here's a photo."

"Well if it helps my kid, give it here. Sure do! I know the kid."

"How can you be so sure?"

"Came in here looking for Black Label. He had to have black. I had it, but I never sold a bottle of it before. So I asked what was so damn special about black label. Most drink the white label or Jack."

"He asked for whiskey, Black Label Jim Beam?"

"He said it was better than Jack. I told him his ass hurt. Then he buys some coke and ice. Makes me a drink in a paper cup. Look here, I don't sell the white no more. He pointed out it's charcoal filtered and aged. I damn near had to go into rehab this last month. I been drinking my own stock."

"You're sure it's him?"

"Oh hell yes. He was here for damn near an hour talked all about the publishers around here rejecting his book. But that it was all going down the drain as we spoke. Funny guy. Hell, I'd've published it. Some blue spot shit about everyone fucking all the time and all at once but forever. I damn near busted my hernia."

"When was this?"

"Oh, about six or seven months ago. Is he missing or something? Hate to see if that young man was in any kind of trouble."

"Did he say anything out of the norm, like he was involved in any type of crime?"

"God, everything he said was out of the norm, but you know I didn't relate it then. I thought he was just talking about our conversation being criminal."

"I don't follow you."

"He said when the cop comes asking, he will be the one to 'drink to blackness.' I thought he was telling me to give the cop a bottle of this stuff to get off the hook for drinking at work. But something about that guy tells me you're the cop."

"I hope I am."

Worthy sat down with the missing persons department of the NY police. Obtaining permission to look at all the files, he entered city hall and requested a search from the records clerk.

"I have reason to believe that the person killed and dumped in the acid on Thirty-Fourth street was in the publishing business. I need a missing persons search for that date."

"That's not a problem, Mr. Worthy. We do have a Cindy R. Smith, who worked at Del Kay Publishers. She didn't show up for work the following day and remains on the missing roster. She was an approval editor for new authors."

"He rapes and kills anyone who rejects him or his belief. What the Hell does he believe in?"

The records clerk replied, "Sounds like the case is close to being solved, if you're right."

"I'm right, but it's only circumstantial evidence, so far. I'll give you all I got in a couple days. Thank you."

"I'll have to report this and especially if you withhold on us."

"I won't. I just have to be sure. He's stick-free Teflon."

This particular killing in New York had brought a sudden strange light to Worthy's prior line of pursuit and general awareness of the *inferma* Mark tangoed with. He now realized this low of low criminal was capable of committing any crime and probably has succeeded at many offenses from childhood. Mark Johnson was not solely a child molester or sex offender. He was living free will, due to a simple but difficult lonely choice. For one mental moment but in thousands of hours of enforcement experience, Worthy had to fundamentally wonder how a man could drift this far from what seemed normal to him. Worthy had to take the how it would be for him to molest his own child, then any child or woman. What would it take for him to molest his child? The first instant moment of those thousand hours of searching was that it would take complete rejection. Worthy realized he would have to have lost who he was to betray his own child, then realized it would not be a betrayal to his seed, only because he would be dislocated from it all, without the average clear light. The *inferma*, the sickness, he realized, would be truly accompanied by evil, further twisting the light of one's once stable mind. Once stable? Had Johnson once been stable, sane? This gave warning and question to all men, just how fragile this immune system was. For the male, it was not so well defended for many. He thought in the next moment, maybe for all men. In the inmate population, many are ill, but in the general population the hidden lingering in us all is that many more are, in fact,

suffering the disease that destroys both the germ and the infected. What normal man had reason to defend against a Goddess' advances for sex? Worthy thought of himself, the line between obeying what your master wants was easy to cross when these were also what you wanted. You wanted it from within you, unlike anything else you wanted. It was your primary reason for living. You wanted her. What would you do to have her? Was it possible you would become sick?

Worthy realized he only contemplated this for his own self-fears, since he concerned himself with nothing of Mark Johnson. In every past investigation, all Detective Worthy desired was just to do his job and arrest lawbreakers. Not in this case, however, and he now realized that he always had this wanton curiosity, while investigating past sex offenders. Johnson had brought Worthy the aware-ness of this madness. He shook it off and snapped out of the moment that was frightening to sanity. Like all males, he ran from the undesirable known danger by changing thought to anything, absolutely anything else. He did not want to enter that door. He did not want to encounter it and, most of all, he could not face it. So it was the same with us all, even to those who did cross that line.

Worthy returned to Eugene, Oregon, to talk with Heather's Mother, Shea. The conversations with all of Worthy's past victims' mothers had been routine to him. Now, this new light, and opened door clearly marked "dangerous" had this detective in a different universe. To converse with Shea now would be partially living the rapist's trail. He desperately tried to keep the conversation to facts that would lead to Johnson's arrest and away from who Mark was.

"Hi, Shea, thank you for having me."

"Anytime. So he's off the hook. Everything for nothing, huh?"

"I'm here to ask you some questions that could bring all of this together."

"I've seen in the news that his business is worth hundreds of thousands of dollars, due to the FBI ruling him out. You guys did nothing but make him famous. I lost my kid. I have no money, no job, a hysterectomy. What else could a twenty-eight-year-old want?"

"Shea, do you remember Mark ever talking about Seattle or any of the cities involved in this acid rape cases?"

"He did talk about the University of Washington up in Seattle a lot. He tried to bullshit me that he played football for the Huskies. I found out from his dad that he didn't. When I confronted him about it, he was very angry. He was pretty upset with his dad for saying so. But he blamed his stepmother, said she broke his elbow, a total fracture. I checked that out and she did. He lost over fifty percent of the strength in his left arm and was rejected from the team. He did favor his

left arm considerably. He would get mad when the team lost, but would party like an animal when they won. He never missed a game."

"How about Las Vegas?"

"That's where he married Joanne. But they split up within a couple of months. Joanne was bisexual. She slept with a girl named Camille. He could not deal with that. He was the one who filed the divorce, claiming her abusive. She later came up with a bunch of false shit about him in retaliation."

"How do you know it was false?"

"Joanne is a chronic liar and has some serious problems that I caught her in. She would do anything sexual. I know that she went down on him in front of other girls, to try and lure a possible lesbian pervert. She did oral sex to him several times, always in the sight of one single female, usually an Asian girl."

Worthy's true curiosity began to probe his fears, and override his male shallows. "Why an Asian girl?"

"She liked them, and they wouldn't freak out or turn them in. But it was more his decision. He has a rejection syndrome. He feels rejected from white women, so he seeks out who he thinks will not reject him."

"How do you know this?"

"One of the girls that saw them was a stripper where I danced. She told me. I asked Mark how he liked it. His answer was just a laugh, you know, like he was blessed to have a sex slave blowing him anytime, anywhere. I also know Mark, he feels like he's a social misfit, since women laugh at his sincere way of getting close. He can't get close by the mainstream male bullshit. So they think he's phony and pan him hard for being fake. But I know Mark; he does mean what he says and it hurts him to be called a liar. It hurts him to the point of acting on this pain in anger or frustration. Also, I know Joanne and her ways; she's like Mark. They're similar, so they attracted each other, but their similarities also showed the weakness they have to maintain a relationship. She was the one who decided what's what and when. He couldn't deal with that. He scrapped her. Then the molesting began on Heather."

"I didn't see any of this in the police reports."

"I know. I thought it would be too much."

"There's a record of this?"

"Yes, the FBI uncovered it recently. He was identified by an Asian girl for masturbating in front of her. She had no witnesses, and he denied it, so they had to release him.

"These are classic signs of a person looking for attention, but I believe he has a different motive. I believe Mark isn't all that sick. I believe he believes in something that drives him to absolute extremes, which is making him sick."

"He was very extreme when it came to being serious. If the subject touched his cleaning business, this man made it a life or death science. He had a lot of seriousness in him, like no man I've ever witnessed. But he could make you laugh over the simple things."

"Like how?"

"Remember when Dairy Queen advertised their fudge and cakes?"

"I do."

"Well, we would pull up to the drive through. The car loaded, Jeremy, Paula, kids, and he'd give the order so cool yet radical. He'd yap out, 'four fuckin cakes' on the speaker and they'd yap back 'four fuckin dollars.' We'd die laughing with him. He was not afraid of anything. Every day was like that, the reason why I went with him. Then it got bad, like the last time I talked to him. He'd use the truth to fuck people up."

"Like how? What did you talk about the last time?"

"He told me that of all the times I did oral sex to him, some of his sperm was still in me somewhere. He said it so accurately, too. I became very ill because of the fact I related it to him being a child molester and that I swallowed him."

"I ahh, I thank you for your time, Shea. I know this seems like follow-up and that he's clear of the law, now, but if I can get your cooperation I believe we can get him."

"What do you want?"

"Write everything down that he ever did that you know was illegal and anything that could connect him to any of these killings. I'll be back in a week. Do we have a deal?"

"I have all the time in the world to do that."

"Not hearsay, now. I want things that could put him at the places of these crimes. Like the Seattle site and his desire for the football program."

"Okay."

Mark was under FBI observation from Reno through the Oregon border, fifteen miles into the desert. The open stretch of Highway 395 provided no cover for the agents. He was on his way home and no longer a suspect. They let him roll. Mark had been conservative in his use of the acid. Three barrels remained, but his desire to rape and taunt was now at the zenith and he'd wished he had fared better in his victims. His human male sex drive was never satisfied. The thought of only having six remaining victims' worth of acid imposed

restrictions on his future methods. Now, with the attention focused elsewhere but his truck containing forensic evidence, he needed a new plan. He quickly discarded the empty barrel in the ravine with the others and collected one new barrel to immediately return to Mexico for safekeeping. He would take Highway 395 right back into Nevada, down through Las Vegas, and over to the border in Tijuana. The Feds had absolutely no idea of his whereabouts and, for the most part, didn't care. He called Sarah on his way from Lakeview, Oregon, where the Feds terminated their watchful eye on him.

"Ultra, Sarah speaking."

"Hi, Sarah, it's Mark."

"How are you?"

"I'm not feeling well, girl. I'll see you in a few days."

"I want you to know that I have every confidence in you, now."

"What does that mean?"

"You're off the hook, with everyone and me. The FBI ruled you out yesterday as an impossibility. The acid rapist struck in De Moines, while you were nearly a thousand miles away when it happened. We're rich! Ultra is a big name in trucking now. You can't believe the calls I've been getting! Contracts, contracts, and more contracts!"

"I told you so, Sarah."

"You sure did."

"Sarah, I ran an advertisement here in Reno. I'm selling the business for half a million. Twenty-five thousand is yours upon sale and you keep your job as head secretary. How's that?"

"Oh, Lord Jesus, this is the day the Lord hath made."

"Okay, Sarah, accept the highest offer in the next four days. I'll be back in four to six days. This flu bug has me really down."

"Take care of yourself, gotta love you!"

Mark could not resist his addiction and made one more stop in Las Vegas. The five hundred dollars he paid for the top-line call girl went back into his pocket, after her immediate severe beating upon entering the sleeper. He drove her to Los Angeles, gagged and bound, stopping frequently to sodomize and manhandle her nearly to death. He searched LA for a dumping site.

"This looks good, Baby. Mateo Street, a nice dark slum and a far cry from the whoredom lights of Vegas, huh Honey? Well, looks like all the spooks are off the street. Let'ss have some conversation, but if you scream, I cut you."

Mark ripped the duct tape from her mouth. The young twenty-one-year-old Aphrodite had been around, but she maintained herself well.

"Look, I know that you don't need money. I'll do exactly what you want. I don't care what it is."

"Do you know who I am?"

"Yes, you're the acid rapist."

"My pictures weren't released. The investigation was kept secret fairly well. I mean people shouldn't know so much about me. I never gave the press a chance to see me. What makes you so sure?"

"The fucking weird bathtub. That fucked up glass cover."

"Yes, that cover used to be very clear. I had such a catbird seat. The acid kinda fogged up the glass. But the view of three Vegas whores, thrashing wildly about in there one at a time, damn that was satisfying. Seeing the first one getting all ate up was enough, but you should've seen the look on the faces of the two that were waiting. When I had to decide which one was next, they wanted to hug, but of course could only rub like lesbians do, you know, being tied together buck naked and all. That was a night. I had to beat ass one at a time. These girls of passion just kept pulling me over. I told 'em I was going to Mexico for the night. One at a time they got in. Vegas is better than Mexico. You know that, don'tcha?"

"One of those girls was my best friend."

"From the looks of you, I'm sure I saved her for last, the tall beauty, tattoo of a peacock on her left shoulder?"

"Yes. Why? Why?"

"Well I saved her for last, because I wanted to screw her while the other lesbian was going down. Came so hard in that moment, think it was an all-time best. I had to use a full two barrels of acid that lengthy night. Didn't think it was going to work out, but by the time the sun came up, they were down the strip. Real costly. Did you mean why I saved her for last or why do I do this?"

"There isn't anything in you. I don't need a reason. I might be a whore, but you know I gave what you wanted. That means you're nothing."

"Wrong."

"I can't see it as being anything."

"The stipulation of money for it."

"You think it's free?"

"Yes, and it will be free someday, always, and anytime. You should have gotten a real job. There's a huge hidden secret in this world. You know it, I know it, and so do the best of men. Males are lesser than females; you should have had compassion on their evolutionary submission. How can you blame someone from birth for being inferior by making him pay for his inherited shortcoming?

Do you kick a cripple in a wheelchair and make him pay for not being able to make it over the street side curb? No, you give him a fucking driveway."

"We're to just give our love away?"

"The best thing you could have done. You're only a whore, because you take the handicap's money. Now me, being the inferior male, my body is stronger, but your mind is much more than mine, so I need to ask you the question."

"You're seriously mental. Life isn't what you've made it. You have no right to take it."

"I'd have no right to take it if you and I were going to the blue places, but where you're going, it's more than a right, because you're going to hell. It's the ultimate payment."

"You'll definitely pay all right, pig. You know that much for certain."

"I want to know, you knew all your life you were above men, you kept it inside you like all women do. How does it feel right now for taking advantage of men and making your choices as to who gets it and who doesn't, when one of the lesser apes like me is about to kill you for that? How does it feel right now that I am making the choices?"

"You're right about women being above men, and real men know and respect this. That's why they kill fucking rapists in prison. Where you are going?"

"You can't answer the reality I asked you. Cat got your tongue? The real truth now. Long ago, women, protective selfish women, labeled rape as a male-dominant control thing. So that is exactly how you women get away without putting out. Men don't rape for control, Honey, they just want a little pussy. You bitches started this male control scapegoat so you wouldn't have to share with the lesser male. You now control him by putting his ass behind bars for what has been rightfully his since the beginning, since we were apes. We used to take that pussy like it was community property. But we got civilized and, you, in fact, are the ones who gained control of men's basic instincts and fundamental needs. Hence: rape was born. Then again, men can get some pussy if they got money, the better the pussy, the more money. Look at the fine bitches driving Mercedes Benzes. Husbands are pros making the big bucks. This is the whole reason why I picked you up. You know, I picked a whore so I could and would rape. Hell knows, a church bitch would have given it to me. But I know you wouldn't have. You choose your men, rejecting and putting those in prison who don't pay for it."

"God fuck you, you can twist, pollute, and mangle. The truth is you are—"

"What, primitive? Not good enough for you? Have to pay a high price for your holiness? You can label me ugly, but check this out. How do you feel when

a dude asks how much it costs to come in your mouth? Does your inventory and pricing make you feel above it all?"

"Yes, you twisted, self-righteous motherfucker, it does!"

"Exactly what I do, too. Exactly. Proved another theory. And I worked my way above you. As in Earth so shall it be in Heaven, but Hell awaits you, and there I shall be your Captain. As in this Earth, so shall I dominate you in the Inferno. Bye for now, bitch. Die, flesh."

Two days later, Mark arrived in La Paz, driving his rig up the long rickety driveway. Maria greeted him.

"You bring your truck!"

"Yeah, my little senorita, we can make a business here in Mexico, driving. I'll park it down in the hole out back so no one knows what we're up to."

"I love you so much, now we can drive all over Mexico and make money too!"

"That's the idea, Hon, just you and me. I can stay tonight but you must drive me to Tijuana starting in the morning, so I can finish business in America. I'll be back a week after that for good with mucho dinero. I sold the business. We're going to be okay forever, Baby."

"Come inside your home."

Maria drove Mark to Tijuana in the Mustang, taking two days. There, he walked through the border unscathed as the gringos are usually not ID'd. From there, he hitched a ride from a local truck stop to Eugene. He greeted Sarah in his office.

"Hi, Sarah, how is it?"

"We have four offers for the sale. One company has upped the bid to six hundred thousand."

"My God, did you do as I asked?"

"Got a cashier's check right here for three hundred thousand from a Mr. Darrel Dimes and the contingency papers for you to sign. The other three hundred is deliverable on transfer."

"God, is my God good! Any cops been around here?"

"None, but the acid rapist struck again in LA, a real big mess. He left the body like in De Moines, only tied to a wooden power pole. Hosed her alive with it and left a message about some Palomino. They think he's trying to conserve the acid, as he is running out."

Mark drifted into himself. "Wanted to be able to see what he was taking."

"Say what?"

Mark snapped out of his place of self-focus. "So they didn't get any evidence, then?"

"Are you kidding? The cop that touched her got burned. She was covered in it and about ten gallons was on the street. You know it was crazy for me to doubt you, ha ha, to think you might have been this freak. They even say you're clear, you being in Lakeview all this time. Where's your truck?"

"I couldn't drive, man. I was sick. I had to leave it in Lakeview."

"Well, Wayne is off tomorrow. Would you like him to pick it up? He could go with Gary on his run?"

"Good idea; that'll work. Let's get this sale going. Call Wells Fargo and have them order the cash for pick up tomorrow. I'll take the check in."

"You want cash?"

Mark ups his offer to Sarah. "You want your thirty thousand?"

"Oh, another raise, please let's do."

Detective Worthy was sticking around Eugene. He spoke with Rainey about the incident with Jerica and the hokie cow story in eastern Oregon. But Worthy took it as seriously as Mark did and sent the heifer's hoof to Paul Harris for testing. The analysis found traces of the incredibly potent Nitric acid. Worthy now obtained Governor-approved immunity for anyone with knowledge that could lead to the arrest of the acid rapist. His first stop was Jeremy and Paula.

"Jeremy, I'm not here to waste a moment of time. If you come totally clean with me, you probably will get a reward. You won't lose Jerica. I've spoke to Rainey. I know you're protecting him. In the long run, you'll be exposed, and America will look at you as Satan's advocate."

Jeremy now let out what he had truly wanted to do years before. "He is the advocate. He is the persuasion. I couldn't say no to him!"

"I know that. I've checked him out. That's what should make you want to punish with a vengeance."

"I thought he was in the clear."

"Come on, Jeremy, how do you think he got cleared."

"By clearing it himself."

"I need you, your kid, the others he's going after right now. For Christ's sake he struck again in L.A."

"I know. He was part of a movie crew. They filmed *Hellraiser Five*, there, on Mateo Street where the girl was found. It was an abandoned police station. I saw it in the news. He worked for a guy named Palomino. Mark brought a fifty-gallon

barrel of the acid here to my home. Cleaned the bathroom with some of it. He left the jar on the toilet, Jerica got into it. That's how it all got started."

"I need sworn statements from all three of you. Let's go. Where did he get the acid?"

"Said he bought it from old man Nick at Scott's."

"Jeremy, go to the police station now with your family. Meet with Rainey. I need to go see Nick. There isn't time to talk. The indictment will take three or four days."

"We're already there, Bill."

While Rainey delightedly took the statements, Worthy arrived at Scott's. Worthy knew full well he needed Nick's testimony, as a second witness, since Paula never actually saw Mark with the acid. Jeremy's testimony alone could not warrant an indictment. He had to do more than convince Nick about Mark. He called for two black and white squad cars to park in front of Nick's store, in sight, for intimidation's sake. Worthy entered the janitorial supply store flashing his badge.

"Nick Henderson?"

"Yes, Sir, officer."

"I'm not going to fuck around with you. We know you received an illegal shipment of nitric acid that you sold to Mark Johnson. If you care to deny it now, you're looking at ten years hard labor. If you confess, you're free, simple as that. I'm on my way out the door with you."

Nick needed reassurances before giving in. "How do I know I'm off?"

Worthy called the plainclothes cops in. "I'll tell you, straight up, here in front of these officers, you will never be charged if you just tell the goddamn truth."

"Well, I didn't know the stuff was nuclear. Hell, the guy who sold it to me gave me a bogus name and address. Some Arabic fella, saying it was a special new cleaning acid."

"How much of this does Johnson have?"

"I'd say five hundred fifty gallons, eleven barrels of it. He came in one day asking for some toilet bowl acid. He had a buddy with him by the name of Wayne. I only had the nuke in stock, so I told him to take one. A few days later, he came back, telling me to seal my lips about the shit and made me pay him to take the rest of it away. He reached into my cash register and took the rest of my cash on hand. He even bought a special portable forklift to move it. I did hear about the kid who got burned."

"Did you hear about the minimum of eleven other women who got smoked?"

"I don't understand."

"Johnson is the acid rapist, Henderson. Sign a sworn statement or go to prison."

"I have a pen right here."

"Who was the Wayne guy?"

"Some fella he worked with. I'm not sure."

"Let me use your phone."

"Here."

Worthy telephoned Sarah at Ultra trucking.

"Ultra Trucking, this is Sarah."

"Yeah, is Wayne in?"

"No, he's on his way to Lakeview."

"Okay, thanks, goodbye."

Worthy had what he always knew. Now he took command of it.

"Shit, you two officers, take Nick downtown and get a full sworn statement. Something about Lakeview, I—"

"He said he was taking the acid way out in the desert, officer." Nick said, recalling Mark's comments about where he was taking the acid.

"Shit yes, the cow. Heather said the snake came out of the blue flowers on Juniper. It's on Juniper! I need your phone again."

Worthy called Rainy.

"Detective Rainey speaking."

"Rainey, I know where Johnson's hid the acid. It's on a place called Juniper in Eastern Oregon on the way to Lakeview. We can call a National Guard unit up and do a search."

"I know the place, Juniper Mountain. It's stark desert. We'll find it within hours. I'm calling the Governor. It makes sense. Heather always mentioned the place. That's only ten miles east off Highway 395 from where we believe Brandy was killed. I mean from the cow hoof and by the report from the Canami transportation manager."

"Rainey?"

"What?"

"Call the chief of police first. Do this right!"

"Yeah, you're right."

"Also, call the state police and stop any Ultra truck en route to Lakeview, and put a guy by the name of Wayne on the radio. I need to speak with Wayne, got it?"

"Talk to you in minutes, Bill."

Worthy used police channels to contact Vince Palomino, the Key Grip movie producer in Los Angeles, where Mark had delighted in leaving this man's name engraved on the last kill.

"This is Vince, how can I help you?"

"Hi, Vince, Detective Worthy here of LAPD. Did you employ a Mark Johnson for a movie shoot?"

"Yeah, ha ha, guy was goofy. He came to my office three times begging me to put him to work on *Hellraiser*. I finally just said okay, because I knew he wouldn't fit in. He left in three days from being humiliated. Just as I suspected he would be. I don't even think he came back for his paycheck."

"What was the deal, I mean why was he humbled?"

"He thought we were all *Hellraiser* freaks in the beginning. He sure was. The rest of the crew belittled him for believing the storyline. It's kind of like he thought we actually were living the movie, a fantasy thing."

"Thanks, Mr. Palomino, good day."

Mark was now closing the sale of his business. He offered the buyers a fifty-thousand-dollar discount to pay five hundred, fifty thousand up front. A notary public was brought in to witness consummation, rather than wait for full closure. He knew he was running out of time. The caller identification at his office displayed Scott's phone number from Worthy's pretentious call for Wayne. Mark was beginning to shake for the first time since Shea had exposed him nearly six years earlier. For a moment, he thought it could be a scare tactic by Rainey to lead him to the acid. Wayne's name brought trembling to Mark, and he made an ingenious escape plan. He closed the deal with the new owner, Mr. Dimes.

"All right, Mr. Dimes. You're now the proud new owner of the tightest transportation company in Oregon. Ultra is yours."

"Well, we sure do appreciate your way of doing things, Mr. Johnson."

"I need to ask you a favor, Mr. Dimes. You have a run tomorrow to Ensenada, Mexico. I was wondering if I could go along. Daniel's driving. We'd like to leave tonight. Do you mind?"

"Well hell no, thata way I know the truck will get there!"

"Okay, you ready, Danny boy?"

"You don't waste time, do you, Mr. Johnson?"

"I want to tell you. You better do exactly like me, here, or the shit will go down the drain. Hustle every day, and it'll keep the pigs at bay."

Mark approached Sarah for the farewell embrace.

"Come here, Sarah, give me some hmmm. I've been waiting six months for that. Here's some small change, Sweetheart."

"Wow, you really did mean it. Thirty thousand dollars, yeah!"

"Always pay it. It keeps you free."

"C'mon, Dan, we got some driving to do."

Dan and Mark started heading south, at the same moment the Oregon National Guard were called out to the acid campground on Juniper Mountain. It was twenty hours to the border from Eugene, but Mark had a detour. Worthy was also hours from getting an indictment and had failed getting state permission to hold Mark for further questioning. Mark was crossing the Oregon-California line at four-thirty p.m., and Worthy had no clue. Mark made a devil's deal with Dan.

"Dan, I need you to do me a favor."

"Anything, man."

"You know I'm packing all this cash. I trust you. How'd you like ten grand right now?"

"Fucking don't even ask that. I'll do anything for that kind of money."

"Give me your driver's license. When the cops pull you over, tell them I got out in Eugene, that I wanted to buy traveler's checks. I told you to go on without me. But you got to be specific. Say I insisted you take me to the church on 6th Street, you got it?"

"No fucking problem, man. I don't care what kind of deal they cut me."

"Here, ten G's. Give me your license and let me out."

"Fuck, way the hell out here?"

"Believe me, Dan. I might not look it, but I can walk to goddamn Mexico in the chill of the worst winter's night for what's coming to my ass. I have the God who has never let me down. See you, brother, and thanks for putting up with my shit for the last eight months. Love you."

"Take care, Acid Rapist. Ten grand seals my lips. I don't care what fucked up shit you're into."

"Don't blow it on the crack, dude."

Mark walked five miles back to the Oregon border and bought a used Buick in Dan's name. He proceeded to Mexico via Nevada, then back through busy Southern California. He knew the Tijuana crossing was the busiest border in the world. It was his safest escape. Worthy sat down with Rainey at the Eugene station, accompanied by the assigned crime unit personnel.

"Look at all this, Worthy. You have witnesses from Pasadena to New York. Now, with Paula, Jeremy, and Nick, we have an indictment right there."

"We need the acid barrels. We need the physical evidence."

"That will get us a conviction, I agree, but we should go for the indictment now!"

"No. I'm not fucking this up, Rainey! We wait for the Guard. I know it's there. Then we have him."

The radio dispatcher informed Worthy that the Sheriff had located Wayne in Lakeview.

"Detective Worthy, we have Wayne Gradall on the radio. The Harney County Sheriff has him on Highway 395."

"All right, pipe it through to me."

"Hello, this is Wayne. You there?"

"Yes Wayne, I'm detective Worthy. I have a question for you. It's very important you tell me the truth about your boss, Mark Johnson. I promise you complete immunity and no harassment."

"Hell, he ain't even my boss, anymore. He sold the business today! Some guy named Dimes bought us out. Johnson sent us on a wild goose chase, saying his truck was in Lakeview. The owner of the Dairy Queen here said that there never was a truck down here. What the hell is he doing?"

"Jesus Christ! Is he still around?"

"I wouldn't be. He got over half a million in cash. He's probably jerking off in his truck halfway to Mexico."

"Fuck! FUCK! Wayne did you go with Mark about eight months ago to Scott's and get a barrel of acid?"

"From an old man named Nick. Yes, shit was so heavy I almost got a hernia."

"Give a written statement of everything you remember that day to the officer there and have him fax it to the Eugene Police, got it?"

"This is deputy Grange, I got it, out."

"Out."

Rainy was losing patience with Worthy.

"That should be enough, Bill. Look, it's dark up there on that mountain now. They won't find it until the morning. Present your evidence now!"

"No, but get every available unit out looking for him. Go to his house, work place, and look for his truck. The National Guard has lights. One more hour, Rainey. If they can't find it by then, it isn't there."

Rainey turned to his crew and barked out the orders to locate Johnson. "You heard him, send it all out."

"I didn't know how smart this guy was, Rainey. He may have beaten me, too. We need to find this bastard, now. The indictment doesn't mean squat if he's across the border. God, this guy is incredible; Mexican citizen by marriage!"

"He did beat me, didn't he?"

"I heard he wrote you a letter when he went to La Paz the first time five years back. At that time, he was wanted on the sodomy charges, taunting you. Why didn't the D.A. go hard on him considering his hardness?"

"We couldn't prove it was him. The letter only had the La Paz postmark on it for ID."

"What did he write?"

"Said that the reason for my failure as a "Dick" was that, when I was a traffic cop, I never looked at oncoming traffic, that I always looked at the car I was following. Gave me a full lecture on speed of the oncoming car, the facial expression of the driver, five pages of what was coming at me. Said one thing that got me was I never noticed the speed of oncoming traffic, because I was a speeder, myself. He went on to say if I had known similarities to that, I would have had a much fuller life."

"If it wasn't for young adult males, my job would be a piece of cake. The addition of this guy causes me to hear the retirement bell. Rainey, you like Mexico?"

"Let's go."

"Where else would he go?"

"Let me call Sarah at Ultra. What the hell."

"Go on."

Detective Rainey regressed to his historical methodology. He telephoned Sarah in deceit.

"Ultra, this is Sarah."

"Hi, Sarah. How do you like your new boss?"

"Oh, he's not at all like Mark, but he's going to work out. Who's this?"

"This is Mark's brother, Allen. Say, I've been trying to get him at home but there's not even an answering machine."

"Oh, he left for Ensenada five or six hours ago with Dan Madden, the tomato run. He didn't tell you he was moving there permanently?"

"Thank you, bye!"

"Shit, he's making his break for it now. He's in an Ultra truck with a Dan Madden to Mexico."

"Notify the California Highway Patrol. That's all we can do. Good job, Rainey. Now I know why he beat you the first time. He knows your tactics, but

I don't think young Mr. Johnson is getting out of California this time. Hell of a good job."

The secretary alerted Worthy of an incoming call.

"Detective Worthy, Captain Bacon from the guard unit on Juniper Mountain is on line 4."

"Put it on the speaker."

"Worthy, here."

"Sir, we found it, and it's been hell to pay. There was one container lying open on its side. One of my men is in serious condition. It spilled down his torso while he was attempting to recover it."

"Goddamn that Johnson son of a bitch. He booby trapped us! Be cautious in your entire search, Bacon. This perp is one badass, taunting, son of a bitch. How many barrels did you find?"

"Two full ones and seven empty, the empty ones were in a ravine. The full ones right where you said to look, in the blue wild flowers."

"Damn, he has the last barrel with him. Anything else, Captain Bacon?"

"There's a fresh carving in a Juniper tree right here where we found the full barrels. Care to hear what it says?"

"Yes, please."

"Says, 'Blue Spot to the born, Blue Spot for many close, the Bright Star has special harvest for few of those.'"

"That's his motivation. He's trying to earn a place. Too many go down for it."

"I'm sorry, Sir?"

"I'll explain later, Bacon. Take care of your man. Rainey, go for the indictment and include this message about a Blue Spot. Now it's on death row."

"Yes! We're famous."

Rainey's motivation was far weaker than Mark's. Worthy discovered exactly what was Mark's force. It would destroy Mark, only if Worthy could get that spoken word to him. The indictment took an hour. The standard international all points bulletin was put out.

The dispatcher updated the detectives. "The Redding City Police have Madden on Interstate Five, Detective Worthy. They're on line two."

"Shit, that means Johnson isn't with him. Wait a minute, don't put it through yet. Odds are this guy is covering for him. What do you know about this Ensenada run, Rainey?"

"I do know the schedule. That run is not supposed to leave Eugene until tomorrow. This guy, Madden, is an ex-con off parole. He's a doper. He would lie for anyone, money or not."

"Shit, this might be one of your days, Rainey. Put Madden through on the speaker."

"Hello."

"Dan Madden?"

"Yep."

"You were seen with Mark Johnson at the border. Where is he now?"

"He's at the church on 6th Street. Said he needed traveler's checks."

"Since when does Satan's church get wheels to the border and hand out traveler's checks?"

"That didn't make much sense to me either."

"Come on, Madden, you know what it's like inside. I'll bet if we search you, your income just ascended a tax bracket or three. Wanna go for it again?"

"Fuck, you are good. I let him out five miles south of the Oregon border for ten grand."

"Why did he have to give you the ten?"

"I can't chew gum right today. He wanted my driver's license. I gave it to him."

"Put the police back on."

"Officer Garner here, Worthy."

"Get a sworn statement from him. Put him back on the road but put a cop in the truck. Take his money as evidence. Don't follow him. Any acid on the truck?"

"Nothing, it's bare."

"Bye."

Worthy flaunted his experience to Rainey. "Johnson just picked the wrong company to testify. Rainey, go to the Oregon State Police. Have them open up every car dealer. Call every person who advertised a car in that area. I think you'll find Johnson is driving Madden's new ride. Time is of the essence, people, let's go. Get every agency on it!"

"You lied to Madden."

"I learned from you."

"How the hell do you know all this?"

"Like Johnson, he's no small-town boy. I grew up on the block too. Seattle's a bad motherfucker, Rainey, but try a day in LA. When a bad motherfucker is on the run, he uses his bad mother fucking brain. We got more fugitives than you have voters."

"He did grow up in Seattle."

"He did not grow up. He was manufactured."

An hour later, dispatch informed Worthy of the latest find. "You're right, Detective Worthy, Knott's Buick sold him a ninety five white Skylark, license KPX 568."

"There you go, now let's not blow this. Send it out sideband throughout California. Keep it off the radio. Considered armed and dangerous; use deadly force."

Four hours passed, leaving Rainey questioning whether Mark had led him off the path.

Mark was moving south on Nevada's Highway 395, just an extension of his Oregon Trail. Mark got spooked to re-enter California and abandoned the Buick. He boarded a Greyhound bus headed for San Diego. Mark always knew that taking costly safe steps was the logic of success. He was lucky, as 395 wound in and out of California. He saw the roadblocks, but they waved the bus on. He knew they would find the Buick in a short time, so he snuck off the bus, while it was taking on passengers in Sacramento. He found Ember's, a strip joint Shea had danced in. He decided to tempt his desire. One lucky dancer got rich, momentarily. She got a room in her name. He left her without a car but in the trunk with a broken neck. He kept the room for three sleepless days.

Dispatch now learned the Buick had been found and alerted Worthy.

"Detective Worthy, a Nevada trooper ran the plates on the Buick. He listed it as abandoned on Nevada 395 South, coming into California at Greystone."

"He still has at least one, maybe two, barrels of the acid and a missing truck. He wouldn't go for Vegas again."

"No, Rainey, he's using all he's got left. The last killing was in L.A. on Mateo Street. The truck is either in L.A. or Mexico. He's hoofing it now or is on public transport. Get all public transportation aware. Call direct to Greystone and find out if they have a bus station or taxi service, some means to get out. I'm on a plane to Tijuana. Stay here, Rainey. If you learned anything, put it to use."

"If he gets across, it's bye-bye, huh."

"Mexicans don't have the death penalty, and they won't allow extradition, unless we agree to a fifteen-year sentence. Combine that with a Mexican five-year citizenship, accompanied by a recent marriage and half a million in cash. You answer that for yourself."

"What are you going to do?"

"He's not getting across. I'm setting up a block. We have the indictment. We have the world's attention. Johnson is a sitting duck, but he will fight with all his know how, until I cuff him."

Mark knew driving down Interstate Five was the safest way out, right through the middle of LA. He just needed to wait. Anything over three-day stays in hotels during a manhunt warrants managers to report it to authorities, especially if everything is room service. The animal was getting weaker in his cage, wishing he had never met Angie, that he would have just settled down in La Paz. He could have stayed if it hadn't been for her extreme fits and cries of her father's abuse. The daily torment, here wretched life and libido made him think about Heather. If he could have only been stronger in his sin, but the sin was so low. He lay down, and regretted the day he had first seen Angie. He could have forgotten Heather and had his Mexico. Now he wished for Heather. How he could be a father, now, seeing what Angie's father had done? He stepped in the Lake of Fire with the Acid, and he could not turn back. Heather was gone. He had to live with his God now.

He telephoned the foster parents, as he was about to leave. He needed his Heather.

"Hello."

"Hi, is this Debbie?"

"Yes, who's calling?"

"This is Gale Stevens from the counselor's office at Day Elementary. May I ask how Heather is doing?"

"She's very well. Would you like to talk to her? I'll put her on."

"Hello!"

"Hi, Heather, that's an energetic hello."

"Yeah. I have lots of energy."

"Heather, is there anyone standing around there who can hear our conversation?"

"Yes, hey go away. He wants to talk to me alone."

"Is it okay now?"

"Sure, what do you want?"

"Heather."

"You sound like my daddy."

"Please don't say anything loud, Sweetheart. I called to tell you how much I love you and I'm so sorry. I wished I had been good, but something in me made me a bad daddy. If I had the chance to do it all again. I now know what to do right."

"Daddy, oh daddy, I can't believe it's you! I love you. Please come home. Come here and get me. I want to go to Mexico with you so bad. . ."

Mark had to interrupt. "I could come, Honey, but I'm really afraid the police will catch me. They will kill me now."

"I know. Mom told me you were in big trouble. But try and come. I hate my new dad and mom."

"Heather, I have a plan. I'll send a woman to your house. She'll bring you here to me. Her name is Angie. She's Mexican with dark skin, but don't be afraid of her. That's the only way we can do it."

"I will. I will do it!"

"Give me the address there."

"1144 Sequoia Court. When will she be here?"

"If you tell anyone, she'll never come. But if you keep it a secret, she'll be there in ten days in a red convertible Mustang. Don't run to her. Wait until she goes around the block, and then walk slowly to her and just get in. Okay?"

"I'll keep it a secret. I will daddy. I love you, I promise."

"If anyone asks you who you talked to on the phone say it was the wrong Heather. The counselor said he had the wrong number, understand?"

"Yes, Daddy, I remember how you teach me. I will be like you when I grow up. I have to go. Debbie's coming. I'm sorry you have the wrong number."

Now Mark had his fight back. He would live to use anyone to make his past correct. The search was toned back for Mark in California. They assumed he'd made the border. But Worthy stayed behind at the border with two other officers on eight-hour shifts. Worthy was certain Mark was still in California and that he would try and slip through at Tijuana.

Mark picked Friday at dusk. So did Worthy. Mark abandoned the car at the last exit and walked across. He pulled his jacket collar up and acted like he's with a group of Mexican nationals, laughing with them and replying with a gringo joke. They were returning from a temporary construction site and had to sign in with Mexican immigration. Mark followed them in to get his papers validated. From experience, he knew they didn't inspect. It was only for records of the individual.

Worthy had never seen Mark personally. Worthy thought he spotted Mark, as he was crossing but wasn't sure. He was wearing a hat and had grown a beard, looking only to himself, blending with other Mexicans in the crowd. But the outdoor backpack only made in Oregon convinced Worthy to draw his pistol, announcing himself.

"*Policia! Policia Extradiciones! Abajo Rapido!*"

The entire crossing became panic-stricken, seeing the gringo policeman holding up the forty-four magnum. Several nationals stormed Worthy, knocking

him to the ground. Mark casually but quickly walked on, not looking to his rear. The Federali's whistles began to screech, and Mark could hear Worthy screaming.

"Stop the rapist! Stop the man with the money in his backpack. He has hundreds of thousands of dollars in his Green backpack! *Dinero en la bolsa verde, mucho dinero en el gringo!*"

Mark felt on total display, as every face was focused on him. He saw the poverty in their eyes wanting to know how to dislodge the back pack. He tightened the strap around his chest. Two men charged him, tearing and ripping at the pack, and several thousand dollars flew into sight, causing a rape scene to ensue. The Federalis fired shots and dispersed the crowd. The money was recovered and Mark was rushed to detention. The same Federali officer from the prior crossing recognized Mark and had the room vacated for personal conversation.

"What is it about you? Now you bring so much money. I want some respect. I know you are a citizen. But this is by far out of my control. This much money means a crime has for sure been committed."

Mark had brought all of his documentation for just this moment.

"Here. it's all legal. I even declared it when I had my passport stamped, see? He stamped it. He didn't look. I sold my business in Oregon. All the papers are there in English and Spanish, notarized. I have done nothing illegal and will give you whatever respect needed."

"I will have a legal aid come in to check this. Why do the police constantly come for you?"

"They want the money. They want it to look like I am a rapist. Does a man with a Mexican wife and have this much money waste his time raping little girls? If you want respect, please show me some for my hard work to bring this money to Mexico for my wife, and I will show you the standard respect you speak of."

"I will get the lawyer first and immigration. Who is the policeman?"

"He's an LA cop. I've spoken to him on the phone before. He hates me because I knew something he did not."

"I'll be talking to him next."

"Come with me, Detective. Who are you?"

"I am Bill Worthy, LAPD."

"You know the last time he was here, the FBI was after him. Did you know they spend time in jail here?"

"I do."

"What makes you any better?"

"I have warrants. He's ours and you know it. I have it all right. . . ."

The papers Worthy was referring to had been ripped from him in the scuffle. "They must be out in the…fuck it, I'll call it in."

"Sit down in here, Mr. Worthy."

"There is no phone here."

"You talk to Johnson before on the telephone?"

"Yes, big fucking deal."

"Wait here. I must lock the door."

The border customs agent for Mexico reviewed Mark's paperwork and informed the authorities that everything was legal. It was not uncommon for so much cash to be hand-carried across the border, but it was common to find out where it came from and where it was going.

"Why did you bring this much cash with you?"

"I don't trust the Mexican banks."

The agents were amused with Mark. "Ha ha, he's an honest Gringo! None of us do either. We don't have money to put in the bank, though."

"If what I'm hearing is right, how much money is enough for an account right here?"

"Let's talk. Are you ever going back to America to make more dollars?"

"If you want I will."

"How about ten percent of everything every time?"

"I'd say that would be a blessing. *Si, muchas gracias*. I will give an extra ten thousand this time."

"Good good. You know we would have taken it all if the policeman from Los Angeles hadn't exposed you."

"I don't understand."

"He made it known. We can't make a taco out of a celebrity. You be careful the next time and come to us first, Gringo, or the others will feed you to the cockroaches. There is one problem left, though. You have to convince me you are not the rapist. I gave my word to the LA cop he'd get his chance with you. If you fail, we then keep all the money and hold you for extradition. The governor will decide on that. Give me the sixty thousand now, so no one knows this, and keep your mouth shut about it. This is the respect part, now you show me you're innocent. Okay, bring in the other Gringo."

Detective Worthy was escorted to the same table where Mark was sitting.

"Please have a seat across the table from Mr. Johnson."

"What the hell is this? He's U.S. material."

"Oh no, he is Mexican-American on the Mexican side. You are on the American side. I say what happens here."

"Fuck you! Take this to your side!"

Worthy pulled out his backup pistol and shoved it to Mark's temple, pulling him by his hair from across the small table.

"Put the gun down! Señor, I will be forced to shoot. Put it down!"

"How's it feel Johnson? Just a second away and the dreams of a blue spot turn into the child molesters Hell? Oh yeah, you don't have any rank, child molester."

"This is the last chance, Worthy. I will shoot."

Mark coolly told the officers in Spanish it was a trick and that Worthy wouldn't shoot.

"No, it is okay. He wants you to shoot him, because he knows you won't kill him. He wants the national attention. That way, they get all the money back and extradite me. If you shoot him, all is lost. It will be in every sector of the news and you will lose every dime. You will have to pay back the sixty thousand I gave you."

The Mexican police lowered their pistols, knowing what Mark said was absolute truth. They'd lose the money and their jobs for accepting the bribe.

Worthy continued his damage on Mark. "You are a demon and have the cleverness, but the Bright Star is dissatisfied. I wouldn't drink to your black. I'm a lighter label, like most. You know, I had a nice long talk with Heather. Yes, you're right, Jesus can never come back in your heart. You're in the ranks of the unforgiven. You have to make the exchange to get above the most lowly. But you failed by being lazy and too careful. You will be in the lesser places of ridicule and torment. You didn't make the required quota. You know how it is in the land of the unjust, if you can't measure up, there are no adjustments. There are two barrels left on the blue flowers, and the Bright Star doesn't like incomplete deals. You're worse off, still at the bottom, but with additional failure. They will still see you as a hideous father performing the lowest deed on his own seed; the worst of the child molesters and now the most molested for your shortcoming. You will probably be a pile of shit, with eyes that you can see all your victims spitting in your stink. Your blue spot will forever be imbedded as lost, and failure will hurt for the pain you run from so hard. Your God must keep his standard. You did not achieve elevation. You sank further in. Look at your life now. That's better than forensic evidence you were so capable of hiding like you do from yourself. But the world sees you, and you know that's why I'm here. Yes, they all gave you up, even Madden! The girl in De Moines will finish her crawl to you in the lake, along with the rest, and everyone that didn't make it to the blue spot. You know you're at the bottom. The Bright Star has a reputation to keep. How's it feel to be stuck in the middle? You can't even go back to the Messiah, blasphemer! It's

the most horrid place where you are. The Bright Star awaits only the pathetic slave he wants to punish for not satisfying the desire. Your darkness has twisted the true light into "mad light." In madness you dwell. Can't let a nobody father loose to molest the hell-bound daughter, because both step-mother and daughter will be following you to castrate your eternal dream of savoring the forbidden poison."

Mark lunged across the table at Worthy, grabbing and shoving the gun barrel into his mouth to shut him up. Without words, he used his lifelong cool and backs down, dropping the gun. Nothing could have shocked the Federalis more. The money was in their bank and it was all they cared to understand.

"I'm going to walk out of here. If anyone dares to contest my God ,it will be me. If anyone answers to my God it will be me. Who said my work is done here? Who said I was finished?"

Worthy had lost his man, but he knew as well as Mark that the damage was done. He was a cripple now. The best were the escapees who only wanted their audience to know that they were the *how*, not the *why*. The *why* was for only the best, the strong who only need prove to themselves. His exposed core would not allow the objective of spiritual reward. Mark was openly exposed to himself, and it shrank him to know the world knew. He would have to start over.

Mark made the cash deposit in his and Angie's Banamex bank account in Tijuana, only accessible in Mexico. He couldn't sleep on the tour bus ride back to La Paz, but he knew he would never have rest in the physical custody of Worthy. He proceeded to worship his God. Maria took him in.

"Mark, I see you look so bad. You look exhausted. Come, you must sleep now."

"I am home forever, my love, forever."

"I go to the bank yesterday. I say nothing, but I think they make a mistake, is so much money in the account. I never see such a big number."

"It's no mistake. It's all yours, love. I put it there for you. I think I can sleep now. It's over."

"You sell the business. It is all finish in America?"

"All finished. I am Mexican now. They cannot touch me. I imagine you must have been surprised to see all that money in your account."

"I have one big surprise for you when you wake up."

"Can you give me a hint?"

"I can have one woman once in a while, Mark?"

"Is that the hint?"

"Well…"

"Definitely, I can't wait to wake up."

"Lay down. You need the bed now. I see you when you wake up."

Mark slept for ten hours. Angie and her friend looked over him.

"I would have awoken by now. Does he always sleep so?"

"No, he run from the police. He is finished running."

"Are you sure about doing this with Mark?"

"Yes, don't worry, I am *positivo*."

"You like my breasts?"

"Mmmm. They are full, bigger than me."

"But yours are natural. Let me kiss them. I want to put them in his lips."

"I want to see that. Come, this will wake him."

They approached Mark and woke him. "Oh my God! I'm tied up."

"In case you're wondering what just happened, you have been abbreviated."

"Rosabla! Where is my God? I've lost my rank, I've lost my place."

"Here, in his lips. Rosabla get the candle, I stop the bloody. You know why, Mark. But it's how. It's called *dirrecion* electronica and the Internet. Every time you call me collect, I see the cities you are in when the bill come for the telephone. I see on the Internet what you do for so long. I am the forensic evidence you don't think of. I see the news, double-you, double-you, double-you, New York times dot com, LA dot com, Seattle dot com, and on and on. You know why, Mark? Because you no change; you no change. I must change you and you are going to live the why of it. In the beginning, I know it is you, but I let you have your revenge because I think you can kill the bug that is up your ass. When you come last time, you know everything there is to know to make the change, but you do not. I gave and give you the attention you wanted. You cannot accept the attention now; it is too late for you, since you have already crossed the line. You have the taste in your mouth, and it can never be satisfied now. De Moines dot com, LA dot com. You no change, Gringo. Now you shall live the *why* of life. Come here, Canella. Come puppy."

Five Years Later

✤

Within the separate offices of Detective Worthy and Rainey an emergency police bulletin out of Mexico flashes over their screens.

"Look at this, Rainey. The Acid Rapist struck in Acapulco: same M.O. same acid, same hemoglobin content, and in a storm drain."

"Christ, those people down there will never figure this freak out."

In Los Angeles, Worthy gets it the same.

"Detective Worthy, you have a collect call from an unidentified caller in Mexico. Should I accept?"

"Put it through."

"The storm drains are the same in Mexico as they are in America."

"Then that means they flow *vamos* to where the fish sleep."

"He no change. He have the most lonely five years. Nothing to satisfy him. He have the very sick pain, the pain of Hell on Earth. He wished he was never born. Heather, please go see Anna. I am on the phone. Excuse me, Detective. He sleep with the fishies now."

"Gracias, Maria. *Y usted tambien ponga depredador abajo?*" Hello,,,

And you also have put the Predator Down? Hello,,,